The
GOSPEL
of
JESUS
CHRIST
Studies in Romans

David Hocking

The
GOSPEL
of
JESUS
CHRIST

David Hocking

Published by HFT Publications
PO Box 3927   Tustin, CA 92781
Copyright 2013 by HFT Publications

TABLE OF CONTENTS

THEME
Righteousness by Faith

The word *"righteousness"* appears 306 times in the Bible, 99 of which are in the New Testament, and 39 times in the Book of Romans (in its various grammatical forms) – but found 52 times in the English translation of the Bible.

The word *"faith"* appears 247 times in the Bible of which 245 of those times are in the New Testament and 38 times in the original language of Romans (in its various grammatical forms) – but listed 63 times in the English translation of the Bible.

The Greek word *dikaiosune* is used 36 times in Romans and related words another 27 times. The Greek word *pistis* appears 244 times in the New Testament of which 39 are used in Romans. The verb *pisteuo* appears 250 times in the New Testament with 21 usages in Romans.

The "GOSPEL OF JESUS CHRIST" is being undermined by weak and often non-Biblical interpretations in our day.

It is time to state clearly what the true gospel of Jesus Christ is all about!

The Book of Romans makes it clear that the righteousness of God is the issue and its reception by humanity is based on faith alone, not on human effort or worthiness.

In many ways, the Book of Romans is like the "constitution of Christianity." It spells out the issues in no uncertain terms and speaks powerfully of God's plan to save humanity from sin, death, and hell.

Serious questions like:

HOW CAN A SINFUL PERSON BE RIGHTEOUS BEFORE A HOLY GOD?

ARE WE MADE RIGHTEOUS BY WHAT WE DO IN LIFE, OR ARE WE SIMPLY DECLARED RIGHTEOUS BY WHAT WE BELIEVE?

These and many more are answered in this wonderful Book!

Chapter 1
INTRODUCTION
Romans 1:1-17

A simple outline of the opening introduction to the Book of Romans speaks of the following:

> The <u>CHARACTER</u> of the gospel
> *(1:1-7)*
> The <u>CONCERN</u> for the gospel
> *(1:8-15)*
> The <u>CONTENT</u> of the gospel
> *(1:16-17)*

The first seven verses contain 126 words in the Greek text and formulate just one sentence! This sentence deals with the <u>MAN</u> who preaches the gospel; the <u>MESSAGE</u> that it contains; and, the <u>MISSION</u> it will accomplish.

THE CHARACTER OF THE GOSPEL
Romans 1:1-7

The <u>MAN</u> who preaches the gospel
Romans 1:1

His <u>ATTITUDE</u> – *"a servant of Jesus Christ"*

His <u>AUTHORITY</u> – *"called to be an apostle"*

His <u>APPOINTMENT</u> – *"separated unto the gospel of God"*

<u>SEVEN CHARACTERISTICS OF THE SERVANT OF THE LORD</u>

The word *"servant"* is the Greek word *doulos* which is used 130 times in the New Testament as a noun, and two verb forms are used an additional 33 times.

In the New Testament, the following are called a *"doulos"* (slave):

MOSES – *Revelation 15:3*
PROPHETS – *Revelation 10:7; 11:18*
JOHN – *Revelation 1:1*
JUDE – *Jude 1*
PETER – *II Peter 1:1*
JAMES – *James 1:1*
EPAPHRAS – *Colossians 4:12*
ALL BELIEVERS – *Revelation 22:3*
PAUL – *Romans 1:1*

JESUS CHRIST – *Philippians 2:7* –
"took upon Him the form of a <u>servant</u> (doulos)"

Jewish rabbis said of this word *doulos* that it was one of the worst insults one man can hurl at another! The Greeks who were proud of their freedom said that the word *doulos* was the opposite of being free. Plato and Aristotle said that it was a derogatory term. In Kittel's Theological Dictionary of the NT, we read: *"In the New Testament, the doulos is the classical picture of bondage and limitation."*

The fact that it is used so often of believers and even used of our Lord Jesus Christ forces us to evaluate our own relationship to such a word! The following facts (seven) reveal the nature of a *doulos*.

1. He obeys his Master without question.
   cf. Matthew 8:9; 10:24; Luke 14:22; John 13;16; 15:20

2. He belongs to his Master.
   cf. I Corinthians 6:19-20; 7:22-25

He was bought with a price and owned by the Master. The *doulos* could not own property, and his family did not belong to him, and no genealogies were kept of his existence and work.

3. He honors his Master.
   cf. I Timothy 6:1; Revelation 19:5

4. He never argues with his Master.
   cf. II Timothy 2:24; Titus 2:9

5. He does what he is commanded to do regardless of any recognition he might want to receive.
   cf. Luke 17:5-10

6. He accepts full responsibility for what the Master has entrusted to him.
   cf. Matthew 25:14, 21, 23

7. He desires to please his Master alone.
   cf. Galatians 6:10; Ephesians 6:5-8; Colossians 3:22-25

The testimony of the Apostle Paul reveals the characteristics of a servant
I Corinthians 9:19-22

"For though I be free from all men, yet have I made myself servant unto all, that I might gain the more. And unto the Jews I became as a Jew, that I might gain the Jews; to them that are under the law, as under the law, that I might gain them that are under the law; To them that are without law, as without law, (being not without law to God, but the law to Christ,) that I might gain them that are without law. To the weak became I as weak, that I might gain the weak: I am made all things to all men, that I might by all means save some."

The <u>MAN</u> who preaches it
Romans 1:1

His <u>ATTITUDE</u> – *"servant of Jesus Christ"* – Greek word: *doulos*

His <u>AUTHORITY</u> – *"called to be an apostle"*

The word *"apostle"* is transliterated from Greek into English without being translated. It refers to a person who is sent by someone with an important

11

message to deliver. The word is used about 70 times in the New Testament.

When we read that Paul was *"called to be an apostle"* – we understand that it was God's decision, the One Who *"called"* him. Galatians 1:1 says: *"Paul, an apostle, not of men, neither by man, but by Jesus Christ, and God the Father, Who raised Him from the dead."*

Acts 9:15-16 gives us the background on this "calling" of God:

> *"Go thy way: for he is a chosen vessel unto Me, to bear My Name before the Gentiles, and kings, and the children of Israel: For I will shew him how great things he must suffer for My Name's sake."*

In Acts 26:15-18, Paul is defending himself before King Agrippa and reviews his personal confrontation on the road to Damascus with Jesus:

> *"I am Jesus Whom thou persecutest. But rise, and stand upon thy feet: for I have appeared unto thee for this purpose, to make thee a minister and a*

*witness both of these things which
thou hast seen, and of those
things in the which I will appear
unto thee; Delivering thee from
the people, and from the Gentiles,
unto whom now I send thee, to
open their eyes, and to turn them
from darkness to light, and from
the power of Satan unto God, that
they may receive forgiveness of
sins, and inheritance among them
which are sanctified by faith that
is in me."*

But, it was not only God's decision, but it was God's direction for Paul as well – when the Lord "called" him, he was *"called to be an apostle."* It meant that Paul was being officially sent by God for a special mission in life.

Yes, Paul's <u>attitude</u> was that of a *"servant of Jesus Christ"* and his <u>authority</u> was that he was *"called to be an apostle."* His particular <u>appointment</u> was indicated by the words *"separated unto the gospel of God."*

In Galatians 1:15-16 we read:

"But when it pleased God, Who separated me from my mother's womb, and called me by His grace, to reveal His Son in me, that I might preach Him among the heathen; immediately I conferred not with flesh and blood."

Paul was *"separated"* from the "womb" and from the "world" for the "work" to which God had called him. His words to Timothy in I Timothy 1:11-17 are quite inspirational and challenging:

"According to the glorious gospel of the blessed God, which was committed to my trust. And I thank Christ Jesus our Lord, Who hath enabled me, for that He counted me faithful, putting me into the ministry; who was before a blasphemer, and a persecutor, and injurious; but I obtained mercy, because I did it ignorantly in unbelief. And the grace of our Lord was exceeding abundant with faith and love which is in Christ Jesus. This is a faithful saying, and worthy of all acceptation, that Christ Jesus

came into the world to save sinners; of whom I am chief. Howbeit for this cause I obtained mercy, that in me first Jesus Christ might shew forth all longsuffering, for a pattern to them which should hereafter believe on Him to life everlasting. Now unto the King eternal, immortal, invisible, the only wise God, be honor and glory forever and ever. Amen.

The <u>MESSAGE</u> it contains
Romans 1:2-4

1. As to its <u>PROMISE</u> – *"which He had promised afore by His prophets in the holy Scriptures"*

There are at least 61 quotations in the Book of Romans from the Jewish Bible, the Old Testament.

2. As to the <u>PERSON</u> of Jesus Christ!

The *"gospel of God"* concerns *"His Son."* The words *"Jesus Christ our Lord"* are not found in any Greek manuscript in verse 3, but they are found at the end of verse 4.

Two issues are found in the words relating to the Person of Jesus Christ our Lord:

(1)   His <u>RELATIONSHIP</u> to King David
        "made of the seed of David according to the flesh"

His <u>preexistence</u> is implied in the word *"made."* The Greek word is *ginomai* which means "to become." We read in John 1:14: *"And the Word was made flesh, and dwelt among us, (and we beheld His glory, the glory as of the only begotten of the Father,) full of grace and truth."* The Greek verb is in the aorist tense and should be translated *"the One Who became."* It indicates a change of condition and assumes His preexistence.

His <u>position</u> as the Messiah of Israel is being proclaimed when we read *"the seed of David."* Luke 1:31-33 makes it quite clear:

> *"And, behold, thou shalt conceive in thy womb, and bring forth a son, and shalt call His Name JESUS. He shall be great, and*

shall be called the Son of the Highest: and the Lord God shall give unto Him the throne of His father David: and He shall reign over the house of Jacob forever; and of His kingdom there shall be no end."

Revelation 22:16 quotes the words of Jesus when He said:

"I Jesus have sent Mine angel to testify unto you these things in the churches. I am the root and the offspring of David, and the bright and morning star."

His <u>presence</u> was fully human – *"according to flesh."* Galatians 4:4 says: *"But when the fullness of the time was come, God sent forth His Son, made of a woman, made under the law."* When Jesus appeared to His disciples after His resurrection, Luke 24:39 quotes His words: *"Behold My hands and My feet, that it is I Myself: handle Me, and see; for a spirit hath not flesh and bones, as ye see Me have."*

(2) His <u>RESURRECTION</u> from the dead – *"declared to be the Son*

*of God with power, according
to the spirit of holiness, by the
resurrection from the dead."*

The Greek word translated *"declared"* is
the word *horisthentos* and means "to
mark out a horizon." The resurrection
clearly revealed Who He is – <u>THE</u> Son of
God!

**HOW DID THE RESURRECTION PROVE
HE IS THE SON OF GOD?**

(1)   He rose by His own power!
John 10:18:
*"No man taketh it from Me, but
I lay it down of Myself. I have
power to lay it down, and I
have power to take it again."*

(2)   It confirmed all that He had
claimed!
Matthew 16:21b:
*"that He must go unto
Jerusalem, and suffer many
things of the elders and chief
priests and scribes, and be
killed, and be <u>raised</u> <u>again</u> the
third day."*

Matthew 20:19:

"And shall deliver Him to the Gentiles to mock, and to scourge, and to crucify Him; and the third day He shall <u>rise again</u>."

(3) It results in our own salvation and future resurrection! Romans 4:24-25:
"But for us also, to whom it shall be imputed, if we believe on Him that raised up Jesus our Lord from the dead; Who was delivered for our offences, and was <u>raised</u> <u>again</u> for our justification."

Romans 10:9:
"That if thou shalt confess with thy mouth the Lord Jesus, and shalt believe in thine heart that God hath raised Him from the dead, thou shalt be saved."

The <u>MISSION</u> it requires
Romans 1:5-7

Its <u>RECEPTION</u> – *"By Whom we have received grace and apostleship, for obedience to the faith among all nations."*

Its <u>REASON</u> – *"for His Name"* – the Greek preposition translated *"for"* is *huper* meaning "in the behalf of."

Its <u>RESPONSE</u>
> Seen in their <u>position</u> – *"the called of Jesus Christ...called to be saints"*

> Seen in their <u>place</u> in the heart of God Himself – *"beloved of God"*

THE CONCERN FOR THE GOSPEL
Romans 1:8-15

The concern of the apostle Paul is easily observed by his <u>PRAYERS</u> noted in verses 8-12.

HIS <u>REJOICING</u>
Romans 1:8 – "I thank my God through Jesus Christ for you all"

1. It was <u>CONTROLLED</u> by his personal relationship to God – *"my God"*

2. It <u>CAME</u> from the access which he had to God – *"through Jesus Christ"*

Hebrews 4:14-16 speaks powerfully of the access we have to the Father – through His Son, our Lord Jesus Christ:

"Seeing then that we have a great high priest, that is passed into the heavens, Jesus the Son of God, let us hold fast our profession. For we have not an high priest which cannot be touched with the feeling of our infirmities; but was in all points tempted like as we are, yet without sin. Let us therefore come boldly unto the throne of grace, that we may obtain mercy, and find grace to help in time of need."

3. It was <u>CENTERED</u> in his intercession for them – *"for you all"*

Philippians 1:3-4 says: *"I thank my God upon every remembrance of you, always in every prayer of mine for you all making request with joy."*

HIS <u>REQUESTS</u>
Romans 1:9-10 (based on four things)

"For God is my witness, Whom I serve with my spirit in the gospel of His Son,

that without ceasing I make mention of you always in my prayers; Making request, if by any means now at length I might have a prosperous journey by the will of God to come unto you.

    1. Based on his <u>SINCERITY</u> – *"For God is my witness"*

Paul spoke similar words in Romans 9:1: *"I say the truth in Christ, I lie not, my conscience also bearing me witness in the Holy Ghost."*

    2. Based on his <u>SERVICE</u> – *"whom I serve with my spirit in the gospel of His Son"*

The Greek word translated *"serve"* is *latreuo* which refers to "religious service" or an act of worship.

Notice that his service was internal, not external – he said in Ephesians 6:6: *"doing the will of God from the heart."*

His service was also spiritual, and not carnal. In Galatians 5:13 he said: *"use not liberty for an occasion to the flesh, but by love <u>serve</u> one another."*

In Colossians 3:24 he said: *"for ye serve the Lord Christ."*

3. Based on his continual SUPPLICATIONS in their behalf – *"without ceasing I make mention of you always in my prayers"*

Paul wrote in I Thessalonians 1:2 – *"making mention of you in my prayers"*

4. Based on his SUBMISSION to the will of God – *"Making request...by the will of God to come unto you"*

HIS REASONS
Romans 1:11-12

"For I long to see you, that I may impart unto you some spiritual gift, to the end ye may be established; That is, that I may be comforted together with you by the mutual faith both of you and me."

1. To EXERCISE a spiritual gift – *"that I may impart unto you some spiritual gift"*

2. To <u>ESTABLISH</u> the believers – *"to the end ye may be established"*

3. To <u>ENCOURAGE</u> them – *"may be comforted together with you"* (evidence of Paul's humility)

Paul's concern for the gospel was not only revealed by his <u>PRAYERS</u> for them but also by his <u>PURPOSES</u>. In Romans 1:13-15 we read:

> *"Now I would not have you ignorant, brethren, that oftentimes I purposed to come unto you, (but was let hitherto,) that I might have some fruit among you also, even as among other Gentiles. I am debtor both to the Greeks, and to the Barbarians; both to the wise, and to the unwise. So, as much as in me is, I am ready to preach the gospel to you that are at Rome also."*

The <u>RESISTANCE</u> to his coming – *"but was let hitherto"*

1. His <u>DESIRE</u> was strong, but unfulfilled – *"For I long to see you"*

2. His <u>DECISION</u> was made on many occasions, but not yet possible – *"oftentimes I purposed to come"*

3. His <u>DETERMINATION</u> was hindered – *"but was let hitherto"*

WHY WAS PAUL "HINDERED" IN HIS SERVICE FOR THE LORD?

Romans 15:20-22 says: *"Yea, so have I strived to preach the gospel, not where Christ was named, lest I should build upon another man's foundation: But as it is written, To whom He was not spoken of, they shall see: and they that have not heard shall understand. For which cause also I have been much hindered from coming to you."*

Paul was "hindered" by the very service in which he was engaged for the gospel.

We also learn in the work of Paul that sickness hindered him and his co-workers. In Philippians 2:25-30 we learn that Epaphroditus was *"sick nigh unto death: but God had mercy on him."* Philippians 2:30 says *"Because for the work of Christ he was nigh unto death, not regarding his life, to supply your lack of service toward me."*

Bad health and specific diseases and sicknesses can certainly hinder the servant of the Lord in his efforts for the gospel.

In II Corinthians 1:8-10 we read: *"For we would not, brethren, have you ignorant of our trouble which came to us in Asia, that we were pressed out of measure, above strength, insomuch that we despaired even of life: But we had the sentence of death in ourselves, that we should not trust in ourselves, but in God which raiseth the dead: Who delivered us from so great a death, and doth deliver: in Whom we trust that He will yet deliver us."*

It seems that the *"trouble"* was quite serious. Paul adds these words in II Corinthians 12:7-10:

"And lest I should be exalted above measure through the abundance of the

revelations, there was given to me a thorn in the flesh, the messenger of Satan to buffet me, lest I should be exalted above measure. For this thing I besought the Lord thrice, that it might depart from me. And He said unto me, My grace is sufficient for thee: for My strength is made perfect in weakness. Most gladly therefore will I rather glory in my infirmities, that the power of Christ may rest upon me. Therefore I take pleasure in infirmities, in reproaches, in necessities, in persecutions, in distresses for Christ's sake: for when I am weak, then am I strong."

In addition to the fact of serving the Lord in some places that would hinder a person from going to other locations, and the hindrance which bad health and constant infirmity or sickness can bring, I Thessalonians 2:18 teaches that the servant of the Lord can be hindered by Satan as well: *"Wherefore we would have come unto you, even I Paul, once and again; but Satan hindered us."*

There are also times in our service for the Lord when we are hindered by the Holy Spirit as well. Acts 16:6-7 says:

"Now when they had gone throughout Phrygia and the region of Galatia, and were forbidden of the Holy Ghost to preach the word in Asia, after they were come to Mysia, they assayed to go into Bithynia: but the Spirit suffered them not."

All of the above factors can "hinder" the servant of the Lord in his desire to preach the gospel.

His <u>REASON</u> for coming to them – *v. 13 "that I might have some fruit among you also, even as among other Gentiles."*

In John 15:16 we read: *"Ye have not chosen Me, but I have chosen you, and ordained you, that ye should go and bring forth fruit, and that your fruit should remain: that whatsoever ye shall ask of the Father in My Name, He may give it you."*

Galatians 5:22-23 speaks of the *"fruit"* which the Holy Spirit produces within the believer, and seems to be that which controls our attitudes. Romans 6:22 speaks of the *"fruit"* that refers to the practices of holiness that control our depravity. We also have the word *"fruit"* referring to the people who come to believe the gospel, controlling our priorities – Romans 16:5 and I Corinthians 16:15.

His <u>RESPONSIBILITY</u> to all men – *v. 14 "I am debtor"*

In terms of <u>ethnicity</u> – *"both to the Greeks, and to the Barbarians"*

In terms of <u>education</u> – *"both to the wise, and to the unwise"*

His <u>READINESS</u> to preach – *v. 15 "So, as much as in me is, I am ready to preach the gospel to you that are at Rome also."*

Acts 20:21-24 records the testimony of Paul as to his readiness to preach the gospel:

> *"Testifying both to the Jews, and also to the Greeks, repentance toward God, and faith toward our Lord Jesus Christ. And now, behold I go bound in the spirit unto Jerusalem, not knowing the things that shall befall me there:*

Save that the Holy Ghost witnesseth in every city, saying that bonds and afflictions abide me. But none of these things move me, neither count I my life dear unto myself, so that I might finish my course with joy, and the ministry, which I have received of the Lord Jesus, to testify the gospel of the grace of God."

In Acts 28:30-31 we have a vivid illustration of Paul's commitment and readiness to preach the gospel:

"And Paul dwelt two whole years in his own hired house, and received all that came in unto him, preaching the kingdom of God, and teaching those things which concern the Lord Jesus Christ, with all confidence, no man forbidding him."

No matter how difficult the circumstances of his life, and the pressure upon him from all sides, he was ready to preach the gospel!

THE CONTENT OF THE GOSPEL
Romans 1:16-17

"For I am not ashamed of the gospel of Christ: for it is the power of God unto salvation to every one that believeth; to the Jew first, and also to the Greek. For therein is the righteousness of God revealed from faith to faith: as it is written, The just shall live by faith."

It is <u>CENTERED</u> in the <u>PERSON</u> of the Messiah!
"the gospel of Christ"

Romans 1:1 calls it *"the gospel of God."* Romans 1:9 refers to it as *"the gospel of His Son."* The phrase *"the gospel of Christ (Messiah)"* is used 11 times in the New Testament.

In Romans 15:19 Paul said *"I have fully preached the gospel of Christ."* In I Corinthians 9:18 he stated *"when I preach the gospel, I may make the gospel of Christ without charge, that I abuse not my power in the gospel."*

In II Corinthians 4:4 Paul said: *"lest the light of the glorious gospel of Christ, Who is the image of God, should shine unto them."* In Philippians 1:27 Paul said: *"Only let your conversation be as it becometh the gospel of Christ."* In I

Thessalonians 3:2 Paul called Timotheus *"our fellow-laborer in the gospel of Christ."*

The gospel is not the true gospel unless it centers in the Person and work of our Lord Jesus Christ!

It is <u>CHARACTERIZED</u> as the <u>POWER</u> of God!
"for it is the power of God unto salvation"

    1. It is <u>SUPERNATURAL</u> power! *"power of God"* – used 14 times in the New Testament.

II Samuel 22:31-33 makes this strong point:

"As for God, His way is perfect; the word of the LORD is tried: He is a buckler to all them that trust in Him. For who is God, save the LORD? and who is a Rock, save our God? God is my Strength and <u>Power</u>: and He maketh my way perfect."

Psalm 62:11 says: *"God hath spoken once; twice have I heard this; that power belongeth unto God."*

Jeremiah 10:12 adds: *"He hath made the earth by His power..."*

Jeremiah 27:5 says: *"I have made the earth, the man and the beast that are upon the ground, by My great power and by My outstretched arm, and have given it unto whom it seemed meet unto Me."*

Jeremiah 32:17 states: *"Ah Lord God! behold, Thou hast made the heaven and the earth by Thy great power and stretched out arm, and there is nothing too hard for Thee."*

The Apostle Paul wrote in I Corinthians 1:18: *"For the preaching of the cross is to them that perish foolishness; but unto us which are saved it is the power of God."*

In I Corinthians 1:24 we read: *"But unto them which are called, both Jews and Greeks, Christ the power of God, and the wisdom of God."* I Corinthians 2:5 adds: *"That your faith should not stand* *in the wisdom of men, but in the <u>power of God</u>.*"

Hebrews 1:3 speaks of God's power when we read: *"Who being the brightness of His glory, and the express image of His Person, and upholding all things by the word of <u>his power</u>, when He had by Himself purged our sins, sat down on the right hand of the Majesty on high."*

I Peter 1:5 adds: *"Who are kept by the <u>power of God</u> through faith unto salvation ready to be revealed in the last time."*

2. It is <u>SAVING</u> power – *"unto salvation"*

The word "salvation" is used 164 times in the Bible of which 45 usages are in the New Testament and 4 in Romans (1:16; 10:10; 11:11; 13:11). The word "saved" is found 57 times in the New Testament and 8 in Romans (5:9, 10; 8:24; 9:27; 10:1, 9, 13; 11:26) and the simple word "save" is used once in Romans 11:14.

It is <u>COMMITTED</u> to all <u>PEOPLE</u> of the world – *"to every one that*

believeth; to the Jew first, and also to the Greek."

1. The <u>PREREQUISITE</u> demands faith – *"to every one that believeth"*

Paul added in Romans 3:22-23:

> *"Even the righteousness of God which is by faith of Jesus Christ unto all and upon all them that believe: for there is no difference: For all have sinned and come short of the glory of God."*

2. The <u>PRIORITY</u> involves reaching Jews – *"to the Jew first"*

We read in John 4:22 the words of our Lord Yeshua to a Samaritan woman: *"Ye worship ye know not what: we know what we worship: for salvation is of the Jews."*

3. The <u>PLAN</u> reaches to all pagans in this world – *"and also to the Greek"* (Hellenist – culturally tied into Greek culture, belief, and practices)

It is <u>CONTROLLED</u> by the <u>PRINCIPLE</u> of the righteousness of God – *"For therein is the righteousness of God revealed from faith to faith"*

    1. **Because God is righteous!** *"the righteousness of God"*

I John 2:29 says: *"If ye know that He is righteous, ye know that every one that doeth righteousness is born of Him."*

    2. **Because Jesus Christ is our righteousness!**

I Corinthians 1:30 says: *"But of Him are ye in Christ Jesus, Who of God is made unto us wisdom, and righteousness, and sanctification, and redemption."* **II Corinthians 5:21 adds:** *"For He hath made Him to be sin for us, Who knew no sin; that we might be made the righteousness of God in Him."*

    3. **Because it is received by faith alone!** *"from faith to faith"*

Romans 10:4 says: *"For Christ is the end of the law for righteousness to every one that believeth."* Galatians 2:16 states: *"Knowing that a man is not justified by the works of the law, but by the faith of Jesus Christ, even we have believed in Jesus Christ, that we might be justified by the faith of Christ, and not by the works of the law: for by the works of the law shall no flesh be justified."*

Philippians 3:8-9 adds: *"Yea doubtless, and I count all things but loss for the excellency of the knowledge of Christ Jesus my Lord: for Whom I have suffered the loss of all things, and do count them but dung, that I may win Christ, and be found in Him, not having mine own righteousness, which is of the law, but that which is through the faith of Christ, the righteousness which is of God by faith."*

The words *"from faith"* are based on the Greek preposition *ek* meaning "out of." The words *"to faith"* use the Greek preposition *eis* meaning "into" or "unto" or "as a result of."

It is <u>CONFIRMED</u> in Biblical PROACY! – *"as it is written, The just shall live by faith"*

These words are taken by way of direct quote from Habakkuk 2:4 – *"Behold, his soul which is lifted up is not upright in him: but the just shall live by his faith."*

    1. It <u>ELIMINATES</u> being justified by the law!

Galatians 3:11 says: *"But that no man is justified by the law in the sight of God, it is evident: for, The just shall live by faith."*

    2. It <u>ENCOURAGES</u> patience as we wait for the fulfillment and complete realization of God's promises!

Hebrews 10:35-39 makes this clear:

"Cast not away therefore your confidence, which hath great recompence of reward. For ye have need of patience, that, after ye have done the will of God, ye might receive the promise. For yet a little while, and He that shall come will come, and will

*not tarry. Now the just shall live by
faith: but if any man draw back, my
soul shall have no pleasure in him. But
we are not of them who draw back unto
perdition; but of them that believe to the
saving of the soul."*

Let's be very clear about the major
argument of the Book of Romans! We
are declared righteous by faith in the
Person and work of Jesus Christ our
Lord! It is not human worth or effort
that saves us – it is Jesus Christ Who
saves us! Not by what we do or have
done, but only by what He has done!

THE PRINCIPLES
OF THE
RIGHTEOUSNESS
OF GOD

Romans 1:18-8:39

Chapter 2
CONDEMNATION
Romans 1:18-3:20

The very first principle of the righteousness of God is that of CONDEMNATION which the Apostle Paul explains in this section of Romans. We are dealing with the problem of how a person can be holy or righteous before a holy and righteous God. We are sinners by nature and practice, and we do not deserve the righteousness of God.

Paul begins by explaining the...
CONDEMNATION of those who REJECT the revelation of God! - *Romans 1:18-32*

Their ACKNOWLEDGEMENT of God in creation was suppressed by their ungodliness and unrighteousness!
Romans 1:18-23

"For the wrath of God is revealed from heaven against all ungodliness and unrighteousness of men, who hold the truth in unrighteousness; Because that

which may be known of God is manifest in them; for God hath shewed it unto them. For the invisible things of Him from the creation of the world are clearly seen, being understood by the things that are made, even His eternal power and Godhead; so that they are without excuse: Because that, when they knew God, they glorified Him not as God, neither were thankful; but became vain in their imaginations, and their foolish heart was darkened. Professing themselves to be wise, they because fools, and changed the glory of the incorruptible God into an image made like to corruptible man, and to birds, and four-footed beasts, and creeping things."

The Greek word translated *"wrath"* is the word *orge* and is used 36 times in the New Testament, of which 11 usages are found in Romans. The term *"wrath of God"* is found in John 3:36, Ephesians 5:6, and Colossians 3:6.

   1. The <u>SUPPRESSION</u> of the truth
       vv. 18-19

"For the invisible things of Him from the creation of the world are clearly

seen, being understood by the things that are made."

By looking at the result that creation brought (*"the things that are made"* – Greek word *poiema* – gives us our English word "poem") we learn of His *"eternal power and Godhead."* We learn two things from creation:

>   (1)   Whoever made it had to be in existence before it was made – *"eternal"*

>   (2)   Whoever made it obviously is bigger than any person – *"power"*

The result of this, the ungodly and unrighteous are *"without excuse"*!

>   2.   The <u>SERIOUSNESS</u> of their rejection – *v. 20* – *"without excuse"*

The <u>power</u> of God is *"clearly seen."*

>   3.   The <u>STEPS</u> leading to their rejection – *vv. 21-23*

"Because that, when they knew God, they glorified Him not as God, neither were thankful; but became vain in their imaginations, and their foolish heart was darkened, professing themselves to be wise, they became fools…"

(1) They <u>REFUSED</u> to glorify God!
"they glorified Him not as God"

In Romans 3:23 we will learn that *"All have sinned and come short of the glory of God."*

(2) They <u>REBELLED</u> against giving thanks to God – *"neither were thankful"*

II Timothy 3 lists the *"perilous times"* that are coming in the future – one of those characteristics is being *"unthankful."*

(3) They <u>REASONED</u> in their own minds as to what might have brought the universe into existence – *"became vain in their imaginations."*

The Greek word is *dialogismois* which is used 14 times as a noun in the New Testament and 16 times as a verb.

> (4)   They <u>REGARDED</u> themselves as intellectually capable – *"professing themselves to be wise"* – cf. I Corinthians 1:19-21
>
> (5)   They <u>REDUCED</u> the Creator to that which has been created – *v. 23 – "changed"*

In Psalm 106:19-22 we read:

"They made a calf in Horeb, and worshipped the molten image. Thus they changed their glory into the similitude of an ox that eateth grass. They forgat God their Savior which had done great things in Egypt; Wondrous works in the land of Ham, and terrible things by the Red Sea."

The result of the failure to glorify and thank God for His creation brought the following upon them:

<u>CONCLUSION:</u>

1. Mental and spiritual darkness is the result of leaving God out of your thinking and behavior! *"their foolish heart was darkened"*

2. Religious paganism is the result of our failure to worship the God of creation! *"they became fools"*

When you reject the God of creation, (which the heart of humanity is designed to worship), – the result when you don't worship God – you create your own image of what you want to worship!

Their <u>ACTIONS</u> prove that they deserve condemnation!
Romans 1:24-27

"Wherefore God also gave them up to uncleanness through the lusts of their own hearts, to dishonor their own bodies between themselves: who changed the truth of God into a lie, and worshipped and served the creature more than the Creator, Who is blessed forever. Amen. For this cause God gave them up unto vile affections: for even their women did change the natural use

*into that which is against nature: And
likewise also the men, leaving the
natural use of the woman, burned in
their lust one toward another; men with
men working that which is unseemly,
and receiving in themselves that
recompence of their error which was
meet."*

Two times in the above verses, we read
"God gave them up." In verse 28, it says
"God gave them over."

They are <u>CONTROLLED</u> by physical desires – *v. 24* -
"uncleanness" (the word is often
associated with sexual sin and demonic
activity – as in *"unclean spirit."*)

Notice two things that result when we
are controlled by sinful desires:

(1)   The <u>DESIRE</u> comes from
within –
"the lusts of their own hearts"

In Mark 7:21-23 our Lord Yeshua taught
this important truth:

*"For from within, out of the heart
of men, proceed evil thoughts,*

adulteries, fornications, murders, thefts, covetousness, wickedness, deceit, lasciviousness, an evil eye, blasphemy, pride, foolishness: All these evil things come from within, and defile the man."

It is easy to blame the environment, or another person for the evil desires that we have; but Jesus said that they *"come from within."*

(2)　The <u>DISHONOR</u> involves their physical bodies – *"to dishonor their own bodies between themselves"*

I Corinthians 6:18 teaches: *"Flee fornication. Every sin that a man doeth is without the body; but he that committeth fornication sinneth against his own body."*

Ephesians 4:18-19 adds: *"Having the understanding darkened, being alienated from the life of God through the ignorance that is in them, because of the blindness of their heart: Who being past feeling have given themselves over unto lasciviousness, to work all uncleanness with greediness."*

They are <u>CONCERNED</u> for the creature rather than the Creator – v. 25

The desire for images, icons, etc., is simply evidence of the idolatry of the human heart. Consider what the LORD GOD of Israel told His people in Deuteronomy 4:15-19:

"Take ye therefore good heed unto yourselves; for ye saw no manner of similitude on the day that the LORD spake unto you in Horeb out of the midst of the fire: Lest ye corrupt yourselves, and make you a graven image, the similitude of any figure, the likeness of male or female, the likeness of any beast that is on the earth, the likeness of any winged fowl that flieth in the air, the likeness of any thing that creepeth on the ground, the likeness of any fish that is in the waters beneath the earth: And lest thou lift up thine eyes unto heaven, and when thou seest the sun, and the moon, and the stars, even all the host of heaven, shouldest be driven to worship them, and serve them, which the LORD thy God hath divided unto all nations under the whole heaven."

These words cover the whole issue of idolatry! In Deuteronomy 4:23-24 the Bible adds:

"Take heed unto yourselves, lest ye forget the covenant of the LORD your God, which He made with you, and make you a graven image, or the likeness of any thing, which the LORD thy God hath forbidden thee. For the LORD thy God is a consuming fire, even a jealous God."

Deuteronomy 4:39 states: *"Know therefore this day, and consider it in thine heart, that the LORD He is God in heaven above, and upon the earth beneath: there is none else."*

They are <u>CORRUPTED</u> by unnatural passions – *vv. 26-27*

"For this cause God gave them up unto vile affections: for even their women did change the natural use into that which is against nature: And likewise also the men, leaving the natural use of the woman, burned in their lust one toward another; men with men working that which is unseemly, and receiving

51

in themselves that recompence of their error which meet."

The words *"For this cause"* in verse 26 refer to the issue of verse 25, which simply strengthens the argument of verses 21-23 – revealing the steps that lead to God's judgment.

The words *"vile affections"* in verse 26 refer to what some translations call "degrading passions" or "shameful lusts."

THREE BASIS ISSUES

    1. A sexual <u>PRINCIPLE</u> is violated!

Verses 26 and 27 refer to *"the natural use."* The word *"use"* is commonly used for sexual intercourse – that which is *"natural"* refers to what God intended.

It is *"natural"* for a man to desire a woman sexually, and also for a woman to desire a man sexually. It is quite "unnatural" for a man to desire a man sexually and for a woman to desire another woman. No matter how the homosexual community tries to change the basic interpretation of this passage,

its clarity and simplicity is without
challenge – even a child can understand!

2. A sexual <u>PLAN</u> of God is ignored!

Verse 27 uses a phrase – *"working that
which is unseemly."* It refers to that
which is without shape, design, or plan.
Leviticus 18:22 states most emphatically
and clearly – *"Thou shalt NOT lie with
mankind, as with womankind: it is
abomination."* This does not mean that
when a man has sex with a woman, it is
permitted or accepted by God. The same
context in Leviticus 18 says in verse 20:
*"Moreover thou shalt not lie carnally
with thy neighbor's wife, to defile
thyself with her."* The sins of adultery,
rape, incest, pre-marital sex, etc., are all
forms of *"fornication"* (Greek: *porneia*)
and sinful practices in the eyes of God.

Leviticus 20:13 also adds: *"If a man also
lie with mankind, as he lieth with a
woman, both of them have committed
an abomination: they shall surely be
put to death; their blood shall be upon
them."*

The death penalty was not practiced
solely for the sin of homosexuality. In

Leviticus 20:10 we read: *"And the man that committeth adultery with another man's wife, even he that committeth adultery with his neighbor's wife, the adulterer and the adulteress shall surely be put to death."*

The obvious teaching of the Bible is that the only safe and honorable sex is within the context of marriage between a man and a woman. Hebrews 13:4 says: *"Marriage is honorable in all, and the bed undefiled: but whoremongers and adulterers God will judge."*

3. A sexual <u>PENALTY</u> is experienced!

Verse 27 says *"receiving in themselves that recompence of their error which was meet."* Instead of being rewarded with sexual satisfaction, a sexual obsession is created that brings dissatisfaction. It is a "penalty" not a reward! It is also possible that sexual disease is intended in addition to the problems of sexual satisfaction or sexual vitality bring reduced.

In the days of the Roman Empire, homosexuality was glorified and made more desirable than heterosexuality. 14

of the first 15 emperors were known to be homosexuals. Nero (for example) married two men in succession and at the time of Paul's writings, he was about to marry a boy named Sporus (recorded in Seutonius's work - <u>LIVES OF THE CAESARS</u>). Plato spoke highly of homosexual love in his work entitled – <u>THE SYMPOSIUM</u>.

The Jewish historian, Flavius Josephus, clearly identifies the sin of Sodom with homosexual practices. In the work called – <u>APOSTOLIC CONSTITUTION</u> – we read this statement: *"Thou shalt not corrupt boys – for this wickedness is contrary to nature and arose from Sodom."*

In the 4th century AD John Chrysostom wrote about homosexuality in the city of Antioch and said: *"There is absolutely nothing more demented or noxious than this wickedness."* Augustine confessed to having contaminated the spring of male friendship with the dirt of lust, and later stigmatized homosexual behavior as against nature and contrary to human custom. Thomas Aquinas declared homosexual acts as *"vices against nature."*

Their <u>ATTITUDES</u> reveal that they deserve the condemnation of God!
Romans 1:28-32

"And even as they did not like to retain God in their knowledge, God gave them over to a reprobate mind, to do those things which are not convenient; Being filled with all unrighteousness, fornication, wickedness, covetousness, maliciousness; full of envy, murder, debate, deceit, malignity; whisperers, backbiters, haters of God, despiteful, proud, boasters, inventors of evil things, disobedient to parents, without understanding, covenant-breakers, without natural affection, implacable, unmerciful: who knowing the judgment of God, that they which commit such things are worthy of death, not only do the same, but have pleasure in them that do them."

According to Romans 1:28, moral deviation leads to mental depravity!

This passage is indeed remarkable in its description of what happens when a person rejects the revelation of God in creation and begins to exchange the glory of the Creator into the creature.

There are 23 characteristics of a
"reprobate mind" placed in the Greek
text into four groupings

1. FIVE THINGS with which a
    reprobate mind is filled!
    "unrighteousness"
    "fornication"
    "wickedness"
    "covetousness"
    "maliciousness"

2. FIVE THINGS that a reprobate
    mind is full of!
    "envy
    "murder"
    "debate"
    "deceit"
    "malignity"

3. EIGHT THINGS that reveal the
    pride of a reprobate mind!
    "whisperers"
    "backbiters"
    "haters of God"
    "despiteful"
    "proud"
    "boasters"
    "inventors of evil things"
    "disobedient to parents"

4. FIVE THINGS that are absent in a reprobate mind!
"without understanding"
"covenant breakers"
"without natural affection"
"implacable"
"unmerciful"

NOTICE TWO THINGS ABOUT THEIR ATTITUDES (verse 32):

1. Their **PRACTICES** continue even though they know what God says about them!

2. Their **PLEASURE** in doing these things is greater when others join them!

IS THERE ANY HOPE?

Absolutely! I Corinthians 6:9-11 makes it powerfully clear!

"Know ye not that the unrighteous shall not inherit the kingdom of God? Be not deceived: neither fornicators, nor idolaters, nor adulterers, nor effeminate, nor abusers of themselves with mankind, nor thieves, nor covetous, nor drunkards, nor revilers,

*nor extortioners, shall inherit the
kingdom of God. And such were some of
you: but ye are washed, but ye are
sanctified, but ye are justified in the
Name of the Lord Jesus, and by the
Spirit of our God."*

These are the words of HOPE –
"SUCH <u>WERE</u> SOME OF YOU"

CONDEMNATION of those who REJECT the revelation of God!
Romans 1:18-32

CONDEMNATION of those who REBUKE others while ignoring their own deeds!
Romans 2:1-16

1. Makes them <u>INEXCUSABLE</u>
   before a just God!
   Romans 2:1-3

*"Therefore thou art inexcusable, O man,
whosoever thou art that judgest: for
wherein thou judgest another, thou
condemnest thyself; for thou that
judgest doest the same things. But we
are sure that the judgment of God is
according to truth against them which*

commit such things. And thinkest thou this, O man, that judgest them which do such things, and doest the same, that thou shalt escape the judgment of God?"

The English word *"judge"* is a very common word, and in the Bible there are eight different grammatical forms of the Greek words. The word *"judge"* is found 758 times in the Bible, of which 201 times are found in the Greek New Testament. Another English word that translates the Greek words is the word "discern" or "discernment" and is used in its various forms about 25 times in the Bible, of which 9 times are found in the New Testament.

The two primary Greek words used are:
    krino – used 167 times
    diakrino – used 25 times

The noun form *krisis* is found 48 more times and refers to the decision or the verdict that is rendered.

The Lord is called *"the righteous Judge"* in II Timothy 4:8 and Hebrews 12:23 speaks of God as *"the Judge of all."* Jesus is called (Acts 10:42) *"the Judge of quick and dead"* and John 5:22 adds:

"The Father judgeth no man, but hath committed all judgment unto the Son." In John 5:27 we read: *"And hath given Him authority to execute judgment also, because He is the Son of man."*

Romans 14:10 and II Corinthians 5:10 speak of the *"judgment seat of Christ."* Psalm 50:6 says *"for God is Judge Himself."*

One of the interesting usages of the word is found in Hebrews 4:12 where the Word of God is a *"discerner of the thoughts and intents of the heart (Greek: kritikos – "critic")."*

Matthew 7:1-5 tells us not to *"judge"* lest we be judged. The reason given is that it makes us blind to our own faults. John 7:24 warns us: *"Judge not according to the appearance, but judge righteous judgment."* Obviously, we are wrong when we draw conclusions based on outward appearance. James 2:1-4 gives us an example of such bad discernment.

The warning about judging others is powerfully given to us in this same book of Romans in chapter 14. In verse 10 of that chapter we read: *"But why dost thou judge thy brother? Or why dost thou set at nought thy brother? For we shall all stand before the judgment seat of Christ."* Verse 4 says: *"Who art thou that judgest another man's servant?"*

The Apostle Paul writes in Romans 14:13: *"Let us not therefore judge one another any more: but judge this rather, that no man put a stumblingblock or an occasion to fall in his brother's way."*

In Colossians 2:16-17 we are told: *"Let no man therefore judge you in meat, or in drink, or in respect of an holyday, or of the new moon, or of the Sabbath days; which are a shadow of things to come; but the body is of Christ."* James 4:12 asks the question: *"Who art thou that judgest another?"*

There are at least three things behind the fact that rebuking others makes us inexcusable before a just God:

    (1)   Their **PRACTICES** condemn them!

Romans 2:1 says *"doest the same things."* The word *"condemnest"* is a compound word in Greek containing the verb "to judge down" (*katakrineis*). Romans 8:1 uses the same word and says that there is no condemnation to those who are believers in Jesus Christ.

John 3:16-18 says: *"For God so loved the world that He gave His only begotten Son, that whosoever believeth in Him should not perish, but have everlasting life. For God sent not His Son into the world to condemn the world; but that the world through Him might be saved. He that believeth on Him is not condemned: but he that believeth not is condemned already, because he hath not believed in the Name of the only begotten Son of God."*

   (2)   The **PRINCIPLE** of God's judgment will condemn them!

Romans 1:2 says that God's judgment is *"according to truth."* The words *"we are sure"* are from the Greek word *oidamen* meaning "know for certain."

Psalm 9:4 speaks of God sitting on His throne and *"judging right."* In verses 7-8 it declares that *"He shall judge the world in righteousness."* In Psalm 96:13

we read: *"He shall judge the world with righteousness, and the people with His truth."* Revelation 19:2 states: *"For true and righteous are His judgments."*

    (3)   The <u>POSSIBILITY</u> of escaping God's judgment is a fallacy of their own thinking!

Romans 2:3 says *"And thinkest thou this, O man..."* Psalm 50:20-21 may be the passage behind the argument of verse 3:

"Thou sittest and speakest against thy brother; thou slenderest thine own mother's son. These things hast thou done, and I kept silence; thou thoughtest that I was altogether such an one as thyself: but I will reprove thee, and set them in order before thine eyes."

    2. Makes them <u>INSENSITIVE</u> to their own need!
        Romans 2:4

"Or despisest thou the riches of His goodness and forbearance and longsuffering; not knowing that the

*goodness of God leadeth thee to
repentance?"*

To "despise" (Greek: *kataphroneis*) is to
look down on it and treat it as common.
When we rebuke others while ignoring
our own need – it makes us quite
insensitive to our own need – we are
ignoring the very fact that leads us to
repentance.

> (1)   They are <u>INDIFFERENT</u> to
> God's character!
> *"despisest thou the riches of
> His goodness and
> forbearance and
> longsuffering"*

His <u>GOODNESS</u> (Greek: *chrestotes* –
used 14 times, 7 of those times with a
companion word *christos* and translated
as *"gracious"* in I Peter 2:3 and *"kind"*
in Ephesians 4:32). It is identified in
Galatians 5:22 as the *"fruit of the
Spirit."* Ephesians 2:7 uses it: *"That in
the ages to come He might shew the
exceeding riches of His grace in His
<u>kindness</u> toward us through Christ
Jesus."* Titus 3:4 says *"But after that the
<u>kindness</u> and love of God our Savior
toward man appeared."*

His <u>FORBEARANCE</u> – from the Greek word *anoche* and used twice in Romans. In Romans 3:25, we read:

"Whom God hath set forth to be a propitiation through faith in His blood, to declare His righteousness for the remission of sins that are past, through the <u>forbearance</u> of God."

His <u>LONGSUFFERING</u> – the Greek word *makrothumias* is used as a noun 14 times and as a verb 14 times. This word also appears as a part of the *"fruit of the Spirit"* in Galatians 5:22. It is also used in Ephesians 4:2: *"With all lowliness and meekness, with <u>longsuffering</u>, forbearing one another in love."* Colossians 3:12 also uses it: *"Put on therefore, as the elect of God, holy and beloved, bowels of mercies, kindness, humbleness of mind, meekness, <u>longsuffering</u>."*

In the wonderful "love chapter" of I Corinthians 13, it is used in verse 4 of that chapter to be one of two basic definitions of God's love: *"Charity <u>suffereth long</u>, and is kind."* God's love is characterized by two attributes: longsuffering and kindness.

(2) They are <u>IGNORANT</u> of how
God's character changes our
lives!
Romans 2:4b – *"not
knowing that the goodness
of God leadeth thee to
repentance"*

3. Makes them <u>INATTENTIVE</u> to the
basis of God's judgment!
Romans 2:5-11

*"But after thy hardness and impenitent
heart treasurest up unto thyself wrath
against the day of wrath and revelation
of the righteous judgment of God; Who
will render to every man according to
his deeds: To them who by patient
continuance in well-doing seek for
glory and honor and immortality –
eternal life: But unto them that are
contentious, and do not obey the truth,
but obey unrighteousness – indignation
and wrath, tribulation and anguish,
upon every soul of man that doeth evil,
of the Jew first, and also of the Gentile;
But glory, honor, and peace, to every
man that worketh good, to the Jew first,
and also to the Gentile: For there is no
respect of persons with God."*

(1)   As to <u>REPENTANCE</u> – *v. 5*

The <u>CONDITION</u> of their hearts – *"thy hardness and impenitent heart"*

The <u>CONSEQUENCES</u> they will face – *"treasurest up unto thyself wrath against the day of wrath and revelation of the righteous judgment of God"*

(2)   As to <u>REWARD</u> – *vv. 6-10*

As to what we <u>DESIRE</u> – *vv. 7-8*

> If we seek for *"glory, honor, and immortality"* the "reward" will be *"eternal life."*
>
> If we refuse to *"obey the truth"* the "reward" will be *"indignation and wrath."*

As to what we <u>DO</u> – *vv. 9-10*

> If we *"doeth evil"* the "reward" is *"tribulation and anguish."*
>
> If we are like the *"man that worketh good"* the "reward" is *"glory, honor, and peace."*

(3)   As to <u>RESPECT</u> of persons –
*v. 11 – "For there is no
respect of persons with God"*

That important truth about our God is
found often in the Bible.

Deuteronomy 10:17 – *"For the LORD
your God is God of gods, and Lord of
lords, a great God, a mighty, and a
terrible, which regardeth not persons,
nor taketh reward."*

II Chronicles 19:7 – *"Wherefore now let
the fear of the LORD be upon you; take
heed and do it: for there is no iniquity
with the LORD our God, nor respect of
persons, nor taking of gifts."*

Acts 10:34 – *"Then Peter opened his
mouth, and said, Of a truth I perceive
that God is no respecter of persons."*

Galatians 2:6 – *"But of these who
seemed to be somewhat, (whatsoever
they were, it maketh no matter to me:
God accepteth no man's person:) for
they who seemed to be somewhat in
conference added nothing to me."*

Ephesians 6:9 – *"And, ye masters, do the same things unto them, forbearing threatening: knowing that your Master also is in heaven; neither is there respect of persons with Him."*

4. Makes them <u>IGNORANT</u> of the judgment of God!
Romans 2:12-16

"For as many as have sinned without law shall also perish without law: and as many as have sinned in the law shall be judged by the law; (For not the hearers of the law are just before God, but the doers of the law shall be justified. For when the Gentiles, which have not the law, do by nature the things contained in the law, these, having not the law, are a law unto themselves: Which shew the work of the law written in their hears, their conscience also bearing witness, and their thoughts the mean while accusing or else excusing one another;) In the day when God shall judge the secrets of men by Jesus Christ according to my gospel."

(1) As to the <u>PRACTICE</u> of the law – *vv. 12-13*

The issue of <u>ACCOUNTABILITY</u> is clear! Verse 12 speaks of those *"without law"* and those *"in the law"* as both being accountable to God.

Romans 3:19 says: *"Now we know that what things soever the law saith, it saith to them who are under the law: that every mouth may be stopped, and all the world may become guilty before God."*

The issue of <u>ACCEPTABILITY</u> before God is also clear! Verse 13 says *"For not the hearers of the law are just before God, but the doers of the law shall be justified."*

Romans 3:20 states: *"Therefore by the deeds of the law there shall no flesh be justified in His sight: for by the law is the knowledge of sin."* Verse 28 adds: *"Therefore we conclude that a man is justified by faith without the deeds of the law."*

> (2)   As to the <u>PRESENCE</u> of
>   conscience – *vv. 14-15*

The <u>EVIDENCE</u> – *"which shew the work of the law written in their hearts, their conscience bearing witness"*

Ecclesiastes 7:22 reminds us: *"For oftentimes also thine own heart knoweth that thou thyself likewise hast cursed others."*

The <u>EFFECT</u> of our conscience – *"their thoughts the mean while accusing or else excusing one another."*

In Romans 1, we are accountable to God for the revelation of His power and presence in CREATION; in Romans 2, we are accountable to God for the impact of our CONSCIENCE upon our thoughts.

>   (3)   As to the <u>PURPOSE</u> of God –
>   *v. 16*

"In the day when God shall judge the secrets of men by Jesus Christ according to my gospel."

Ecclesiastes 3:17 says: *"I said in mine heart, God shall judge the righteous and the wicked: for there is a time there for every purpose and for every work."*

In Ecclesiastes 11:9 we are reminded: *"Rejoice, O young man, in thy youth; and let thy heart cheer thee in the days of thy youth, and walk in the ways of thine heart, and in the sight of thine eyes: but know thou, that for all these things God will bring thee into judgment."*

Ecclesiastes 12:14 summarizes the arguments of its pages with these words: *"For God shall bring every work into judgment, with every secret thing, whether it be good, or whether it be evil."*

The <u>MOTIVES</u> of all humanity are known to God and will be judged by God – *"secrets of men."* In Jeremiah 17:9-10 we read: *"The heart is deceitful above all things, and desperately wicked: who can know it? I the LORD search the heart, I try the reins, even to give every man according to the fruit of his doings."*

Psalm 139:1-6 makes it abundantly clear: *"O LORD, Thou hast searched me and known me. Thou knowest my downsitting and mine uprising, Thou understandest my thought afar off.*

Thou compasseth my path and my lying down, and art acquainted with all my ways. For there is not a word in my tongue, but, lo, O LORD, Thou knowest it altogether. Thou hast beset me behind and before, and laid Thine hand upon me. Such knowledge is too wonderful for me; it is high, I cannot attain unto it."

The <u>MESSAGE</u> by which all will be judged is stated to be *"according to my gospel."*

In summary, God's judgment is:

Romans 2:2 – INFALLIBLE
Romans 2:3 – INEVITABLE
Romans 2:11 – IMPARTIAL
Romans 2:16 - INFINITE

CONDEMNATION OF THOSE WHO REJECT THE REVELATION OF GOD – Romans 1:18-32

CONDEMNATION OF THOSE WHO REBUKE OTHERS WHILE IGNORING THEIR OWN DEEDS – Romans 2:1-16

CONDEMNATION OF THOSE WHO RELY UPON THEIR OWN STANDARDS OF RIGHTEOUSNESS
Romans 2:17-3:8

The word *"Jew"* comes from the word *"Judah"* – one of the 12 tribes, and seems to have been used after the Assyrian captivity of the ten northern tribes. It is used 32 times in the Bible and 10 usages are in the Old Testament, and 8 of those in the Book of Esther.

The plural word *"Jews"* is used 257 times in the Bible of which 175 usages are in the New Testament, and 139 of those in the Gospel of John and the Book of Acts.

The word *"Hebrew"* or *"Hebrews"* is used 47 times while the word *"Israelites"* appears 19 times. The number one description of these chosen people is the *"children of Israel"* and is found 644 times in the Bible.

In the Gospel of John in particular, the term *"the Jews"* is used often to refer to the religious leaders, not the common people.

The issue in this section of Romans deals with the importance of inward commitment over mere outward performance. This will be illustrated in two areas: Jewish <u>claims</u> and Jewish <u>circumcision</u>.

Personal <u>CLAIMS</u> to be righteous are hypocritical when they are not backed up by a godly lifestyle! Romans 2:17-24

1. The <u>PRIDE</u> of such claims does not fool God!
   Romans 1:17-20

"Behold, thou art called a Jew, and restest in the law, and makest thy boast of God, and knowest His will, and approvest the things that are more excellent, being instructed out of the law; And art confident that thou thyself art a guide of the blind, a light of them which are in darkness, an instructor of the foolish, a teacher of babes, which hast the form of knowledge and of the truth in the law."

Obadiah 3-4 reminds us: *"The pride of thine heart hath deceived thee, thou that dwellest in the clefts of the rock, whose habitation is high; that saith in his heart, Who shall bring me down to the ground? Though thou exalt thyself as the eagle, and though thou set thy nest among the stars, thence will I bring thee down, saith the LORD."*

Pride indeed deceives us!

> (1) In terms of your <u>ACKNOWLEDGEMENT</u> of God and His Word! *vv. 17-18*

Their <u>RELATIONSHIP</u> to God as His chosen people was behind the pride and self-confidence they had. As verse 17 says: *"makest thy boast of God."* But, according to Psalm 135:4: *"For the LORD hath chosen Jacob unto Himself and Israel for His peculiar treasure."* It was God's decision, and was not based on personal worthiness or self-efforts.

Their <u>REGARD</u> for God's will and commands made them believe that they had special favor with God – *v. 18.*

The words *"being instructed"* - refer to what is known as "catechism." Psalm 119:98-100 says:

"Thou through Thy commandments hast made me wiser than mine enemies: for they are ever with me. I have more understanding than all my teachers: for Thy testimonies are my meditation. I understand more than the ancients, because I keep Thy precepts."

> (2) In terms of your <u>ATTITUDES</u> toward other people – *vv. 19-20*

Proverbs 26:12 says: *"Seest thou a man wise in his own conceit? There is more hope of a fool than of him."* Isaiah 5:21 adds: *"Woe unto them that are wise in their own eyes, and prudent in their own sight!"*

FOUR THINGS THAT MADE THEM FEEL SUPERIOR TO OTHERS:

1. A GUIDE to the blind!

In Matthew 23:16-22, our Lord condemned those who thought this about themselves in relation to others:

"Woe unto you, ye blind guides, which say, whosoever shall swear by the temple, it is nothing; but whosoever shall swear by the gold of the temple, he is a debtor! Ye fools and blind: for whether is greater, the gold, or the temple that sanctifieth the gold? And, whosoever shall swear by the altar, it is nothing; but whosoever sweareth by the gift that is upon it, he is guilty. Ye fools and blind: for whether is greater, the gift, or the altar that sanctifieth the gift? Whoso therefore shall swear by the altar, sweareth by it, and by all things thereon. And whoso shall swear by the temple, sweareth by it, and by him that dwelleth therein. And he that shall swear by the temple sweareth by it, and by him that dwelleth therein. And he that shall swear by heaven sweareth by the throne of God, and by Him that sitteth thereon."

Our Lord was proclaiming these matters to the religious leaders of His day — *"scribes and Pharisees."*

   2. A LIGHT to those in darkness!

   3. An INSTRUCTOR of the foolish!

John 7:47-49 records the answer of the Pharisees to the officers: *"Then answered them the Pharisees, Are ye also deceived? Have any of the rulers or of the Pharisees believed on Him? But this people who knoweth not the law are cursed."* That was the attitude of the religious leaders toward the common people.

I Corinthians 3:18 says: *"Let no man deceive himself. If any man among you seemeth to be wise in this world, let him become a fool, that he may be wise."*

    4. A TEACHER of babes!

Our Lord said a fascinating thing about this attitude of the religious leaders in Matthew 11:25: *"I thank Thee, O Father, Lord of heaven and earth, because Thou hast hid these things from the wise and prudent, and hast revealed them unto babes."*

    2. The **PROBLEM** of such claims is seen when a person's conduct does not match what he or she claims! Romans 2:21-24

(1)   The <u>REASONS</u> behind this problem – *vv. 21-23*

"Thou therefore which teachest another, teachest thou not thyself? Thou that preachest a man should not steal, dost thou steal? Thou that sayest a man should not commit adultery, does thou commit adultery? Thou that abhorrest idols, dost thou commit sacrilege? Thou that makest thy boast of the law, through breaking the law dishonorest thou God?"

They <u>DISREGARD</u> their own need for instruction – *v. 21a.*

Psalm 50:16-23 could easily have been the text that the Apostle Paul was thinking about when he spoke these words about their attitudes:

"But unto the wicked God saith, What hast thou to do to declare My statutes, or that thou shouldest take My covenant in thy mouth? Seeing thou hatest instruction, and castest My words behind thee. When thou sawest a thief, then thou consentest with him, and hast been partaker with adulterers.

Thou givest thy mouth to evil, and thy tongues frameth deceit. Thou sittest and speakest against thy brother; thou slenderest thine own mother's son. These things hast thou done, and I kept silence; thou thoughtest that I was altogether such as one as thyself: but I will reprove thee, and set them in order before thine eyes. Now consider this, ye that forget God, lest I tear you in pieces, and there be none to deliver. Whoso offereth praise glorifieth Me: and to him that ordereth his conversation aright will I shew the salvation of God."

They <u>DISOBEY</u> what God forbids! - *vv. 21-22*

     (1)   In the case of STEALING – *v. 21*

As Isaiah 56:11 says: *"Yea, they are greedy dogs which can never have enough, and they are shepherds that cannot understand: they all look to their own way, every one for his gain, from his quarter."*

Ezekiel 22:12 agrees: *"In thee have they taken gifts to shed blood; thou hast taken usury* (interest) *and increase, and thou hast greedily gained of thy neighbors by extortion, and hast forgotten Me, saith the Lord GOD."*

The indictment against stealing is strong in Amos 8:4-7:

"Hear this, O ye that swallow up the needy, even to make the poor of the land to fail, saying, When will the new moon be gone, that we may sell corn? And the Sabbath, that we may set forth wheat, making the ephah small, and the shekel great, and falsifying the balances by deceit? That we may buy the poor for silver, and the needy for a pair of shoes; yea, and sell the refuse of the wheat? The LORD hath sworn by the excellency of Jacob, Surely I will never forget any of their works."

Micah 3:11 adds: *"The heads thereof judge for reward, and the priests thereof teach for hire, and the prophets thereof divine for money: yet will they lean upon the LORD, and say, Is not the LORD among us? None evil can come upon us."*

      (2)   In the case of ADULTERY – *v. 22*

Jeremiah 9:2-3 proclaims this ugly truth: *"Oh that I had in the wilderness a lodging place of wayfaring men; that I might leave My people, and go from them! For they be all adulterers, an assembly of treacherous men. And they bend their tongues like their bow for lies: but they are not valiant for the truth upon the earth; for they proceed from evil to evil, and they know not Me, saith the LORD."*

In Ezekiel 22:8-12 we read this solemn fact:

"Thou hast despised Mine holy things, and hast profaned My Sabbaths. In thee are men that carry tales to shed blood: and in thee they eat upon the mountains: in the midst of thee they commit lewdness. In thee have they discovered their fathers' nakedness: in thee have they humbled her that was set apart for pollution. And one hath committed abomination with his neighbor's wife; and another hath lewdly defiled his daughter in law; and another in thee hath humbled his sister, his father's daughter. In thee have they taken gifts to shed blood; thou hast taken usury and increase, and thou

*hast greedily gained of thy neighbors
by extortion, and hast forgotten Me,
saith the Lord GOD."*

     **(3)   In the case of SACRILEGE!
             (rob temples)**

Jeremiah 7:8-11 comments:

*"Behold, ye trust in lying words, that
cannot profit. Will ye steal, murder,
and commit adultery, and swear
falsely, and burn incense unto Baal,
and walk after other gods whom ye
know not; And come and stand before
Me in this house, which is called by My
Name, and say, We are delivered to do
all these abominations? Is this house,
which is called by My Name, become a
den of robbers in your eyes? Behold,
even I have seen it, saith the LORD."*

They <u>DISHONOR</u> God! – v. 23

*"Thou that makest thy boast of the law,
through breaking the law dishonorest
thou God?"*

**Jeremiah 8:8-9 says: *"How do ye say,
We are wise, and the law of the LORD is
with us? Lo, certainly in vain made He***

it; the pen of the scribes is in vain. The wise men are ashamed, they are dismayed and taken: lo, they have rejected the word of the LORD; and what wisdom is in them?"

(2)   The <u>RESULT</u> of this problem
        – v. 24

"For the Name of God is blasphemed among the Gentiles through you, as it is written."

We read in II Samuel 12:14 these words from the time of King David: *"Howbeit, because by this deed thou hast given great occasion to the enemies of the LORD to blaspheme, the child also that is born unto thee shall surely die."*

David's sin of adultery with Bathsheba resulted in an *"occasion"* for the enemies of the LORD to *"blaspheme."* The result? The child died.

Isaiah 52:5 says: *"Now therefore, what have I here, saith the LORD, that My people is taken away for nought? They howl, saith the LORD; and My Name continually every day is blasphemed."*

When Jerusalem was destroyed by Babylon, the result was great suffering and sorrow by the people left in the land to handle agricultural needs and pay tribute to Babylon. The Book of Lamentations was written by Jeremiah about their suffering and in Lamentations 2:15-16 we read:

"All that pass by clap their hands at thee; they hiss and wag their head at the daughter of Jerusalem, saying, Is this the city that men call The perfection of beauty, the joy of the whole earth? All thine enemies have opened their mouth against thee: they hiss and gnash the teeth: they say, We have swallowed her up: certainly this is the day that we looked for; we have found, we have seen it."

Physical <u>CIRCUMCISION</u> does not guarantee one's position before God! *Romans 2:25-29*

"For circumcision verily profiteth, if thou keep the law: but if thou be a breaker of the law, thy circumcision is made uncircumcision. Therefore if the uncircumcision keep the righteousness of the law, shall not his uncircumcision

be counted for circumcision? And shall not uncircumcision which is by nature, if it fulfill the law, judge thee, who by the letter and circumcision dost transgress the law? For he is not a Jew, which is one outwardly; neither is that circumcision, which is outward in the flesh: But he is a Jew, which is one inwardly; and circumcision is that of the heart, in the spirit, and not in the letter; whose praise is not of men, but of God."

Jewish rabbis have taught: *"No circumcised man will be lost."* And *"Abraham stands at the gates of hell, seeing that no circumcised man is cast into it."*

1. The <u>PROFIT</u> of circumcision – *v. 25a – "For circumcision verily profiteth, if thou keep the law"*

The Apostle Paul wrote in Galatians 5:1-3 these powerful words about circumcision:

"Stand fast therefore in the liberty wherewith Christ hath made us free, and be not entangled again with the yoke of bondage. Behold, I Paul say

unto you, that if ye be circumcised, Christ shall profit you nothing. For I testify again to every man that is circumcised, that he is a debtor to do the whole law."

In Galatians 6:15 clearly states: *"For in Christ Jesus, neither circumcision availeth any thing, nor uncircumcision, but a new creature."*

    2. The <u>POWER</u> of circumcision alone to make one righteous – *vv. 26-27*

"Therefore if the uncircumcision keep the righteousness of the law, shall not his uncircumcision be counted for circumcision? And shall not uncircumcision which is by nature, if it fulfill the law, judge thee, who by the letter and circumcision dost transgress the law?"

Jeremiah 9:25-26 says of the future:

"Behold, the days come, saith the LORD, that I will punish all them which are circumcised with the uncircumcised; Egypt, and Judah, and Edom, and the children of Ammon, and Moab, and all that are in the utmost corners, that

dwell in the wilderness: for all the house of Israel are uncircumcised in the heart."

The Apostle Peter added these words in Acts 10:34-35:

"Then Peter opened his mouth, and said, Of a truth I perceive that God is no respecter of persons: But in every nation he that feareth Him, and worketh righteousness, is accepted with Him."

   3. The <u>PURPOSE</u> of circumcision – Genesis 17:9-14

"And God said unto Abraham, Thou shalt keep My covenant therefore, thou, and thy seed after thee in their generations. This is My covenant, which ye shall keep, between Me and you and thy seed after thee; Every man child among you shall be circumcised. And ye shall circumcise the flesh of your foreskin; and it shall be a token of the covenant betwixt Me and you. And he that is eight days old shall be circumcised among you, every man child in your generations, he that is born in the house, or bought with

money of any stranger, which is not of thy seed. He that is born in thy house, and he that is bought with thy money, must needs be circumcised: and My covenant shall be in your flesh for an everlasting covenant. And the uncircumcised man child whose flesh of his foreskin is not circumcised, that soul shall be cut off from his people; he hath broken My covenant."
(cf. Joshua 5:1-9)

      (1)   It was a sign of faith (on the part of the parents who believed God's promise to Abraham).

      (2)   It was a sign of separation – from sin and the world.

  4. The <u>PLACE</u> where circumcision takes place – *v. 29* – *"of the heart, in the spirit, and not in the letter"*

Deuteronomy 10:16 taught: *"Circumcise therefore the foreskin of your heart, and be no more stiffnecked."*

Deuteronomy 30:6 adds: *"And the LORD thy God will circumcise thine heart, and the heart of thy seed, to love the LORD thy God with all thine heart, and with all thy soul, that thou mayest live."*

Stephen said in Acts 7:51: *"Ye stiffnecked and uncircumcised in heart and ears, ye do always resist the Holy Ghost: as your fathers did, so do ye."*

The Apostle Paul said in Philippians 3:3: *"For we are the circumcision which worship God in the spirit, and rejoice in Christ Jesus, and have no confidence in the flesh."*

So far in looking at the CONDEMNATION of those who rely upon their own standards of righteousness (Romans 2:17-3:8), we have seen two basic issues:

Personal <u>CLAIMS</u> are hypocritical when they are not backed up by a godly lifestyle!
Romans 2:17-24

Physical <u>CIRCUMCISION</u> is insufficient to make a person righteous before God!
Romans 2:25-29

And now we come to a third issue:

Personal <u>CONDUCT</u> does not affect the nature and character of God and His judgment!
Romans 3:1-8

Notice the opening words of Romans 3:1:
"What advantage then hath the Jew?
Or what profit is there of
circumcision?"

Jews felt advantaged for three reasons:
  (1) As a son of Abraham
  (2) As one who possessed God's law
  (3) As one who was circumcised

The question deals with the credibility of God – if there is no advantage in being Jewish, and if circumcision has no value, then why did God choose the Jews out of all nations to be His special people, and why did He give them circumcision as the sign of the Abrahamic covenant?

Deuteronomy 7:6-9 speaks of God's choosing of Israel:

"For thou art an holy people unto the LORD thy God: the LORD thy God hath chosen thee to be special people unto Himself, above all people that are upon the face of the earth. The LORD did not set His love upon you, nor choose you, because ye were more in number than any people; for ye were the fewest of all people: But because the LORD loved you, and because He would keep the oath which He had sworn unto your fathers, hath the LORD brought you out with a mighty hand, and redeemed you out of the house of bondmen, from the hand of Pharaoh king of Egypt. Know therefore that the LORD thy God, He is God, the faithful God, which keepeth covenant and mercy with them that love Him and keep His commandments to a thousand generations."

Deuteronomy 26:18-19 says:

"And the LORD hath avouched thee this day to be His peculiar people, as He hath promised thee, and that thou shouldest keep all His commandments; And to make thee high above all nations which He hath made, in praise, and in name, and in honor; and that thou

mayest be an holy people unto the LORD thy God, as He hath spoken."

Psalm 135:4 adds: *"For the LORD hath chosen Jacob unto Himself, and Israel for a peculiar treasure."*

Isaiah 41:8-10 says:

"But thou, Israel, art My servant, Jacob whom I have chosen, the seed of Abraham My friend. Thou whom I have taken from the ends of the earth, and called thee from the chief men thereof, and said unto thee, Thou art My servant; I have chosen thee, and not cast thee away. Fear thou not; for I am with thee; be not dismayed; for I am thy God: I will strengthen thee; yea, I will help thee; yea, I will uphold thee with the right hand of My righteousness."

1. The great <u>PRIVILEGE</u> in being Jewish and circumcised – Romans 3:1-2

"What advantage then hath the Jew? Or what profit is there of circumcision? Much every way: chiefly, because that unto them were committed the oracles of God."

(1)   The immediate <u>RESPONSE</u> from Paul – *"much every way"* or "in every respect" Greek: *tropos* – used 13 times.

(2)   The primary <u>REASON</u> – *"chiefly"* – they have been given *"the oracles of God"* Greek: *logia* – used 4 times.

Acts 7 records Stephen's message and in verse 37 he refers to Moses, and says in verse 38: *"This is he, that was in the church* (Greek: *ekklesia* – assembly) *in the wilderness with the angel which spake to him in the Mount Sinai, and with our fathers: who received the <u>lively oracles</u> to give unto us.*

Hebrews 5:12 also refers to the *"first principles of the <u>oracles of God</u>."* I Peter 4:11 refers to one of the spiritual gifts as a speaking gift and says: *"If any man speak, let him speak as the <u>oracles of God</u>."*

Two things are involved:
    The <u>protection</u> of the Scriptures (they were placed in the Ark of the covenant)

The <u>publishing</u> of those Scriptures to the world

Deuteronomy 4:5-8 says:

"Behold, I have taught you statutes and judgments, even as the LORD my God commanded me, that ye should do so in the land whither ye go to possess it. Keep therefore and do them; for this is your wisdom and your understanding in the sight of the nations, which shall hear all these statutes, and say, Surely this great nation is a wise and understanding people. For what nation is there so great, who hath God so nigh unto them, as the LORD our God is in all things that we call upon Him for? And what nation is there so great, that hath statutes and judgments so righteous as all this law, which I set before you this day?"

No doubt about it — the great privilege in being Jewish and circumcised is the fact that God gave them His *"oracles."*

2. The difficult <u>PROBLEMS</u> that are created by this advantage — Romans 3:3-8

There are three "IF" clauses in this passage in verses 3, 5, and 7.

(1)   As to the <u>FAITHFULNESS</u> of God – 3:3-4

"For what IF some did not believe? Shall their unbelief make the faith of God without effect? God forbid: yea, let God be true, but every man a liar; as it is written, That Thou mightiest be justified in Thy sayings, and mightiest overcome when Thou art judged."

The <u>QUESTION</u>: How does the unbelief of some Jews affect the faithfulness of God?

The Greek text in verse 3 begins with the *"what if"* and grammatically uses the word *ei* followed by the indicative mood and should be translated in English by the words "IF and it is so!"

The <u>ANSWER:</u> It does not affect it one bit! A strong contrast is used here between God and humanity in terms of reliability. The quotation is from Psalm 51:4: *"Against Thee, Thee only, have I sinned, and done this evil in Thy sight: that Thou mightiest be justified when*

98

Thou speakest, and be clear whey Thou judgest."

This issue of God's reliability or faithfulness is presented powerfully in Psalm 89:30-37:

"If his children (seed of David) forsake My law, and walk not in My judgments; If they break My statutes, and keep not My commandments; Then will I visit their transgression with the rod, and their iniquity with stripes. Nevertheless My lovingkindness will I not utterly take from him, nor suffer My faithfulness to fail. My covenant will I not break, nor alter the thing that is gone out of My lips. Once have I sworn by My holiness that I will not lie unto David. His seed shall endure forever, and his throne as the sun before Me. It shall be established forever as the moon, and as a faithful witness in heaven."

    (2)   As to the <u>RIGHTEOUSNESS</u> of God — 3:5-6

"But if our unrighteousness commend the righteousness of God, what shall we say? Is God unrighteous Who taketh

vengeance? (I speak as a man) God forbid: for then how shall God judge the world?"

The <u>QUESTION</u> – Is God unrighteous by bringing judgment on those whose unrighteousness commends His righteousness?

The <u>ANSWER</u> – Of course not! How then could God judge the world?

The last part of verse 4 is a quote from Psalm 51:4 concerning David's sin – was it saying that David's sin was committed in order that God might be recognized as being *"just"?* Or, is it saying that the unbelief of some Jews actually reinforces the faithfulness of God or makes it more obvious?

But, if God is not the just Judge of the whole world, then He is not God at all! If He is unjust in any way, how can He judge the world?

Genesis 18:25 says: *"Shall not the Judge of all the earth do right?"*

Deuteronomy 32:4 adds: *"He is the Rock, His work is perfect: for all His ways are judgment: a God of truth and without iniquity, just and right is He.*"

The question is asked by one of Job's friends, Bildad the Shuhite, in Job 8:3: "*Doth God pervert judgment? Or doth the Almighty pervert justice?*" Job 34:12 is a response from Job's friend, Elihu: "*Yea, surely God will not do wickedly, neither will the Almighty pervert judgment.*"

(3)   As to the <u>JUSTICE</u> of God –
       3:7-8

"*For if the truth of God hath more abounded through my lie unto His glory; why yet am I also judged as a sinner? And not rather, (as we be slanderously reported, and as some affirm that we say,) Let us do evil, that good may come? Whose damnation is just.*"

The <u>QUESTION</u>: How can God judge me as a sinner if my sin brings Him glory?

The reasoning here goes something like this: What advantage is it to have the oracles of God entrusted to you, and your unfaithfulness to those oracles brings glory to God's faithfulness, and then God judges you as a sinner?

The <u>ANSWER</u>: Those who would argue such a point prove they deserve the judgment of God!

God's character needs nothing from us, least of all our sin to make them stand out in contrast. God rightly judges the sinner, and especially those to whom His word was given.

SO, WHAT ADVANTAGE IS IT TO BE ENTRUSTED WITH THE ORACLES OF GOD?

First – <u>IF</u> your obedience or disobedience to what it says does not affect what God has promised in it? (3:3-4)

Second – <u>IF</u> God will judge you even though your unrighteousness demonstrates His righteousness? (3:5-6)

Third – <u>IF</u> God regards you as a sinner even though your sin brings Him glory? (3:7-8)

Not all questions deserve an answer! The need to be condemned at the point that they insinuate something is wrong with the character of God. Who are we to question the God Who made us?

SO, WHAT IS THE ADVANTAGE?

The great advantage of having the law of God is that it brings the knowledge of sin and shows us our need of a Savior!

Galatians 3:24: *"Wherefore the law was our schoolmaster to bring us unto Christ, that we might be justified by faith."*

Principle #1 – CONDEMNATION
Romans 1:18-3:20

CONDEMNATION of those who REJECT the revelation of God!
Romans 1:18-32

CONDEMNATION of those who REBUKE others while ignoring their own deeds!
Romans 2:1-16

CONDEMNATION of those who RELY upon their own standards of righteousness!
Romans 2:17-3:8

CONDEMNATION of all who REFUSE to follow the way of the LORD!
Romans 3:9-20

"What then?" – used in verse 1 and now in verse 9.

The <u>PRINCIPLE</u> of condemnation is declared – v. 9 – *"they are all under sin"*

In Galatians 3 we have this stated in three ways:
> 3:10 – *"under the curse"*
> 3:22 – *"all under sin"*
> 3:23 – *"under the law"*

Romans 3:9 – *"What then? are we better than they? No, in no wise: for we have before proved both Jews and Gentiles, that they are all under sin."*

While Romans 3:1-8 shows a Jewish advantage, it does not mean that the Jews are better in terms of being justified before God!

The <u>PROOF</u> of Scripture is presented – *vv. 10-18*

"As it is written, There is none righteous, no, not one: There is none that understandeth, there is none that seeketh after God. They are all gone out of the way, they are together become unprofitable; there is none that doeth good, no, not one. Their throat is an

open sepulcher; with their tongues they have used deceit; the poison of asps is under their lips: Whose mouth is full of cursing and bitterness: Their feet are swift to shed blood: Destruction and misery are in their ways: And the way of peace have thy not known: There is no fear of God before their eyes."

The question of "Who is righteous?" is answered four times in the above passage by the simple word *"none"* and two times by the words *"no, not one."*

> 1. Our <u>CHARACTER</u> does not reflect the righteousness of God! - v. 10

"As it is written" – this phrase appears many times in the Dead Sea Scrolls but is only used with canonical Scriptures.

"As it is written, There is none righteous, no, not one."

Isaiah 64:6 says: *"But we are all as an unclean thing, and all our righteousnesses are as filthy rags; and we all do fade as a leaf; and our iniquities, like the wind, have taken us away."*

Romans 10:3 states: *"For they being ignorant of God's righteousness, and going about to establish their own righteousness, have not submitted themselves unto the righteousness of God."*

2. Our <u>CONFORMITY</u> to God's will and Word is lacking! – vv. 11-12a

"There is none that understandeth, there is none that seeketh after God. They are all gone out of the way, they are together become unprofitable"

I Corinthians 2:14 – *"But the natural man receiveth not the things of the Spirit of God: for they are foolishness unto him: neither can he know them, because they are spiritually discerned."*

3. Our <u>CAPACITY</u> for good is non-existent! – *v. 12b* – *"there is none that doeth good, no, not one"*

We read in Psalm 14:1-3:

"The fool hath said in his heart, There is no God. They are corrupt, they have done abominable works, there is none that doeth good. The LORD looked

down from heaven upon the children of men, to see if there were any that did understand, and seek God. They are all gone aside, they are all together become filthy: there is none that doeth good, no, not one."

    4. Our <u>CONVERSATION</u> is uncontrolled! – *vv. 13-14*

"Their throat is an open sepulcher; with their tongues they have used deceit; the poison of asps is under their lips"

Psalm 5:9 says: *"For there is no faithfulness in their mouth; their inward part is very wickedness; their throat is an open sepulcher; they flatter with their tongue"*

Psalm 10:7 adds: *"His mouth is full of cursing and deceit and fraud: under his tongue is mischief and vanity"*

Psalm 140:3 teaches: *"They have sharpened their tongues like a serpent; adders' poison is under their lips"*

    5. Our <u>CONDUCT</u> is destructive! vv. 15-16

"Their feet are swift to shed blood: Destruction and misery are in their ways."

Perhaps the Apostle Paul was thinking about this passage in Isaiah 59:1-7:

"Behold, the LORD's hand is not shortened, that it cannot save; neither His ear heavy, that it cannot hear: But your iniquities have separated between you and your God, and your sins have hid His face from you, that He will not hear. For your hands are defiled with blood, and your fingers with iniquity; your lips have spoken lies, your tongue hath muttered perverseness. None calleth for justice, nor any pleadeth for truth: they trust in vanity, and speak lies; they conceive mischief, and bring forth iniquity. They hatch cockatrice's eggs, and weave the spider's web; he that eateth of their eggs dieth, and that which is crushed breaketh out into a viper. Their webs shall not become garments, neither shall they cover themselves with their works: their works are works of iniquity, and the act of violence is in their hands. Their feet run to evil, and they make haste to shed innocent blood: their thoughts are

thoughts of iniquity; wasting and destruction are in their paths."

6. Our <u>CONTENTMENT</u> is totally lacking! v. 17 – *"and the way of peace have they not known"*

It was Isaiah 59:8 that said: *"The way of peace they know not; and there is no judgment in their goings: they have made them crooked paths: whosoever goeth therein shall not know peace."*

Jeremiah 6:14 says: *"They have healed also the hurt of the daughter of My people slightly, saying, Peace, peace; when there is no peace."*

Jeremiah 8:11 repeats the above indictment: *"For they have healed the hurt of the daughter of My people slightly, saying, Peace, peace; when there is no peace."*

7. Our <u>COMMITMENT</u> to God is missing! – *v. 18* – *"There is no fear of God before their eyes"*

Psalm 36:1 says: *"The transgression of the wicked saith within my heart, that there is no fear of God before his eyes."*

Proverbs 16:6 says: *"By mercy and truth iniquity is purged: and by the fear of the LORD, men depart from evil."*

The <u>PURPOSE</u> of the law is proclaimed – *vv. 19-20*

"Now we know that what things soever the law saith, it saith to them who are under the law: that every mouth may be stopped, and all the world may become guilty before God. Therefore by the deeds of the law there shall no flesh be justified in His sight: for by the law is the knowledge of sin."

At least three things in the above passage make it clear as to the purpose of the law.

1. It <u>DECLARES</u> the guilt of every person!

2. It <u>DEMONSTRATES</u> the impossibility of salvation by works!

3. It <u>DESCRIBES</u> the nature of sin!

A quick review of the principle of <u>CONDEMNATION</u> in Romans 1:18-3:20

clearly shows that no one escapes it regardless of their background, knowledge, culture, or advantages.

1:18-32 – light of CREATION
2:1-16 – light of CONSCIENCE
2:17-3:8 – light of COMMANDMENTS
3:9-18 – light of CONDUCT

The words of our Lord Yeshua in John 3:16-18 are powerful:

"For God so loved the world that He gave His only begotten Son, that whosoever believeth in Him should not perish, but have everlasting life. For God sent not His Son into the world to condemn the world; but that the world through Him might be saved. He that believeth on Him is not condemned: but he that believeth not is condemned already, because he hath no believed in the Name of the only begotten Son of God."

Yes, the whole world stands condemned before God and in need of a Savior!

Chapter 3
JUSTIFICATION
Romans 3:21-5:21

The first principle of the righteousness of God is that of CONDEMNATION which the argument of Romans was in verses 1:18-3:20. We come now to the second principle – JUSTIFICATION which is found in Romans 3:21 to 5:21.

JUSTIFICATION is <u>DEPENDENT</u> upon the work of Jesus Christ! Romans 3:21-31

Romans 3:21 begins with the words *"But now..."* These are words of great contrast! In contrast with the principle of condemnation and our inability to be righteous before God based on our depravity and sin, we now come to the wonderful and essential truth of the gospel of our Lord Jesus Christ – what He has done for us is the ground upon which true salvation and justification is based.

The <u>NEED</u> for the righteousness of God – vv. 21-23

"But now the righteousness of God without the law is manifested, being witnessed by the law and the prophets; Even the righteousness of God which is by faith of Jesus Christ unto all and upon all them that believe: for there is no difference: For all have sinned, and come short of the glory of God."

The *"righteousness of God"* means three things:
God is righteous!
God demands righteousness!
God provides righteousness!

1. It is <u>REVEALED</u> by the law and prophets – *v. 21* – *"being witnessed by the law and the prophets"*

The law reveals it through the sacrificial system of the Mosaic Law. The prophets reveal it by their prophecies of the Messiah.

2. It is <u>RECEIVED</u> by all who believe – v. 22 – *"unto all and upon all them that believe: for there is no difference"*

Some Greek manuscripts leave out the words *"upon all."* But, we believe the words belong in the text. The words *"unto all"* describe the <u>EXTENT</u> of it, and the words *"upon all"* deal with the <u>EFFECT</u> of it.

There is no distinction made in the family of God – *"no difference."* All are equal in God's eyes, based on faith in the Lord Yeshua and His work of salvation.

3. It is <u>REQUIRED</u> because all have sinned – v. 23

The Greek word translated *"sinned"* is the word *hamartia* which refers to shooting an arrow at a target and missing the central mark. We all have sinned by missing the mark of the *"glory of God."* We do not become sinners by sinning; we sin because we already are sinners – born in sin.

In Psalm 51:5, David said: *"Behold I was shapen in iniquity, and in sin did my mother conceive me."*

The <u>NECESSITY</u> of the righteousness of God Romans 3:24-26

"Being justified freely by His grace through the redemption that is in Christ Jesus: whom God hath set forth to be a propitiation through faith in His blood, to declare His righteousness for the remission of sins that are past, through the forbearance of God; To declare, I say, at this time His righteousness: that He might be just, and the Justifier of him which believeth in Jesus."

1. It requires a <u>PURCHASE</u> – v. 24 *"through the redemption that is in Christ Jesus"*

The word *"redemption"* is from the Greek word *apolutrosis* which is used 10 times in the New Testament. Ephesians 1:7 says: *"In Whom we have <u>redemption</u> through His blood, the forgiveness of sins, according to the riches of His grace."* Colossians 1:14 adds: *"In Whom we have redemption through His blood, even the forgiveness of sins."*

Hebrews 9:15 states: *"and for this cause He is the Mediator of the New Testament, that by means of death, for the <u>redemption</u> of the transgressions that were under the first testament,* *they which are called might receive the promise of eternal inheritance."*

When Romans 3:24 says *"justified freely"* it sounds like it is "without cost." The Greek word translated *"freely"* is *dorean* which is used 9 times in the New Testament. One fascinating usage is found in John 15:25 where we read: *"But this cometh to pass, that the word might be fulfilled that is written in their law, They hated me <u>without a cause</u>."*

It is possible that the point behind the usage of *dorean* in this passage is that there is no cause in us that brought us salvation and the righteousness of God!

    2. It requires a <u>PROPITIATION</u> –
       v. 25a – *"a propitiation through faith in His blood"*

The Greek word that is translated by the English word *"propitiation"* is the word *hilasteerion* – "mercy seat." It is also used in I John 2:2: *"And He is the propitiation for our sins: and not for ours only, but also for the sins of the whole world."* A form of the word in Greek *hilasmos* is also found in I John 4:9-10:

"In this was manifested the love of God toward us, because that God sent His only begotten Son into the world, that we might live through Him. Herein is love, not that we loved God, but that He loved us, and sent His Son to be the propitiation for our sins."

The word *"propitiation"* (referring to the Mercy Seat – the gold lid of the Ark of the Covenant) refers to the satisfaction of the wrath of God against our sin! When the blood of one of two goats was taken into the Holy of Holies by the High Priest (and only him!) on the Day of Atonement (Yom Kippur), the blood was put on the lid of the Ark (called the Mercy Seat). The wrath of God exercised by the two Cherubim (angels designed out of gold on the lid of the Ark) was appeased or satisfied when the blood of the goat was placed there.

Another goat (called the *"Azazel")* was released while still alive – into the wilderness and no one was to go after it. This happened after the High Priest confessed the sins of his people while holding on to the live goat – it pictured the removal of our sins by God's grace and mercy! This was pictured and symbolized by our Lord (according to Hebrews 13:12) when the Bible says: *"Wherefore Jesus also, that He might sanctify the people with His own blood, suffered without* (outside) *the gate."*

It is interesting to read the translation of the New American Standard Bible in Romans 3:25: *"as a propitiation in His blood through faith"* – but – the actual text reads: *"faith in His blood"* – that is very important because it is His blood, NOT our faith that provides propitiation.

    3. It requires <u>PATIENCE</u> – vv. 25c-26 *"to declare His righteousness for the remission of sins that are past, through the forbearance of God; To declare, I say, at this time His righteousness: that He might be just, and the Justifier of him which believeth in Jesus."*

Romans 2:4 spoke of God's *"forbearance"* in His *"goodness"* that leads us *"to repentance."*

The word *"remission"* in verse 25 as used in the King James Version of the Bible does not reflect the precise meaning of the Greek term *paresin* – it means "passed over" or "overlooked."

It is found in Acts 17:30-31:
"And the times of this ignorance God <u>winked at</u> (overlooked); but now commandeth all men everywhere to repent: Because He hath appointed a day, in the which He will judge the world in righteousness by that Man Whom He hath ordained; whereof He hath given assurance unto all men, in that He hath raised Him from the dead."

The <u>NATURE</u> of the righteousness of God – Romans 3:27-31

1. It <u>EXCLUDES</u> boasting – *v. 27*

"Where is boasting then? It is excluded. By what law? Of works? Nay: but by the law of faith."

I Corinthians 1:29 says: *"That no flesh should glory in His presence."*

2. It <u>ELIMINATES</u> righteousness by law – v. 28

"Therefore we conclude that a man is justified by faith without the deeds of the law." The word *"conclude"* is from the Greek word *logizomai* which is used 42 times in the New Testament, 19 of which are in Romans and 11 in chapter 4!

3. It <u>ENABLES</u> God to be God of both Jews and Gentiles – vv. 29-30

"Is He the God of the Jews only? Is He not also of the Gentiles? Yes, of the Gentiles also: Seeing it is one God, which shall justify the circumcision by faith, and uncircumcision through faith."

Paul's discussion of this issue is very clear in Ephesians 2:11-18:

"Wherefore remember, that ye being in time past Gentiles in the flesh, who are called Uncircumcision by that which is called the Circumcision in the flesh made by hands; That at that time ye were without Christ, being aliens from the commonwealth of Israel, and strangers from the covenants of promise, having no hope, and without God is the world: But now in Christ

Jesus ye who sometimes were far off are made nigh by the blood of Christ. For He is our peace, Who hath made both one, and hath broken down the middle wall of partition between us; Having abolished in His flesh the enmity, even the law of commandments contained in ordinances; for to make in Himself of twain one new man, so making peace; And that He might reconcile both unto God in one body by the cross, having slain the enmity thereby: And came and preached peace to you which were afar off, and to them that were nigh. For through Him we both have access by one Spirit unto the Father."

The ones who were *"afar off"* are the Gentiles; the ones who were *"nigh"* are the Jewish people. This was made quite clear in the Temple itself as there was a wall between them, and the Jewish people were closer to the Holy Place than were the Gentiles. The word *"both"* is referring to Jew and Gentile – they are now BOTH in one body!

> 4. It <u>ESTABLISHES</u> the law – v. 31 – *"Do we then make void the law through faith? God forbid: yea, we establish the law."*

HOW DOES IT DO THAT?

    (1)   **By paying the penalty of our sin which is death!**

    (2)   **By leading us to the Messiah! Galatians 3:24**

    (3)   **By making it possible for believers to fulfill the law!**

Romans 8:3-4 says: *"For what the law could not do, in that it was weak through the flesh, God sending His own Son in the likeness of sinful flesh, and for sin, condemned sin in the flesh: That the righteousness of the law might be fulfilled in us, who walk not after the flesh, but after the Spirit."*

THE QUESTION IS: HOW CAN A SINFUL PERSON BE RIGHTEOUS BEFORE A HOLY GOD?

JUSTIFICATION is the act of God by which He declares a sinful person righteous because of his dependence upon the Person and work of His Son, the Messiah of Israel – the great Redeemer!

JUSTIFICATION is not only DEPENDENT upon the Person and work of Jesus Christ, it is also...

DESCRIBED in the life of Abraham himself –Romans 4:1-25

Romans 4:1 begins: *"What shall we say then?"* Also found in 6:1; 7:7; 9:14, 20; In Romans 3:5 we read *"What shall we say?* In Romans 11:1, 11 – *"I say then"* – The words *"But I say"* in Romans 10:18-19. One of the fascinating things about the structure of Romans in the Greek language is the usage of the word *"then"* - 42 times and the word *"therefore"* which is found 27 times.

In the Textus Receptus (early Greek manuscript upon which the King James English translation was based) chapter four of Romans is one long paragraph. The most natural break is at verse 16 with the word *"Therefore."*

The key word is *"counted"* or *"reckoned"* or *"imputed."* The Greek word *logizomai* appears 42 times in the New Testament but 19 of those usages are in Romans – with 11 usages in

Romans 4. The word means "to count" or "to calculate" – a mathematical term. God has calculated the number of our sins versus the finished work of His Son, our Lord Jesus Christ, and has decided that His death equals our sins as an adequate and sufficient payment!

In the beautiful song – "IT IS WELL WITH MY SOUL," one of the stanzas reads: *"My sin, O the bliss of this glorious thought: My sin, not in part, but the whole – is nailed to the cross, and I bear it no more – Praise the Lord, praise the Lord, O my soul!"*

It is <u>REWARDED</u> without works! Romans 4:1-8

"What shall we say then that Abraham our father, as pertaining to the flesh, hath found? For if Abraham were justified by works, he hath whereof to glory; but not before God. For what saith the scripture? Abraham believed God, and it was counted unto him for righteousness. Not to him that worketh is the reward not reckoned of grace, but of debt. But to him that worketh not, but believeth on Him that justifieth the ungodly, his faith is counted for

righteousness. Even as David also describeth the blessedness of the man, unto whom God imputeth righteousness without works, saying, Blessed are they whose iniquities are forgiven, and whose sins are covered. Blessed is the man to whom the Lord will not impute sin."

1. The <u>PROBLEM</u> of works

In James 2:21-24 we have a commentary on this chapter in Romans:

"Was not Abraham our father justified by works, when he had offered Isaac his son upon the altar? Seest thou how faith wrought with his works and by works was faith made perfect? And the scripture was fulfilled which saith, Abraham believed God, and it was imputed unto him for righteousness: and he was called the Friend of God. Ye see then how that by works a man is justified, and not by faith alone."

In Romans 4:1 we have the phrase *"pertaining to the flesh"* – Is it referring to Abraham as our physical ancestor, or is it speaking about his works? The parallel statement in verse 2, *"justified by works,"* is proof that the phrase is referring to his works.

2. The <u>PROOF</u> of Scripture

Romans 4:3 quotes Genesis 15:6 when it says *"Abraham believed God, and it was counted unto him for righteousness."*

In Galatians 3:6-9 we read:
"Even as Abraham believed God, and it was accounted to him for righteousness. Know ye therefore that they which are of faith, the same are the children of Abraham. And the scripture, foreseeing that God would justify the heathen through faith, preached before the gospel unto Abraham, saying, In thee shall all nations be blessed. So then they which be of faith are blessed with faithful Abraham."

3. The <u>PRINCIPLE</u> involved

Romans 4:4-5 – *"Now to him that worketh is the reward not reckoned of grace, but of debt. But to him that worketh not, but believeth on Him that justifieth the ungodly, his faith is counted for righteousness."*

NOTE: In the footnotes of the Confraternity edition of the New Testament by the Roman Catholic Church, we read this remarkable statement:

"We should distinguish between justification and salvation. We cannot be saved without good works, and accordingly, St. Paul repeatedly insists on the necessity of avoiding sin and doing good. But justification, that is the infusion of sanctifying grace, cannot be merited by us; it is an entirely gratuitous gift of God. The justification of which St. Paul here speaks is the infusion of sanctifying grace which alone renders a person supernaturally pleasing in the sight of God. This cannot be obtained either by the observance of the law or by any other work of unregenerate man."

Interestingly, Cardinal Eugene Tisserant, President of the Pontifical Biblical Commission, congratulated the American Committee for their splendid translation!

4. The <u>PROMISE</u> of God's blessing

Romans 4:6-8 – *"Even as David also describeth the blessedness of the man, unto whom God imputeth righteousness without works, saying, Blessed are they whose iniquities are forgiven, and whose sins are covered. Blessed is the man to whom the Lord will not impute sin."*

The words *"Even as"* are from the Greek word *kathaper* which is a stronger word than *kathos* (used often) – it means "exactly as" – in total agreement!

Psalm 32:1-2 says: *"Blessed is he whose transgression is forgiven, whose sin is covered. Blessed is the man unto whom the LORD imputeth not iniquity, and in whose spirit there is no guile."*

> **(1)** As to <u>RIGHTEOUSNESS</u> – v. 6 - *"the blessedness of the man"*
>
> **(2)** As to <u>REMOVAL</u> – v. 7 *"Blessed are they"*
>
> **(3)** As to <u>REMEMBRANCE</u> – v. 8 – *"Blessed is the man"*

It is <u>RECEIVED</u> without circumcision!
Romans 4:9-12

"Cometh this blessedness then upon the circumcision only, or upon the uncircumcision also? For we say that faith was reckoned to Abraham for righteousness. How was it then reckoned? When he was in circumcision, or in uncircumcision? Not in circumcision, but in uncircumcision. And he received the sign of circumcision, a seal of the righteousness of the faith which he had yet being uncircumcised: that he might be the father of all them that believe, though they be not circumcised; that righteousness might be imputed unto them also: And the father of circumcision to them who are not of the circumcision only, but who also walk in the steps of that faith of our father Abraham, which he had being yet uncircumcised."

1. The <u>EXAMPLE</u> of Abraham

Abraham was not circumcised when he *"believed God."* Here are the facts:

Genesis 12:4 – 75 years old when he left Haran to go to Canaan.

Genesis 15:6 – Abraham believed God!

Genesis 17:26 – he was circumcised along with his son, Ishmael, at age 99!

Genesis 21:5 – he was 100 years old when Isaac was born – a year after his circumcision.

    2. The <u>EVIDENCE</u> of circumcision – *v. 11a – "the sign – a seal of the righteousness of faith"*

Circumcision is the result, NOT the cause!

    3. The <u>EXPLANATION</u> of these circumstances – *v. 11b – "that he might be the father of all them that believe"*

The Jewish Talmud says *"Ye shall not eat of the Passover unless the seal of Abraham be in your flesh."*

Circumcision was considered so powerful that if an Israelite who practiced idolatry was going to hell

(Gehenna), his circumcision had to be removed first!

It was <u>REALIZED</u> without the law! Romans 4:13-15

"For the promise, that he should be the heir of the world, was not to Abraham, or to his seed, through the law, but through the righteousness of faith. For if they which are of the law be heirs, faith is made void, and the promise made of none effect: Because the law worketh wrath: for where no law is, there is no transgression."

> 1. Because the <u>PROMISE</u> came previously – *v. 13*

Galatians 3:16-18 says: *"Now to Abraham and his seed were the promises made. He saith not, And to seeds, as of many; but as of one, and to thy seed, which is Christ. And this I say, that the covenant, that was confirmed before of God in Christ, the law, which was four hundred and thirty years after, cannot disannul, that it should make the promise of none effect. For if the inheritance be of the law, it is no more of promise: but God gave it to Abraham by promise."*

The big issue? WHAT IS ABRAHAM'S SEED?

(1)   Primarily – ISAAC

Genesis 17:18-21 – *"And Abraham said unto God, O that Ishmael might live before thee! And God said, Sarah thy wife shall bear a son indeed; and thou shalt call his name Isaac: and I will establish My covenant with him for an everlasting covenant, and with his seed after him. And as for Ishmael, I have heard thee: Behold, I have blessed him, and will make him fruitful, and will multiply him exceedingly; twelve princes shall he beget, and I will make him a great nation. But My covenant will I establish with Isaac, which Sarah shall bear unto thee at this set time in the next year."*

(2)   Racially - JEWS

Romans 2:29 says: *"But he is a Jew, which is one inwardly; and circumcision is that of the heart, in the*

*spirit, and not in the letter; whose
praise is not of men, but of God."*

    (3)   Preeminently – MESSIAH

Galatians 3:16 – *"Now to Abraham and
his seed were the promises made. He
saith not, And to seeds, as of many; but
as of one, and to thy seed, which is
Christ* (Messiah)."*

    (4)   Ultimately – ALL BELIEVERS

Galatians 3:29 – *"And if ye be Christ's,
then are ye Abraham's seed, and heirs
according to the promise."*

  **2. Because of the <u>PROBLEMS</u> that
would be created – *vv. 14-15***

    **(1)   Faith would be worthless (no
value)! – v. 14a – *"faith is
made void"***

    **(2)   Promise would be ineffective
– v. 14b – *"the promise made
of none effect"***

    **(3)   Law would not achieve its
purpose – v. 15 – *"the law
worketh wrath: for where
no law is, there is no
transgression."***

JUSTIFICATION IS <u>DEPENDENT</u> UPON THE WORK OF JESUS CHRIST – Romans 3:21-31

JUSTIFICATION IS <u>DESCRIBED</u> IN THE LIFE OF ABRAHAM - Romans 4:1-25

It is <u>REWARDED</u> without works! Romans 4:1-8

It is <u>RECEIVED</u> without circumcision! Romans 4:9-12

It is <u>REALIZED</u> without the law! Romans 4:13-15

It has <u>RESULTED</u> through faith! Romans 4:16-25

Romans 4:16 begins: *"Therefore it is of faith, that it might be by grace"*

1. The <u>REASON</u>

Romans 4:16-18: *"Therefore it is of faith, that it might be by grace; to the end the*

*promise might be sure to all the seed;
not to that only which is of the law, but
to that also which is of the faith of
Abraham; who is the father of us all, (As
it is written, I have made thee a father
of many nations,) before Him Whom he
believed, even God, Who quickeneth the
dead and calleth those things which be
not as though they were. Who against
hope believed in hope, that he might
become the father of many nations,
according to that which was spoken, So
shall thy seed be."*

If it was based on our works, then the
promise would not be sure! It was based
on the following three things:

      (1)   Based on God's <u>PROVISION</u>
             "by grace"

Grace guarantees what works can never
do! Ephesians 2:7 says: *"That in the
ages to come He might shew the
exceeding riches of His grace in His
kindness toward us through Christ
Jesus."*

      (2)   Based on God's <u>POWER</u>

His power is seen in the <u>resurrection</u> – *"even God, Who quickeneth the dead."*

His power is seen in <u>creation</u> – *"and calleth those things which be not as though they were."*

> **(3)** **Based on God's <u>PROMISE</u>** *"who against hope believed in hope"*

Promises depend on the character and reliability of the One Who made them – it demands only faith as a response!

Hebrews 6:13 – *"For when God made promise to Abraham, because He could swear by no greater, He sware by Himself, saying, Surely blessing I will bless thee, and multiplying I will multiply thee. And so, after he had patiently endured, he obtained the promise. For men verily swear by the greater: and an oath for confirmation is to them an end of all strife. Wherein God, willing more abundantly to shew unto the heirs of promise the immutability of His counsel, confirmed it by an oath: That by two immutable things, in which it was impossible for God to lie, we might have a strong consolation, who have fled for refuge to lay hold upon the hope set before us: Which hope we have as an anchor of the soul, both sure and stedfast, and which entereth into that within the veil; Whither the Forerunner is for us entered, even Jesus, made a High Priest forever after the order of Melchizedec."*

Verse 18 says: *"according to that which was spoken"* – God's Word is the issue! Hebrews 11:11 says of Sarah: *"because she judged Him faithful Who had promised."*

2. The <u>RESPONSE</u> of Abraham to the obstacles he faced.

Romans 4:19-21 – *"And being not weak in faith, he considered not his own body now dead, when he was about an hundred years old, neither yet the deadness of Sarah's womb: He staggered not at the promise of God through unbelief but was strong in faith, giving glory to God; And being fully persuaded that, what He had promised, He was able also to perform."*

(1) The <u>CONDITION</u> of his body and his wife's womb — v. 19
"being not weak in faith"

Genesis 17:15-21 tells us:

"And God said unto Abraham, As for Sarai thy wife, thou shalt not call her name Sarai, but Sarah shall her name be. And I will bless her, and give thee a son also of her: yea, I will bless her, and she shall be a mother of nations; kings of people shall be of her. Then Abraham fell upon his face, and laughed, and said in his heart, Shall a child be born unto him that is an hundred years old? And shall Sarah, that is ninety years old, bear? And Abraham said unto God, O that Ishmael might live before thee! And God said, Sarah thy wife shall bear thee a son indeed; and thou shalt call his name Isaac: and I will establish My covenant with him for an everlasting covenant, and with his seed after him. And as for Ishmael, I have heard thee: Behold, I have blessed him, and will make him fruitful, and will multiply him exceedingly; twelve princes shall he beget, and I will make him a great nation. But My covenant will I

establish with Isaac, which Sarah shall bear unto thee at this set time in the next year."

Genesis 18:11-14 adds:

"Now Abraham and Sarah were old and well stricken in age; and it ceased to be with Sarah after the manner of women. Therefore Sarah laughed within herself, saying, After I am waxen old shall I have pleasure, my lord being old also? And the LORD said unto Abraham, Wherefore did Sarah laugh, saying, Shall I of a surety bear a child, which am old? Is anything too hard for the LORD? At the time appointed I will return unto thee, according to the time of life, and Sarah shall have a son."

The story is indeed amazing, and it is critical to the argument about how a sinful person can become righteous before a holy God!

> (2)   His <u>CONFIDENCE</u> in God's promise never wavered! – vv. 20-21

"He staggered not at the promise of God through unbelief; but was strong in

faith, giving glory to God; And being fully persuaded that, what He had promised, He was able to perform."

His confidence was seen in his <u>ACCEPTANCE</u> of what God said – *"staggered not at the promise of God through unbelief"* – It was the Apostle Paul in Acts 27:25 who manifested the same kind of confidence as Abraham when he said to the sailors fighting a vicious storm: *"Wherefore, sirs, be of good cheer: for I believe God, that it shall be even as it was told me."*

His confidence was also seen in his <u>ATTITUDE</u> – *"giving glory to God"* – Daniel's three friends, Shadrach, Meshach, and Abed-nego, said to King Nebuchadnezzar (Daniel 3:17-18): *"If it be so, our God Whom we serve is able to deliver us from the burning fiery furnace, and He will deliver us out of thine hand, O king. But if not, be it known unto thee, O king, that we will not serve thy gods, nor worship the golden image which thou hast set up.*

We also observe the confidence of Abraham in his <u>ASSURANCE</u> – *"being fully persuaded."*

3. The <u>RESULTS</u> – vv. 22-25

"And therefore it was imputed to him for righteousness. Now it was not written for his sake alone, that it was imputed to him; But for us also, to whom it shall be imputed, if we believe on Him that raised up Jesus our Lord from the dead; Who was delivered for our offences, and was raised again for our justification."

The results for Abraham are clearly stated in verse 22 – *"imputed to him for righteousness."* Faith does not merit salvation, but simply accepts it from God's gracious hand!

The results for all who believe are stated in the last three verses of Romans 4. The reason we can be declared righteous as Abraham was is twofold:

(1)　Jesus Christ was *"delivered for our offences"*

(2)　Jesus Christ was *"raised again for our justification"*

The death and resurrection of our Lord
has made it all possible! Hallelujah!

JUSTIFICATION is...

<u>DEPENDENT</u> upon the work of Jesus Christ – 3:21-31

<u>DESCRIBED</u> in the life of Abraham – 4:1-25

<u>DECLARED</u> IN THE REWARDS OF OUR SALVATION!
Romans 5:1-11

Those "REWARDS" include at least two
major issues:

A right <u>RELATIONSHIP</u> with God
5:1-5

A wonderful <u>REDEMPTION</u>
5:6-11

In Romans 5:1 it begins with the word *"Therefore"* – it assumes the point has been established by the discussion about Abraham in chapter 4.

A right <u>RELATIONSHIP</u> with God!
Romans 5:1-5

"Therefore being justified by faith, we have peace with God through our Lord Jesus Christ: By Whom also we have access by faith into this grace wherein we stand, and rejoice in hope of the glory of God. And not only so, but we glory in tribulations also: knowing that tribulation worketh patience; and patience, experience; and experience, hope: And hope maketh not ashamed; because the love of God is shed abroad in our hearts by the Holy Ghost which is given unto us."

1. The <u>GROUND</u> upon which our relationship with God is based! v. 1a – *"being justified by faith"*

The words *"being justified"* are aorist passive in Greek and refer to the moment of our salvation.

JUSTIFICATION can be described as having five major facts:

The <u>SOURCE</u> is God, not man! Romans 8:33 says: *"It is God that justifieth"*

The <u>REASON</u> is God's grace, not our merit or worthiness! Romans 3:24 – *"Being justified freely by His grace"*

The <u>MEANS</u> is faith, not our works! Romans 3:28 – *"Therefore we conclude that a man is justified by faith without the deeds of the law"*

The <u>PRICE</u> is the blood of Jesus Christ, not our performance! Romans 5:9 – *"being now justified by His blood"*

The <u>RESULTS</u> are *"peace with God"* and *"saved from wrath"* Romans 5:1 – *"we have peace with God"* Romans 5:9 – *"saved from wrath through Him"*

The words of Romans 5:1 that say *"we have"* is a present tense in Greek – it refers to a constant and continuous possession.

2. The <u>GUARANTEE</u> of our position in Jesus Christ – v. 2a – *"By Whom also we have access by*

faith into this grace wherein we stand" – We are not saved by God's grace and then preserved by human effort!

The Greek word for *"access"* is *"prosagogen"* and is found seven times in the New Testament (three times as a noun, and four times as a verb).

Access to God was an awesome thing in the Old Testament under the Mosaic Law.

In Exodus 19:12-13 we read: *"And thou shalt set bounds unto the people round about, saying, Take heed to yourselves, that ye go not up into the mount, or touch the border of it: whosoever toucheth the mount shall be surely put to death: There shall not an hand touch it, but he shall surely be stoned, or shot through; whether it be beast or man, it shall not live: when the trumpet soundeth long, they shall come up to the mount."*

In Exodus 19:21 the LORD said to Moses: *"Go down, charge the people, lest they break through unto the LORD to gaze, and many of them perish."* Exodus

20:21 we read: *"And the people stood afar off, and Moses drew near unto the thick darkness where God was."*

3. The <u>GIVING</u> of hope for the future *"and rejoice in <u>hope</u> of the glory of God"*

Colossians 1:27 reads: *"To whom God would make known what is the riches of the glory of this mystery among the Gentiles; which is Christ in you, the <u>hope</u> of glory."*

Romans 8:18 says: *"For I reckon that the sufferings of this present time are not worthy to be compared with the <u>glory</u> which shall be revealed in us."*

Romans 9:23 adds: *"And that He might make known the riches of His <u>glory</u> on the vessels of mercy, which he had afore prepared unto <u>glory</u>."*

II Corinthians 4:17-18: *"For our light affliction, which is but for a moment, worketh for us a far more exceeding and eternal weight of <u>glory</u>; While we look not at the things which are seen: for the things which are seen are* *temporal; but the things which are not seen are eternal."*

Titus 2:13: *"Looking for that blessed <u>hope</u> and the glorious appearing of our great God and Savior Jesus Christ."*

I Peter 4:12-13: *"Beloved, think it not strange concerning the fiery trial which is to try you, as though some strange thing happened unto you: But rejoice, inasmuch as ye are partakers of Christ's sufferings; that, when His <u>glory</u> shall be revealed, ye may be glad also with exceeding joy."*

I Peter 5:10: *"But the God of all grace, Who hath called us unto His eternal <u>glory</u> by Christ Jesus, after that ye have suffered awhile, make you perfect, stablish, strengthen, settle you."*

I John 3:1-3: *"Behold, what manner of love the Father hath bestowed upon us, that we should be called the sons of God: therefore the world knoweth us not, because it knew Him not. Beloved, now are we the sons of God, and it doth not yet appear what we shall be: but we know that, when He shall appear, we shall be like Him, for we shall see Him* *as He is. And every man that hath this* *hope* *in him purifieth himself, even as He is pure. "*

Charles H. Gabriel wrote this song:
When all my labors and trials are o'er, and I am safe on that beautiful shore; Just to be near the dear Lord I adore, will through the ages be *glory* *for me. "*

CHORUS: *O that will be* *glory* *for me, glory* *for me,* *glory* *for me; when by His grace I shall look on His face: That will be* *glory*, *be* *glory* *for me. "*

When by the gift of His infinite grace, I am accorded in heaven a place – Just to be there and to look on His face – will through the ages be *glory* *for me!*

4. The <u>GLORY</u> of our present trials – vv. 3-5

"And not only so, but we glory in tribulations also: knowing that tribulation worketh patience; and patience, experience; and experience, hope: And hope maketh not ashamed; because the love of God is shed abroad

in our hearts by the Holy Ghost which is given unto us."

The Greek word translated *"tribulations"* is the word *thlipsis* which is used 45 times in the New Testament. It refers to the pressure we are under – used of squeezing olives and grapes.

John 16:33 – *"These things I have spoken unto you, that in Me ye might have peace. In the world ye shall have <u>tribulation</u>: but be of good cheer; I have overcome the world."*

On Paul's first missionary journey, he reported back to the church from which he was sent – Acts 14:22 says: *"Confirming the souls of the disciples, and exhorting them to continue in the faith, and that ye must through much <u>tribulation</u> enter into the kingdom of God."*

II Corinthians 4:17-18 says: *"For our light <u>affliction</u>, which is but for a moment, worketh for us a far more exceeding and eternal weight of glory; While we look not at the things which are seen, but at the things which are not see: for the things which are seen are* *temporal; but the things which are not see are eternal."*

        (1)   **Seen in the <u>PATIENCE</u> that results from the pressure we are under!**
                  "knowing that tribulation worketh patience"

The Greek word is *hupomonen.* We read in James 1:2-4: *"My brethren, count it all joy when ye fall into divers temptations; Knowing this, that the trying of your faith worketh <u>patience</u>. But let <u>patience</u> have her perfect work, that ye may be perfect and entire, wanting nothing."*

James 1:12 says: *"Blessed is the man that endureth <u>temptation</u>: for when he is tried, he shall receive the crown of life, which the Lord hath promised to them that love Him."*

Matthew 5:10-12 reads: *"Blessed are they which are persecuted for righteousness' sake: for theirs is the kingdom of heaven. Blessed are ye, when men shall revile you, and persecute you, and shall say all manner of evil against you falsely, for My sake.*

Rejoice, and be exceeding glad: for great is your reward in heaven: for so persecuted they the prophets which were before you."

    (2)   Seen in the <u>PROOF</u> of our character before God that comes from the trials we endure!
            "and patience, experience"

The Greek word *dokimen* refers to the result of something being tested and then proven to be valuable!

I Peter 1:6-7 says: *"Wherein ye greatly rejoice, though now for a season, if need be, ye are in heaviness through manifold <u>temptations</u>: that the <u>trial</u> of your faith, being much more precious than of gold that perisheth, though it be <u>tried</u> with fire, might be found unto praise and honor and glory at the appearing of Jesus Christ."*

    (3)   Seen in the <u>PROMISES</u> which God gives to those who suffer!
            "and experience, hope; and hope maketh not ashamed"

His promises give us no reason to be embarrassed or to shrink back!

> (4) Seen in the <u>PRESENCE</u> of God's Holy Spirit!
> *"because the love of God is shed abroad in our hearts by the Holy Ghost which is given unto us"*

The words *"shed abroad"* are from a Greek word meaning "poured out."

A wonderful <u>REDEMPTION</u>! Romans 5:6-11 — *"saved from wrath"*

> 1. The <u>REALIZATION</u> of our spiritual condition – *"without strength"*

The Greek word *asthenon* is used as a noun 21 times, and as a verb 42 times (*astheneo*). In Matthew 26:41 we read: *"Watch and pray, that ye enter not into temptation: the spirit indeed is willing, but the flesh is <u>weak</u>."*

> 2. The <u>RECOGNITION</u> of God's timing – *"in due time"* – v. 6

Galatians 4:4 reads: *"But when the fullness of time was come, God sent forth His Son, made of a woman, made under the law."*

The phrase *"Christ died for the ungodly"* uses the Greek preposition *huper* – translated *"for"* – literally meaning "in the behalf of." A fascinating usage of this is found when two passages about our Lord's *"ransom"* are compared:

Matthew 20:28 – *"a ransom for many"* The Greek preposition is *anti* - meaning "in the stead of" – a word of substitution. The text reads in Greek *"a ransom in the stead of THE many"* – meaning the many who will believe in Him.

But, in I Timothy 2:6 we read *"a ransom for all"* - the Greek word is *huper* – meaning "in the behalf of" – a word of sufficiency.

Two aspects of our Lord's death are blended together in discussing the meaning of His death as a *"ransom."*

It is a <u>SUBSTITUTION</u> only for those who believe on Him!

It is a <u>SUFFICIENCY</u> for all, both believer and non-believer!

When Romans 5:6 says *"Christ died for the ungodly"* – His death was sufficient for all, but it will only be efficient for those who believe!

   3. The <u>REASON</u> for His death – vv. 7-8 – *"His love toward us"*

"For scarcely for a righteous man will one die: yet peradventure for a good man some would even dare to die. But God commandeth His love toward us, in that, while we were yet sinners, Christ died for us."

John 3:16 is known and loved by many people: *"For God so loved the world that He gave His only-begotten Son, that whosoever believeth in Him, should not perish, but have everlasting life."*

I John 4:9-10 adds: *"In this was manifested the love of God toward us, because that God sent His only begotten Son into the world, that we might live*

*through Him. Herein is love, not that
we loved God, but that He loved us, and
sent His Son to be the propitiation for
our sins."*

WHAT A WONDERFUL REDEMPTION!

    4. The <u>RESULT</u> of His blood – v. 9a
        "being now justified by His blood"

His blood is the means by which we can
be declared righteous before a holy God!
His blood was and is the payment for
our sin – praise the Lord!

    5. The <u>RESCUE</u> from wrath – v. 9b
        "saved from wrath through Him"

The word *"saved"* in various forms of
the word is found 356 times in the Bible
of which 127 times are in the New
Testament.

John 3:36 says: *"He that believeth on
the Son hath everlasting life: and he
that believeth not the Son shall not see
life; but the wrath of God abideth on
him."*

I Thessalonians 1:10 also says: *"And to
wait for His Son from heaven, Whom*

*He raised from the dead, even Jesus,
which delivered us from the wrath to
come."*

    6. Our <u>RECONCILIATION</u> to God!
        v. 10

*"For if, when we were enemies, we were
reconciled to God by the death of His
Son, much more, being reconciled, we
shall be saved by His life."* Notice the
following four things from this verse:

      (1)   Our <u>PROBLEM</u> – *"we were
                enemies"*

Colossians 1:20-22 teaches: *"And,
having made peace through the blood of
His cross, by Him to reconcile all things
unto Himself; by Him, I say, whether
they be things in earth, or things in
heaven. And you, that were sometime
alienated and enemies in your mind by
wicked works, yet now hath He
reconciled in the body of His flesh
through death, to present you holy and
unblameable and unreproveable in His
sight."*

      (2)   His <u>PART</u> – *"by the death of
                His Son"*

II Corinthians 5:18-20 says: *"And all things are of God, Who hath reconciled us to Himself by Jesus Christ, and hath given to us the ministry of reconciliation; To wit, that God was in Christ, reconciling the world unto Himself, not imputing their trespasses unto them; and hath committed unto us the word of reconciliation. Now then we are ambassadors for Christ, as though God did beseech you by us: we pray you in Christ's stead, be ye reconciled to God."*

Ephesians 2:14-16 adds: *"For He is our peace, Who hath made both one, and hath broken down the middle wall of partition between us; Having abolished in His flesh the enmity, even the law of commandments, contained in ordinances; for to make in Himself of twain one new man, so making peace; And that He might reconcile both unto God in one body by the cross, having slain the enmity thereby."*

   (3)   His <u>PROMISE</u> – *"we shall be saved"*

   (4)   His <u>PROVISION</u> – *"by His life"*

7. Our <u>REJOICING</u> in God – v. 11

The opening phrase *"And not only so, but..."* contains the Greek conjunction *alla* a word of strong contrast!

> (1)   The <u>PERSON</u> Who makes it possible – *"through our Lord Jesus Christ"*

> (2)   The present <u>POSSESSION</u> that fills us with joy! *"by Whom we have now received the atonement"*

The last word *"atonement"* is the Greek word for *"reconciliation."* The text says that believers have *"<u>NOW</u> received"* it!

JUSTIFICATION is...

<u>DEPENDENT</u> upon the work of Jesus Christ – 3:21-31

<u>DESCRIBED</u> in the life of Abraham – 4:1-25

<u>DECLARED</u> in the rewards of our salvation – 5:1-11

<u>DEMONSTRATED</u> in the results of the fall – 5:12-21

> 1. The <u>CONSEQUENCE</u> which one man's sin brought upon the whole world! vv. 12-14

"Wherefore, as by one man sin entered into the world, and death by sin; and so death passed upon all men, for that all have sinned: (For until the law sin was in the world: but sin is not imputed when there is no law. Nevertheless death reigned from Adam to Moses, even over them that had not sinned after the similitude of Adam's transgression, who is the figure of Him that was to come."

The opening word *"Wherefore"* is the Greek phrase *dia touto* which means "because of this" or "on account of this" – referring to what we were told in verses 1-11 – that we have been reconciled to God by the death of His Son.

(1)   The <u>ENTRANCE</u> of sin – v. 12a

It came through one man, namely – ADAM. It is described as <u>THE</u> sin! I Timothy 2:13-14 speaks of this fact when we read: *"For Adam was first formed, then Eve. And Adam was not deceived, but the woman being deceived was in the transgression."*

Sin did not originate with Adam; it merely entered the world through him. Sin originated with Satan. I John 3:8 says: *"He that committeth sin is of the devil; for the devil sinneth from the beginning."*

(2)   The <u>EFFECT</u> of that one sin – *"and death by sin"*

The Greek text says *"and through THE sin, THE death."* The singular usage of the word *"sin"* points to the depravity which resulted, not simply the acts of sinning.

Adam's sin was a deliberate decision to disobey the known revealed will of God. His wife was deceived, but Adam was not – he disobeyed with the full knowledge

that what he was doing was in violation
of God's will. Our depravity is not the
result of sinning, but the cause of it.

    (3)   The <u>EXPERIENCE</u> of all men
               *"and so death passed upon
               all men"*

<u>NOTE:</u> Adam did not die physically the
day he disobeyed God; but he did die
spiritually, and was separated from
fellowship with God.

    (4)   The <u>EXECUTION</u> of the law
               *"until the law sin was in the
               world; but sin is not
               imputed when there is no
               law"*

Our sinful acts in breaking God's law do
not bring the consequence of death – but
rather it is our sinful nature that causes
it.

    (5)   The <u>EXPLANATION</u> for the
               reality of death – v. 14

*"Nevertheless death reigned from Adam
to Moses, even over them that had not
sinned after the similitude of Adam's*

transgression, who is the figure of Him that was to come."

From *"Adam to Moses"* people still experienced physical death even when they did not sin in the same way as did Adam. The reason, therefore, did not lie in the knowledge of the law and therefore the breaking of it, nor did it lie in the similarity of people sinning like Adam did: The reason was that Adam was a *"type"* of the One Who was coming!

    2. The <u>CONTRAST</u> between Adam and Christ – Romans 5:15-17

"But not as the offence, so also is the free gift. For if through the offence of one many be dead, much more the grace of God, and the gift by grace, which is by one man, Jesus Christ, hath abounded unto many. And not as it was by one that sinned, so is the gift: for the judgment was by one to condemnation, but the free gift is of many offences unto justification. For if by one man's offence death reigned by one; much more they which receive abundance of grace and of the gift of righteousness shall reign in life by one, Jesus Christ."

(1)   A contrast between one man's offence and one man's free gift – v. 15

The Greek word for *"offence"* is the word *paraptoma* and refers to a "fall." The words *"If through..."* come from a Greek grammatical usage (*ei* with the indicative) that should read "if and it is so" or "since" – the free gift is the Greek word *charisma* and emphasizes God's grace is behind it all. The second word *"gift"* is the Greek *dorea* and is used in reference to righteousness.

The words *"much more"* appear in verses 15, 17, and 20 – The difference being emphasized is GRACE!

In terms of Adam's sin – many died! In terms of Christ's gift – many have received grace!

WHAT A CONTRAST!

(2)   A contrast between condemnation and justification – v. 16

The Greek text has the construction *men...de* – meaning "on the one hand...but on the other hand.

On the one hand, if was *"out of"* one act of disobedience that condemnation came. But, on the other hand, it was *"out of"* many offences that justification came – it was a *"free gift"* – the Greek word is *charisma* – a gift of God's grace made this possible!

> (3) A contrast between
> death and life – v. 17

Once again the *"if"* clause should read "if and it is so" or "since." The text reads *"<u>THE</u> death"* – it reigned over all men through one man's disobedience; but those who receive God's grace and the gift of <u>THE</u> righteousness, shall all reign *"in life by one, Jesus Christ."*

Once again, it is God's grace that makes it possible – praise the Lord!

> 3. The <u>COMPARISON</u> between Adam and Christ – *vv. 18-21*

"Therefore as by the offence of one judgment came upon all men to

condemnation; even so by the righteousness of one the free gift came upon all men unto justification of life. For as by one man's disobedience many were made sinners, so by the obedience of one shall many be made righteous. Moreover the law entered, that the offence might abound. But where sin abounded, grace did much more abound: That as sin hath reigned unto death, even so might grace reign through righteousness unto eternal life by Jesus Christ our Lord."

In both cases, it was one person and one act that brought the results – v. 18

In both cases, many people were affected by one act – v. 19

In both cases, the consequences abound – vv. 20-21

When the law came, sin increased – cf. Romans 7:7-11. When Jesus came, grace super-abounded! The Greek word *"huperperisseuo"* makes the point powerfully!

NOTICE AGAIN THE CONTRASTS:
Adam vs. Christ

Condemnation vs. Justification
Disobedience vs. Obedience
Law vs. Grace
Sin vs. Righteousness
Death vs. Life

Chapter 4
SANCTIFICATION
Romans 6:1-7:25

In Romans 6, the word *"sin"* appears 17 times; In Romans 7, the word *"law"* is used 19 times. In Romans 6 forms of the first person singular appear just once; but in Romans 7, they appear 47 times!

OUR <u>REALIZATION</u> OF CERTAIN FACTS
Romans 6:1-10

"What shall we say then? Shall we continue in sin, that grace may abound? God forbid. How shall we, that are dead to sin, live any longer therein? Know ye not, that so many of us as were baptized into Jesus Christ were baptized into His death? Therefore we are buried with Him by baptism into death: that like as Christ was raised up from the dead by the glory of the Father, even so we also should walk in newness of life. For if we have been planted together in the likeness of His death, we shall be also in the likeness of his resurrection: Knowing this, that our old man is

crucified with Him, that the body of sin might be destroyed, that henceforth we should not serve sin. For he that is dead is freed from sin. Now if we be dead with Christ, we believe that we shall also live with Him: Knowing that Christ being raised from the dead dieth no more; death hath no more dominion over Him. For in that He died, He died unto sin once: but in that He liveth, He liveth unto God."

1. The <u>PROBLEMS</u> that develop — vv. 1-2

Three questions:
"What shall we say then?
"Shall we continue in sin, that grace may abound?
"How shall we, that are dead to sin, live any longer therein?

The phrase *"What shall we say then?"* is used in Romans 6:15, 7:7, and 8:31 in this section dealing with sanctification.

The "PROBLEMS" deal with God's <u>PURPOSES</u> and with our <u>PRACTICE</u>.

(1)   As to God's <u>PURPOSES</u>

Romans 6:1 is connected to what was said in Romans 5:20 – *"where sin abounded, grace did much more abound."* The question naturally follows: *"Shall we continue in sin, that grace may abound?"*

God's grace does not abound because we sin; it abounds in spite of our sin and even if we don't sin!

Justification and Sanctification are inseparable – both are rooted in the finished work of Jesus Christ on the cross. When we become Christians, we are separated immediately from the control and consequences of sin.

Hebrews 12:14 says: *"Follow peace with all men, and holiness* (sanctification), *without which no man shall see the Lord."*

According to I Corinthians 6:9-11, all true believers are already *"sanctified."*

"Know ye not that the unrighteous shall not inherit the kingdom of God? Be not deceived: neither fornicators, nor idolaters, nor adulterers, nor effeminate, nor abusers of themselves

with mankind, nor thieves, nor covetous, nor drunkards, nor revilers, nor extortioners, shall inherit the kingdom of God. And such were some of you: but ye are washed, but ye are sanctified, but ye are justified in the Name of the Lord Jesus, and by the Spirit of our God."

In Hebrews 10:10 it says: *"By the which will we are sanctified through the offering of the body of Jesus Christ once for all."* In Hebrews 10:14 it adds: *"For by one offering He hath perfected forever them that are sanctified."*

Jesus said in His prayer to His Father in John 17:17: *"Sanctify them through Thy truth: Thy word is truth."* The word *"sanctify"* is in the aorist tense in the Greek language. The same is found in Ephesians 5:26 where we read: *"That He might sanctify and cleanse it with the washing of water by the word."*

Some Bible teachers argue that sanctification is always a continual process in the lives of believers. While that is certainly understandable, the above verses do not teach that, because of the use of the aorist tense – it refers to what happened in the past, in a moment of time. At the moment of a person's conversion (born again), that person is justified (declared righteous) and sanctified (separated from the control and consequences of sin).

(2)   As to our <u>PRACTICE</u> – v. 2

"How shall we, that are dead to sin, live any longer therein?"

Sin did not die; we died to its control over us! The opening words of verse 2 – *"God forbid!"* emphasizes "May it NEVER be!" Paul uses it 14 times in his letters, 9 of which are in the Book of Romans – 3:4, 6, 31; 6:2, 15; 7:7, 13; 9:14; 11:1, 11.

This is a wonderful fact of our relationship to Jesus Christ, but one which is difficult to understand and apply. It is clear from the Bible that we still have a sin nature (depravity). I John 1:8 says; *"If we say that we have no sin, we deceive ourselves, and the truth is not in us."* According to I John 1:10 it is also clear that we still do sin (individual acts) – *"If we say that we have not sinned, we make Him a liar, and His word is not in us."*

However, it is also clear that genuine believers do not make a practice of sinning. I John 3:9 says: *"Whosoever is born of God doth not commit sin; for his seed remaineth in him: and he cannot sin, because he is born of God."* Also, in I John 5:18 we read: *"We know that whosoever is born of God sinneth not; but he that is begotten of God keepeth himself, and that wicked one toucheth him not."*

When the Bible says that a genuine believer does not *"commit sin"* it uses the present tense in Greek and means "does not make a practice of sinning."

    2. The <u>PRINCIPLES</u> that deliver us vv. 3-10

    (1)   The principle of <u>BAPTISM</u>

Romans 6:3-5 – *"Know ye not, that so many of us as were baptized into Jesus Christ were baptized into His death? Therefore we are buried with Him by baptism into death: that like as Christ as raised up from the dead by the glory*

*of the Father, even so we also should
walk in newness of life. For if we have
been planted together in the likeness of
His death, we shall be also in the
likeness of His resurrection."*

The word *"baptism"* in its various forms
is used 126 times in the New Testament.
There are also 21 usages in the Greek
Old Testament (Septuagint). A related
word *"to wash"* (Greek: *louo*) is used 10
times in the New Testament and 46
times in the Greek Old Testament.

> *Louo* – describes the effect of
> washing = cleansing
> *Baptizo* – describes the method
> of washing = dipping

There are five kinds of *"baptism"* in the
Bible:

FIGURATIVE – used in I Corinthians
10:2 – *"and were all baptized unto
Moses in the cloud and in the sea"*

SUFFERING – used in Matthew 20:22-23
*"Ye know not what ye ask. Are ye able
to drink of the cup that I shall drink of,
and to be baptized with the baptism
that I am baptized with? They say unto
Him, We are able. And He saith unto*

them, Ye shall drink indeed of My cup, and be _baptized_ with the _baptism_ that I am _baptized_ with: but to sit on My right hand, and on My left, is not Mine to give, but it shall be given to them for whom it is prepared of My Father."

FIRE – used in Matthew 3:11-12: _"I indeed _baptize_ you with water unto repentance: but He that cometh after me is mightier than I, Whose shoes I am not worthy to bear: He shall _baptize_ you with the Holy Ghost, and with _FIRE_: Whose fan is in His hand, and He will thoroughly purge His floor, and gather His wheat into the garner; but He will burn up the chaff with unquenchable fire."_

SPIRIT – used in Acts 1:5: _"For John truly _baptized_ with water; but ye shall be _baptized_ with the Holy Ghost not many days hence."_

WATER – used in Acts 8:36-38: _"And as they went on their way, they came unto a certain water; what doth hinder me to be _baptized_? And Philip said, If thou believest with all thine heart, thou mayest. And he answered and said, I believe that Jesus Christ is the Son of_

God. And he commanded the chariot to stand still: and they went down both into the water, both Philip and the eunuch; and he <u>baptized</u> him."

Three things about the principle of *"baptism"* in Romans 3-5:

The <u>REALITY</u> of the symbol – v. 3
"Know ye not, that so many of us as were baptized into Jesus Christ were baptized into His death?"

The <u>REASON</u> for this truth – v. 4
"Therefore we are buried with Him by baptism into death: that like as Christ was raised up from the dead by the glory of the Father, even so we also should walk in newness of life."

The <u>REASSURANCE</u> of new life – v. 5
"For if we have been planted together in the likeness of His death, we shall be also in the likeness of His resurrection."

WHY SHOULD TRUE BELIEVERS BE BAPTIZED IN WATER?

Four reasons:

Because it is a Divine <u>COMMAND</u>!

Matthew 28:19 says *"Go ye therefore, and teach all nations, baptizing them in the Name of the Father, and of the Son, and of the Holy Ghost."*

Because it is a public <u>CONFESSION</u>!
I Peter 3:21 – *"The like figure whereunto even baptism doth also now save us (not the putting away of the filth of the flesh, but the answer of a good conscience toward God,) by the resurrection of Jesus Christ."*
(Also, compare Acts 8:35-38 when Philip baptized the Ethiopian eunuch in water)

Because it is a symbolic <u>CLEANSING</u>!
Acts 2:38 – *"Then Peter said unto them, Repent, and be baptized every one of you in the Name of Jesus Christ for the remission of sins, and ye shall receive the gift of the Holy Ghost."*

Acts 22:16 adds: *"And now why tarriest thou? Arise, and be baptized, and wash away thy sins, calling on the Name of the Lord."*

Because it is a spiritual <u>CELEBRATION</u>!
That's what we have here from Romans 6:3-5 – We have died, been buried, and

have been resurrected to a new life in
Jesus Christ!

Romans 6:5 begins with the words *"for
IF…"* In the Greek grammar it is the
word *ei* with the indicative mood of the
verb – we should translate "Since" or
"It's a fact" – We have been planted
together in the *"likeness of His death"*
(pictured by being placed under water –
the water represents a coffin – the
principle of death to the old life) and this
guarantees that one day we shall be
planted together *"in the likeness of His
resurrection"* (pictured by our coming
up out of the water!)

Baptism represents death, burial, and
resurrection!

(2)   The principle of
        CRUCIFIXION – vv. 6-8

*"Knowing this, that our old man is
crucified with Him, that the body of sin
might be destroyed, that henceforth we
should not serve sin. For he that is dead
is freed from sin. Now if we be dead
with Christ, we believe that we shall
also live with Him."*

NOTE: The words *"Knowing this"* are found in verses 3, 6, and 9. These are facts that we are to know.

FACTS ABOUT OUR CRUCIFIXION:

The <u>PLACE</u> of the cross in our deliverance.

Romans 6:6 says *"our old man is crucified with Him"*

Galatians 2:20-21 says: *"I am crucified with Christ: nevertheless I live; yet not I, but Christ liveth in me: and the life which I now live in the flesh I live by the faith of the Son of God, Who loved me, and gave Himself for me. I do not frustrate the grace of God: for if righteousness come by the law, then Christ is dead in vain."*

The <u>POWER</u> of sin has been defeated at the cross.

Romans 6:6 — *"that the body of sin might be destroyed"*

The Greek word translated *"destroyed"* is *katargeo*, a word used 44 times in the New Testament and in Romans 3:3, 31; 4:4; 6:6; 7:2, 6.

The **PURPOSE** is to deliver us from slavery to sin.

Romans 6:6 says *"that henceforth we should not serve sin."*

The **POSITION** we now have before God.

Romans 6:7 says: *"For he that is dead is freed from sin"* – the Greek text uses the word *"justified"* – and should be translated *"has been justified"* (a perfect passive grammatical form).

The **PROMISE** we can now count on.

Romans 6:8 – *"Now if we be dead with Christ, we believe that we shall also live with Him."* The *"if"* clause (again" means "Since" or "If and it is so."

Colossians 3:1-4 states clearly:

"If ye than be risen with Christ, seek those things which are above, where Christ sitteth on the right hand of God. Set your affection on things above, not on things on the earth. For ye are dead, and your life is hid with Christ in God. When Christ, Who is our life, shall appear, then shall ye also appear with Him in glory."

In Romans 6 we have three basic principles in verses 1-10:
      BAPTISM
      CRUCIFIXION

And, number 3 -

    (3)   The principle of
           RESURRECTION – vv. 9-10

"Knowing that Christ being raised from the dead dieth no more; death hath no more dominion over Him. For in that He died, He died unto sin once: but in that He liveth, He liveth unto God."

The <u>FACT</u> of His victory
"dieth no more" – Death is no longer ruling – *"have not more dominion over Him."*

Hebrews 2:14-18 reinforces this great truth:

"Forasmuch then as the children are partakers of flesh and blood, He also Himself likewise took part of the same; that through death He might destroy him that had the power of death, that is, the devil; and deliver them who through fear of death were all their lifetime subject to bondage. For verily He took not on Him the nature of angels; but He took on Him the seed of Abraham. Wherefore in all things it behooved Him to be made like unto His brethren, that He might be a merciful and faithful high priest in things pertaining to God, to make reconciliation for the sins of the people. For in that He Himself hath suffered being tempted, he is able to succor them that are tempted."

The <u>FINALITY</u> of His victory
"He died unto sin once"

Hebrews 9:23-28 presents this powerful case:

"It was therefore necessary that the patterns of things in the heavens should be purified with these; but the heavenly

things themselves with better sacrifices than these. For Christ is not entered into the holy places made with hands, which are the figures of the true; but into heaven itself, now to appear in the presence of God for us: Nor yet that He should offer Himself often, as the high priest entereth into the holy place every year with blood of others; For then must He often have suffered since the foundation of the world: but now once in the end of the world hath He appeared to put away sin by the sacrifice of Himself. And as it is appointed unto men once to die, but after this the judgment: So Christ was once offered to bear the sins of many; and unto them that look for Him shall He appear the second time without sin unto salvation."

And, in Hebrews 10:10-14 we read:

"By the which will we are sanctified through the offering of the body of Jesus Christ once for all. And every priest standeth daily ministering and offering oftentimes the same sacrifices, which can never take away sins: But this Man, after He had offered one sacrifice for sins forever, sat down on

the right hand of God; From henceforth expecting till His enemies be made His footstool. For by one offering He hath perfected forever them that are sanctified."

The <u>FUTURE</u> of His victory
"but in that He liveth, He liveth unto God" – that is, He continues to live – praise God!

Our <u>RESPONSIBILITY</u> to these facts
Romans 6:11-23

The word *"Likewise"* that begins this section means simply "in the same way."

    1. The <u>COUNTING</u> we must do!

The Greek word *logizomai* is found 42 times in the New Testament – 19 of those times are in the Book of Romans!

Many believers find it hard to believe what Romans 6 teaches! Why do we find it so hard?

        (1)   Because of the presence and practice of sin.

(2)   Because it does not require
       any effort on our part to
       make it true.

(3)   Because it is not visible or
       physical, but rather –
       spiritual.

(4)   Because of the power of
       temptation upon our minds
       and hearts.

I Corinthians 10:13 – *"There hath no
temptation taken you but such as is
common to man: but God is faithful,
Who will not suffer you to be tempted
above that ye are able; but will with the
temptation also make a way to escape,
that ye may be able to bear it."*

   2. The <u>CONTROL</u> we must have!

Romans 6:12 says: *"Let not sin therefore
reign in your mortal body, that ye
should obey it in the lusts thereof."*

We cannot blame it on others or on our
circumstances! How does sin *"reign"* in
your body?

(1)   By <u>REFUSING</u> to glorify
       God!
       Romans 1:21-23; 3:23

(2)   By <u>REBELLING</u> against the
       known will of God!
       I Samuel 15:22-23;
       I Thessalonians 4:3, 7-8;
       I John 3:4

(3)   By <u>RESISTING</u> the
       opportunity to do good!
       James 4:17

(4)   By <u>REACTING</u> with anger
       instead of kindness!
       Ephesians 4:26-27, 30-32

(5)   By <u>RESPONDING</u> to its
       desires and enticements!
       Ephesians 2:1-3;
       I John 2:15-17

It is our response to temptation that is
the problem! Verse 12 said: *"that ye
should obey it in the lusts thereof."*
cf. James 1:13-15; I Peter 2:11-12

  3. The <u>COMMITMENT</u> we must
     make!

In Romans 6:13-16 we read the following:

"Neither yield ye your members as instruments of unrighteousness unto sin: but yield yourselves unto God, as those that are alive from the dead, and your members as instruments of righteousness unto God. For sin shall not have dominion over you: for ye are not under the law, but under grace. What then? shall we sin, because we are not under the law but under grace? God forbid. Know ye not, that to whom ye yield yourselves servants to obey, his servants ye are to whom ye obey; whether of sin unto death, or of obedience unto righteousness?

(1) Our <u>RESPONSIBILITY</u> is to yield to God, not to sin!

The Greek word translated *"yield"* is the word *paristemi* which is used 46 times in the New Testament and literally means "to stand alongside of." Instead of keeping our distance from potential sinful situations, we often get as close as we can, trusting ourselves to be strong enough to resist! How foolish we are!

(2)   Our <u>RECOGNITION</u> of the importance of the body in expressing our commitment!

I Corinthians 6:18-20 emphasizes this crucial understanding:

"Flee fornication. Every sin that a man doeth is without (outside) *the body; but he that committeth fornication sinneth against his own body. What? Know ye not that your body is the temple of the Holy Ghost which is in you, which ye have of God, and ye are not your own? For ye are bought with a price: therefore glorify God in your body, and in your spirit, which are God's."*

Notice that we are urged to run away from committing fornication (sexual sin) – obviously involving the physical body.

A simple illustration is the use of our tongue. James 3:8 says *"But the tongue can no man tame; it is an unruly evil, full of deadly poison."* Verse 6 claims: *"the tongue is a fire, a world of iniquity: so is the tongue among our members, that it defileth the whole body, and setteth on fire the course of nature; and it is set on fire of hell."*

    (3)   Our <u>REALIZATION</u> of what it means to be *"under grace."*

It means that sin has lost its ability to dominate our lives!

Romans 6:14 – *"For sin shall not have dominion over you: for ye are not under the law, but under grace."*

It means that we are not *"under the law"*!

It means that we are not free to sin! Our freedom from the law's control does NOT mean that we are free to sin whenever we desire to do so!

    (4)   The <u>RESULTS</u> we experience are based solely upon what we choose to obey!

If we choose to obey sinful desires, we will experience its consequences – death! If we choose to obey God's Word and will – the result is righteousness!

4. The <u>CONSEQUENCES</u> we must face!

Romans 6:17-23 says:
"But God be thanked, that ye were the servants of sin, but ye have obeyed from the heart that form of doctrine which was delivered you. Being then made free from sin, ye became the servants of righteousness. I speak after the manner of men because of the infirmity of your flesh: for as ye have yielded your members servants to uncleanness and to iniquity unto iniquity; even so now yield your members servants to righteousness unto holiness. For when ye were the servants of sin, ye were free from righteousness. What fruit had ye then in those things whereof ye are not ashamed? For the end of those things is death. But now being made free from sin, and become servants to God, ye have your fruit unto holiness, and the end everlasting life. For the wages of sin is death; but the gift of God is eternal life through Jesus Christ our Lord."

　　　　(1)　　A <u>REASON</u> to be thankful!

Romans 6:17 says: *"But God be thanked, that ye were the servants of sin, but ye have obeyed from the heart that form of doctrine which was delivered you."*

The <u>SOURCE</u> is God – *"But God be thanked"*

The <u>SINCERITY</u> of your heart was and is crucial – *"ye have obeyed <u>from</u> the heart"*

The <u>SCRIPTURES</u> were obeyed – *"that form of doctrine which was delivered you"*

(2) A <u>REALITY</u> that now exists in every true believer!

Romans 6:18 states: *"Being then made free from sin, ye became the servants of righteousness."*

(3) A <u>RESPONSIBILITY</u> that continues after we are saved!

Romans 6:19 says: *"even so now yield your members servants to righteousness unto holiness"*

Our <u>DEPRAVITY</u> is real!
"because of the infirmity of your flesh"

The Greek word for *"infirmity"* is *astheneian* which literally means "without strength" and also is used in Matthew 26:41 – *"the spirit is willing but the flesh is <u>weak</u>"*

Our <u>DECISIONS</u> are critical!
"for as ye have yielded...even so now yield your members..."

> The <u>standards</u> by which we make our decisions – Is it by *"uncleanness"* and *"iniquity"* OR is it by *"righteousness"*?

The Apostle Paul wrote in Ephesians 5:3-7 these words:

"But fornication, and all uncleanness, or covetousness, let it not be once named among you, as becometh saints; Neither filthiness, nor foolish talking, nor jesting, which are not convenient: but rather giving of thanks. For this ye know, that no whoremonger, nor unclean person, nor covetous man, who is an idolater, hath any inheritance in the kingdom of Christ and of God. Let

no man deceive you with vain words: for because of these things cometh the wrath of God upon the children of disobedience. Be not ye therefore partakers with them."

Similar words appear in Colossians 3:5-8:

"Mortify therefore your members which are upon the earth; fornication, uncleanness, inordinate affection, evil concupiscence and covetousness, which is idolatry: for which things' sake the wrath of God cometh on the children of disobedience: In the which ye also walked some time, when ye lived in them. But now ye also put off all these: anger, wrath, malice, blasphemy, filthy communication out of your mouth."

It is very clear in the above two passages that the decisions we make are very critical!

The **SLAVERY** that results from the decisions we make are also quite serious! It is either *"unto iniquity"* or *"unto holiness."* The Greek word for *"iniquity"* is "lawlessness."

(4)   A <u>REMINDER</u> of the
past – vv. 20-21

*"For when ye were the servants of sin,
ye were free from righteousness. What
fruit had ye then in those things
whereof ye are now ashamed? For the
end of those things is death."*

Our <u>freedom</u> was *"from righteousness"*
and the <u>fruit</u> brought us shame!
Ephesians 5:11 speaks of the *"unfruitful
works of darkness."* Notice the <u>future</u>
which such lifestyles will bring – *"the
end of those things is death."*

Proverbs 14:12 says: *"There is a way
which seemeth right unto a man, but
the end thereof are the ways of death."*

(5)   A <u>RESULT</u> we can
expect! vv. 22-23

*"But now being made free from sin, and
become servants to God, ye have your
fruit unto holiness, and the end
everlasting life. For the wages of sin is
death; but the gift of God is eternal life
through Jesus Christ our Lord."*

THE PRINCIPLE OF SANCTIFICATION

Our <u>REALIZATION</u> of certain facts! Romans 6:1-10

Our <u>RESPONSIBILITY</u> to these facts! Romans 6:11-23

But, our understanding is not complete until we deal with a third matter:

Our <u>RELATIONSHIP</u> to the Law! Romans 7:1-25

The opening words of chapter seven say *"Know ye not, <u>brethren</u>"* – the recipients of his remarks must be Messianic Jews! The word *"brethren"* is used 231 times in the New Testament, 109 of which are used by Paul himself. He uses it 14 times in Romans, and the singular form *"brother"* another 36 times in this book.

The evidence that the recipients are Jews is found in Romans 7:1 – *"for I speak to them that know the law."*

In Romans 6, the key word was "SIN" – but in Romans 7, the key word is "LAW"!

The word *"law"* is found 523 times in the Bible of which 223 times are in the New Testament. Paul uses it 148 times, including 78 times in Romans, and 23 times in chapter 7 alone!

The ILLUSTRATION of marriage
Romans 7:1-6

"Know ye not, brethren, (for I speak to them that know the law,) how that the law hath dominion over a man as long as he liveth? For the woman which hath an husband is bound by the law to her husband so long as he liveth; but if the husband be dead, she is loosed from the law of her husband. So then if, while her husband liveth, she be married to another man, she shall be called an adulteress: but if her husband be dead, she is free from that law; so that she is no adulteress, though she be married to another man. Wherefore, my brethren, ye also are become dead to the law by the body of Christ; that ye should be married to another, even to Him Who is

raised from the dead, that we should bring forth fruit unto God. For when we were in the flesh, the motions of sins, which were by the law, did work in our members, to bring forth fruit unto death. But now we are delivered from the law, that being dead wherein we were held; that we should serve in newness of spirit, and not in the oldness of the letter."

The <u>EXPLANATION</u>

In the first three verses, Paul gives an explanation dealing with the illustration of marriage. In verses 4-6 he gives us the application. There are three issues in the first three verses:

1. The <u>DURATION</u> of the law – *"the law hath dominion over a man as long as he liveth"*

In marriage, the wife is *"bound by the law to her husband so long as he liveth."* This, of course, is referring to God's law. In Matthew 19:4-6 we read the words of our Lord Yeshua:

"Have ye not read, that He which made them at the beginning made them male

and female, and said, For this cause shall a man leave father and mother, and shall cleave to his wife: and they twain shall be one flesh? Wherefore they are no more twain, but one flesh. What therefore God hath joined together, let not man put asunder."

The permission to remarry – *"loosed from the law of her husband"* is based upon his death. I Corinthians 7:39 says: *"The wife is bound by the law as long as her husband liveth; but if her husband be dead, she is at liberty to be married to whom she will; only in the Lord."*

Are there any "exceptions"?

Our Lord Yeshua said in Matthew 5:31-32: *"It hath been said, whosoever shall put away his wife, let him give her a writing of divorcement: But I say unto you, That whosoever shall put away his wife, saving for the cause of fornication, causeth her to commit adultery: and whosoever shall marry her that is divorced committeth adultery."*

It would appear that *"fornication"* (refers to sexual immorality) is a possible exception to the bondage of the law concerning marriage.

Yeshua also said in Matthew 19:9: *"And I say unto you, Whosoever shall put away his wife, except it be for fornication, and shall marry another, committeth adultery: and whoso marrieth her which is put away doth commit adultery."*

Another possible exception is the one the Apostle Paul mentioned in I Corinthians 7:12-15 when he discussed a marriage where one person is a believer and the other is not. If the unbelieving partner does not want to stay married to the believer and leaves the relationship, the believing partner is *"not under bondage in such cases."*

The issue of "irreconcilable differences" is not one of the "exceptions."

2. The <u>DELIVERANCE</u> from the law — *"if the husband be dead, she is loosed from the law of her husband"*

3. The **DISOBEDIENCE** to the law – *"if, while her husband liveth, she be married to another man, she shall be called an adulteress"*

Adultery is more than having sex with a married person who is not your spouse! At its essential core, it is an act of unfaithfulness to God's law – including the issue of divorce.

The **APPLICATION**

Verse 4 begins *"Wherefore, my brethren"* and records the application to what Paul said about marriage and the law.

1. The **PRINCIPLE**

The words of verse 4 are clear: *"ye also are become dead to the law by the body of Christ."*

The law's penalty for violating it is death, but the death of the Messiah paid for that penalty, thus breaking the law's power over us – we are now free!

Hebrews 2:14-15 says: *"Forasmuch then as the children are partakers of flesh and blood, He also Himself likewise took part of the same; that through death He might destroy him that had the power of death, that is, the devil; and deliver them who through fear of death were all their lifetime subject to bondage."*

I John 3:8 adds: *"He that committeth sin is of the devil; for the devil sinneth from the beginning. For this purpose the Son of God was manifested, that He might destroy the works of the devil."*

2. The <u>PURPOSE</u>

The words of verse 4 are *"that we should bring forth fruit unto God."* In the illustration of marriage it would be like having a child from that marriage union.

3. The <u>PAST</u>

Verse 5 states: *"For when we were in the flesh."*

> (1)   The <u>REALIZATION</u> of what was working in us – v. 5a *"the motions of sins"*

The Greek word translated *"motions"* is the word *pathemata* which, interestingly, is used of the suffering of our Lord (Romans 8:18; Galatians 5:24; I Peter 5:9). This word is speaking of the damage which sin does!

> (2) The <u>RESULTS</u> that are produced – *"to bring forth fruit unto death"*

James 1:14-16 says: *"But every man is tempted when he is drawn away of his own lust, and enticed. Then when lust hath conceived, it bringeth forth sin: and sin, when it is finished, bringeth forth death. Do not err, my beloved brethren."*

4. The <u>PRESENT</u>

Verse 6 begins with the wonderful words *"But now..."* These words are used by the Apostle Paul 26 times in his letters. In Romans we find them used in 3:21; 6:22; 7:6; and 16:26.

> (1) The spiritual <u>REALITY</u> we must understand and believe!

We read in verse 6: *"But now we are delivered from the law, that being dead wherein we were held..."*

> **(2)   The spiritual <u>REASON</u> this has occurred!**

Verse 6 continues: *"that we should serve in newness of spirit, and not in the oldness of the letter."*

These words are not referring to chronological time; the words *"newness"* and *"oldness"* are referring to that which is "fresh" in contrast to that which is "worn."

<u>The INSTRUCTION of the law</u>
Romans 7:7-14
"What shall we say then?"

Romans 6:1 – the issue of grace
Romans 6:15 – the issue of freedom
Romans 7:7 – the issue of sin

If the inclination to sin comes through the law (as implied in 7:5), then isn't the law something sinful? A second question will arise when we come to verse 13. The point being, if the law is as he says in verse 12, then why can't the law make us holy?

1. The law **REMOVES** our ignorance of sin – *v. 7*

"Is the way sin? God forbid. Nay, I had not known sin, but by the law: for I had not known lust, except the law had said, Thou shalt not covet."

The problem of *"lust"* or *"coveting"* – the Greek noun *epithumia* appears 38 times and the verb another 16 times.

Consider its usage:
Matthew 5:27-28
John 8:44
Romans 1:24; 6:12; 13:14
I Corinthians 10:6
Galatians 5:16-17
Colossians 3:5
I Thessalonians 4:5
II Timothy 2:22
James 1:13-15
I Peter 2:11
I John 2:15-17

2. The law <u>RESURRECTS</u> our sinful desires – *vv. 8-11*

But sin, taking occasion by the commandment, wrought in me all manner of concupiscence. For without the law sin was dead. For I was alive without the law once: but when the commandment came, sin revived, and I died. And the commandment, which was ordained to life, I found to be unto death. For sin, taking occasion by the commandment, deceived me, and by it slew me."

(1) Sin <u>STIRS</u> the evil desires, NOT the law – *v. 8a*

(2) Sin <u>STAYS</u> hidden and unknown without the teaching of God's law – *v. 8b*

(3) Sin <u>SLAYS</u> us by using the law – *v. 11*

3. The law <u>REQUIRES</u> the penalty of death – *v. 10*

The words *"shall surely be put to death"* are found 28 times in God's law.

Hebrews 10:28 says: *"He that despised Moses' law died without mercy under two or three witnesses."*

4. The law **REFLECTS** the character of God Himself – *v. 12*

"Wherefore the law is holy, and the commandment holy, and just, and good." Paul calls it *"the law of God"* in verses 22, 25, and 8:7. Our Lord Yeshua referred to it as *"the commandment of God"* in *Matthew 15:3, 6.*

> (1) It is not sinful at all – *"holy"*
> (2) It is fair in what it demands – *"just"*
> (3) It is beneficial to us – *"good"*

It protects our lives, property, and families.

5. The law **REMINDS** us of how terrible sin is – v. 13

"Was then that which is good made death unto me? God forbid. But sin, that it might appear sin, working death in me by that which is good; that sin by

the commandment might become
exceeding sinful."

6. The law <u>REVEALS</u> our carnality – *v. 14*

"For we know that the law is spiritual:
but I am carnal, sold under sin."

7. The law <u>REINFORCES</u> our need of a Savior, and that justification and sanctification are by faith in the finished work of the Messiah!

Galatians 2:19-21: *"For I through the*
law am dead to the law, that I might
live unto God. I am crucified with
Christ: nevertheless I live; yet not I, but
Christ liveth in me: and the life which I
now live in the flesh I live by the faith of
the Son of God, Who loved me, and gave
Himself for me. I do not frustrate the
grace of God: for if righteousness come
by the law, then Christ is dead in vain."

Galatians 3:24 – *"Wherefore the law*
was our schoolmaster (tutor) *to bring*

us unto Christ, that we might be justified by faith."

The IMPOSSIBILITY of keeping the law
Romans 7:15-25

1. The DIFFICULTY we have

(1) Our PRACTICE does not reveal our values!

Romans 7:15 – "For that which I do I allow not: for what I would, that do I not; but what I hate, that do I."

Romans 7:19 – "For the good that I would I do not: but the evil which I would not, that I do."

(2) Our PERFORMANCE does not reveal our desires!

Romans 7:18 – "for to will is present with me; but how to perform that which is good I find not."

2. The DECISION we face

(1) The <u>PRINCIPLE</u> of the law is validated – *v. 16* – *"it is good"*

Ecclesiastes 7:20 – "For there is not a just man upon earth, that doeth good, and sinneth not."

(2) The <u>PRESENCE</u> of sin is real – *v. 17* – *"sin that dwelleth in me"*

Psalm 51:5 – "Behold, I was shapen in iniquity, and in sin did my mother conceive me."

Isaiah 64:6 – "But we are all as an unclean thing, and all our righteousnesses are as filthy rags; and we all do fade as a leaf; and our iniquities like the wind, have taken us away."

(3) The <u>POWER</u> of the flesh is helpless – *v. 18a* – *"in me (that is, in my flesh) dwelleth no good thing"*

Job 14:4 – "Who can bring a clean thing out of an unclean? Not one."

Job 15:14-16 – "What is man, that he should be clean? And he which is born of a woman, that he should be righteous? Behold, he putteth no trust in his saints; yea, the heavens are not clean in his sight. How much more abominable and filthy is man, which drinketh iniquity like water?"

Job 25:4-6 – "How then can man be justified with God? or how can he be clean that is born of a woman? Behold even to the moon, and it shineth not; yea, the stars are not pure in his sight. How much less man, that is a worm? And the son of man, which is a worm?

3. The <u>DISCOVERY</u> we make

There are four laws operating in every believer's life!

(1)   The law of the <u>FLESH</u> (*"members"*)

Two things are clear about the *"law of the flesh"*:

It <u>BATTLES</u> the mind – *v. 23a*
"warring against the law of my mind"

210

It **BRINGS** us into bondage to sin –
v. 23b – "bringing me into captivity to the law of sin which is in my members"

II Timothy 2:25-26 – "In meekness instructing those that oppose themselves; if God peradventure will give them repentance to the acknowledging of the truth; And that they may recover themselves out of the snare of the devil, who are taken captive by him at his will."

(2)   The law of the **MIND**

It **DESIRES** to do good – *v. 18 – "for to will is present with me"* and *v. 19a – "for the good that I would"*

It **DELIGHTS** in the law of God – *v. 22 "For I delight in the law of God after the inward man."*

Psalm 1:1-2 – "Blessed is the man that walketh not in the counsel of the ungodly, nor standeth in the way of sinners, nor sitteth in the seat of the scornful. But his delight is in the law of the LORD; and in His law doth he meditate day and night."

Psalm 19:8-10 – "The statutes of the LORD are right, rejoicing the heart: the commandment of the LORD is pure, enlightening the eyes. The fear of the LORD is clean, enduring forever: the judgments of the LORD are true and righteous altogether. More to be desired are they than gold, yea, than much fine gold: sweeter also than honey and the honeycomb."

Psalm 40:8 – "I delight to do Thy will, O my God: yea, thy law is within my heart."

Psalm 119:16 – "I will delight myself in Thy statutes: I will not forget Thy word."

Psalm 119:24 – "Thy testimonies also are my delight and my counselors."

Psalm 119:35 – "Make me to go in the path of Thy commandments, for therein do I delight."

Psalm 119:47 – "And I will delight myself in Thy commandments, which I have loved."

Psalm 119:97 – O how love I Thy law! It is my meditation all the day."

Psalm 119:174 – "I have longed for Thy salvation, O LORD; and Thy law is my delight."

(3)   The law of <u>GOD</u>

It is <u>PERFECT</u> - *Romans 7:12 – "Wherefore the law is holy, and the commandment holy, and just, and good."*

Romans 7:14 – "For we know that the law is spiritual..."

It is <u>PURPOSEFUL</u> – *Psalm 19:11 – "Moreover by them is Thy servant warned: and in keeping of them there is great reward"*

It is <u>POWERFUL</u> – *Psalm 119:9-11 – "Wherewithal shall a young me cleanse his way? By taking heed thereto according to Thy word. With my whole heart have I sought Thee: O let me now wander from Thy commandments. Thy word have I hid in mine heart, that I might not sin against Thee."*

(4)   The law of <u>SIN</u>

It <u>DWELLS</u> in the believer

Romans 7:17 – "sin that dwelleth in me"

Romans 7:20 – "sin that dwelleth in me"

Romans 7:21 – "evil is present with me"

Romans 7:23 – "the law of sin which is in my members"

It <u>DOMINATES</u> the believer

Romans 7:23 – "bringing me into captivity to the law of sin which is in my members"

Romans 6:12 – "Let not sin therefore reign in your mortal body, that ye should obey it in the lusts thereof."

Romans 7:11 – "For sin, taking occasion by the commandment, deceived me, and by it slew me."

4. The <u>DELIVERANCE</u> we need

Romans 7:24-25 – "O wretched man that I am! Who shall deliver me from the body of this death? I thank God through Jesus Christ our Lord. So then with the mind I myself serve the law of God; but with the flesh the law of sin."

LAW OF THE MIND – LAW OF GOD
LAW OF THE FLESH – LAW OF SIN

(1) <u>REALIZE</u> your sinful condition – *"wretched men that I am!"*

(2) <u>RESPOND</u> to our only Savior from sin – *"I thank God through Jesus Christ our Lord!"*

(3) <u>RECOGNIZE</u> the facts that reveal our need of the Holy Spirit's power and control – *"So then with the mind I myself serve the law of God: but with the flesh the law of sin."*

Chapter 5
SECURITY
Romans 8:1-39

The <u>PRINCIPLES</u> of the
RIGHTEOUSNESS of GOD

CONDEMNATION – *1:18-3:20*
JUSTIFICATION – *3:21-5:21*
SANCTIFICATION – *6:1-7:25*

SECURITY – *8:1-39*

This marvelous chapter is foundational
to the Christian life. It answers the
dilemma that chapter 7 left us with –
Who is going to deliver us from the fact
of sin that dwells within us? How are we
going to have victory over the carnality
that plagues us all?

Our SECURITY is stated clearly in this
chapter – in *Romans 8:1* we read:
*"There is therefore now no
condemnation to those who are in
Christ Jesus, who walk not after the
flesh, but after the Spirit."*

In *Romans 8:38-39* the chapter ends with: *"For I am persuaded, that neither death, nor life, nor angels, nor principalities, nor powers, nor things present, nor things to come, nor height, nor depth, nor any other creature, shall be able to separate us from the love of God which is in Christ Jesus our Lord."*

Romans 8:1 – NO CONDEMNATION!
Romans 8:39 – NO SEPARATION!

Our SECURITY is given by the presence and power of the Holy Spirit!
Romans 8:1-17

Our SECURITY is grounded in our hope!
Romans 8:18-25

Our SECURITY is guaranteed by four amazing facts!
Romans 8:26-39

OUR SECURITY IS GIVEN BY THE PRESENCE AND POWER OF THE HOLY SPIRIT!

Romans 8:1-17

The key word of Romans 6 is "SIN." The key word of Romans 7 is "LAW." The key word of Romans 8 is "SPIRIT."

This key word is used 22 times in its various forms in this chapter, and 19 of those times read *"the Spirit of God."*

The chapter begins with the words *"There is therefore now…"* The Greek words *ara nun* probably refer to the first seven chapters – because we have been justified by faith, that is, declared righteous by the Person and work of our blessed Lord Yeshua, we have some wonderful results of our position in Jesus Christ.

1. **The wonderful <u>RESULTS</u> of our position in Jesus Christ!** *Romans 8:1-2*

"There is therefore now no condemnation to them which are in Christ Jesus, who walk not after the flesh, but after the Spirit. For the law of the Spirit of life in Christ Jesus hath

made me free from the law of sin and death."

The phrase *"in Christ"* is found 77 times in the New Testament, and in 40 of those places were read *"in Christ Jesus."*

I Corinthians 15:22 says: "in Christ Jesus shall all be made alive."

(1)   NO <u>CONDEMNATION</u>!

The Greek adverb in verse one is what we call an "emphatic negative" and is a word of time.

(2)   NO <u>CARNALITY</u> dominating our lifestyle!

We are often told by various commentators and authors that the words of verse 1 – *"who walk not after the flesh, but after the Spirit"* are not a part of the original Greek text. It appears in the studies of well-respected Bible teachers. We are told that it is not found in the earliest manuscripts of Romans or in most modern translations.

However, the truth is that the only manuscripts that leave the phrase out are Codex Sinaiticus and Codex Vaticanus. The majority of manuscripts contain the reading, and it is quoted by early church leaders and writings. The phrase is repeated in verse four because it is teaching a very important truth about a true, genuine believer, in contrast with an unbeliever who merely professes to belong to the Lord!

       (3)   NO <u>CONTROL</u> by sin and death!

John 8:32-36 says: *"And ye shall know the truth, and the truth shall make you free. They answered Him, We be Abraham's seed, and were never in bondage to any man: how sayest Thou, Ye shall be made free? Jesus answered them, Verily, verily, I say unto you, Whosoever committeth sin is the servant of sin. And the servant abideth not in the house forever: but the Son abideth ever. If the Son therefore shall make you free, ye shall be free indeed."*

2. The marvelous <u>REASON</u> why these results are made possible!

Romans 8:3 – "For what the law could not do, in that it was weak through the flesh, God sending His own Son in the likeness of sinful flesh, and for sin, condemned sin in the flesh."

(1)   The <u>INABILITY</u> of the law

The verse says that the law had no power because it was *"weak through the flesh."* The word in Greek for *"weak"* is *asthenos* – the law is unable to do what was thought possible because of human depravity and carnality.

(2)   The <u>INITIATIVE</u> of God

The phrase that brings joy and hope is *"God sending His own Son."* On ten occasions Jesus referred to His Father as the One Who *"hath sent Me."*

(3)   The <u>INCARNATION</u> of Jesus Christ

The simple words *"in the likeness of sinful flesh"* is not referring to His *"flesh"* but rather to ours! He did NOT have *"sinful flesh"* – it was only a *"likeness."*

II Corinthians 5:21 says: *"For He hath made Him to be sin for us, Who knew no sin; that we might be made the righteousness of God in Him."*

Hebrews 2:14-15 – "Forasmuch then as the children are partakers of flesh and blood, He also Himself likewise took part of the same; that through death He might destroy him that had the power of death, that is, the devil; And deliver them who through fear of death were all their lifetime subject to bondage."

Hebrews 4:15 – "For we have not an high priest which cannot be touched with the feeling of our infirmities; but was in all points tempted like as we are, yet without sin."

(4)   The <u>IMPACT</u> of His coming

Romans 7:3 – "condemned sin in the flesh."

Hebrews 10:10-14 – "By the which will we are sanctified through the offering of the body of Jesus Christ once for all. And every priest standing daily ministering and offering oftentimes the same sacrifices, which can never take away sins; But this Man, after He had offered one sacrifice for sins forever, sat down on the right hand of God; From henceforth expecting till His enemies be made His footstool. For by one offering He hath perfected forever them that are sanctified."

3. The amazing <u>REALITY</u> in the life of every true believer!

Romans 8:4 – "That the righteousness of the law might be fulfilled in us, who walk not after the flesh, but after the Spirit."

The <u>ABILITY</u> to do what God wants us to do is made possible by the presence and power of the Holy Spirit – *"might be fulfilled in us."*

The <u>ASSURANCE</u> that we are *"in Christ Jesus"* is based on a lifestyle that follows the Holy Spirit, not the flesh!

The word *"walk"* is used in its various forms in English 93 times, of which 34 are used by Paul.

The <u>CHARACTERISTICS</u> of those who walk after the flesh

Romans 8:5-8 – "For they that are after the flesh do mind the things of the flesh; but they that are after the Spirit, the things of the Spirit. For to be carnally minded is death; but to be spiritually minded is life and peace. Because the carnal mind is enmity against God: for it is not subject to the law of God, neither indeed can be. So then they that are in the flesh cannot please God."

They <u>FILL</u> their minds with carnal thoughts!

"they that are after the flesh do mind the things of the flesh"

II Corinthians 10:3-5 – "For though we walk in the flesh, we do not war after the flesh: For the weapons of our warfare are not carnal, but mighty through God to the pulling down of strong holds; Casting down imaginations, and every high thing that exalted itself against the knowledge of God, and bringing into captivity every thought to the obedience of Christ."

Philippians 2:5 – "Let this mind be in you, which was also in Christ Jesus."

Colossians 3:1-4 – "If ye than be risen with Christ, seek those things which are above, where Christ sitteth on the right hand of God. Set you affection on things above, not on things on the earth. For ye are dead, and your life is hid with Christ in God. When Christ, Who is our life, shall appear, then shall ye also appear with Him in glory."

They <u>FACE</u> the future without hope!

Romans 8:6 – "For to be carnally minded is death; but to be spiritually minded is life and peace."

When carnality dominates the mind, it leads to death, death to everything that is good and productive and glorifying to the Lord. Your future is uncertain and lacks the kind of hope which spiritual-mindedness brings to a person's life.

They <u>FIGHT</u> against God and His law!

Romans 8:7 – "the carnal mind is enmity against God: for it is not subject to the law of God, neither indeed can be."

One of the most insightful passages on this matter is found in James 4:1-10:

"From whence come wars and fightings among you? come they not hence, even of your lusts that war in your members? Ye lust, and have not: ye kill, and desire to have, and cannot obtain: ye fight and war, yet ye have not, because ye ask not. Ye ask, and receive not, because ye ask amiss, that ye may consume it upon your lusts. Ye adulterers and adulteresses, know ye not that the friendship of the world is enmity with God? whosoever therefore will be a friend of the world is the enemy of God. Do ye think that the scripture saith in vain, The spirit that dwelleth in us lusteth to envy? But He giveth more grace. Wherefore He saith, God resisteth the proud, but giveth grace unto the humble. Submit yourselves therefore to God. Resist the devil, and he will flee from you. Draw night to God, and He will draw nigh to you. Cleanse your hands, ye sinners;

and purify your hearts, ye double-minded. Be afflicted, and mourn, and weep: let your laughter be turned to mourning, and your joy to heaviness. Humble yourselves in the sight of the Lord, and He shall lift you up."

Reading the above passage over and over again will strengthen your understanding and bring relief from the control of self and sin. Read carefully the words that admonish us to deal with carnality! Understand that submission to God and humility before Him are fundamental in our struggles against God and His Word.

They <u>FAIL</u> to please God in whatever they think, say, and do!

Romans 8:8 – "So then they that are in the flesh cannot please God."

The <u>CHARACTERISTICS</u> of a person controlled by the flesh (carnality) are:
1. They <u>FILL</u> their minds with carnal thoughts!
2. They <u>FACE</u> the future without hope!
3. They <u>FIGHT</u> against God and His law!

4. They <u>FAIL</u> to please God in whatever they think, say, and do!

HOW DOES A PERSON PLEASE GOD?

The Bible gives at least nine answers to this basic question. Putting them all together gives us a realization of what it is to be spiritual, and not carnal!

   1. PROCLAIMING the true gospel!

I Corinthians 1:21 – "it <u>pleased</u> God by the foolishness of preaching to save them that believe."

   2. BELIEVING that God will reward those who seek Him!

Hebrews 11:6 – "But without faith it is impossible to <u>please</u> Him; for he that cometh to God must believe that He is, and that He is a Rewarder of them that diligently seek Him."

   3. OBEYING whatever God says!

Colossians 3:20 – "Children, obey your parents in all things: for this is well <u>pleasing</u> unto the Lord."

I John 3:22 – "And whatsoever we ask, we receive of Him, because we keep His commandments, and do those things that are <u>pleasing</u> in His sight."

4. STAYING away from sexual sin!

I Thessalonians 4:1-3 – "Furthermore then we beseech you, brethren, and exhort you by the Lord Jesus, that as ye have received of us how ye ought to walk and to <u>please</u> God, so ye would abound more and more. For ye know what commandments we gave you by the Lord Jesus. For this is the will of God, even your sanctification, that ye should abstain from fornication."

5. REFUSING to please men!

Galatians 1:10 – "For do I now persuade men, or God? or do I seek to <u>please</u> men? For if I yet <u>pleased</u> men, I should not be the servant of Christ."

6. GIVING to others in time of need!

Philippians 4:18 – "But I have all, and abound: I am full, having received of Epaphroditus the things which were *sent from you, an odor of a sweet smell, a sacrifice acceptable, <u>well-pleasing</u> to God."*

7. **PRAISING and GIVING THANKS to God!**

Psalm 69:30-31 – "I will praise the Name of God with a song, and will magnify Him with thanksgiving. This also shall <u>please</u> the LORD better than an ox or bullock that hath horns and hoofs."

8. **KEEPING your priorities straight!**

II Timothy 2:3-4 – "Thou therefore endure hardness as a good soldier of Jesus Christ. No man that warreth entangleth himself with the affairs of this life; that he may <u>please</u> Him Who hath chosen him to be a soldier."

9. **BEARING the infirmities of the weak!**

Romans 15:1-3 – "We then that are strong ought to bear the infirmities of the weak, and not to <u>please</u> ourselves. Let every one of us <u>please</u> his neighbor for his good to edification. For even

Christ <u>pleased</u> not Himself; but, as it is written, The reproaches of them that reproached thee fell on Me."

The <u>CONFIDENCE</u> for those who walk in the Spirit!

Romans 8:9-11 – "But ye are not in the flesh, but in the Spirit, if so be that the Spirit of God dwell in you. Now if any man have not the Spirit of Christ, he is none of His. And if Christ be in you, the body is dead because of sin; but the Spirit is life because of righteousness. But if the Spirit of Him that raised up Jesus from the dead dwell in you, He that raised up Christ from the dead shall also quicken your mortal bodies by His Spirit that dwelleth in you."

Once again we notice that the key word of chapter 8 is "SPIRIT" – used 21 times. The word *"Spirit"* appears 505 times in the Bible, of which 261 times are in the New Testament. The term *"Holy Spirit"* is found 3 times in the Old Testament, but 94 times in the New Testament. The phrase *"the Spirit of God"* appears 26 times in the Bible, of which 12 times are in the New Testament. When the definite article (*"the"*) appears in front of the word (*"THE Spirit"*) it usually refers to the Holy Spirit, and is so used 275 times in the Bible, of which 163 times are in the New Testament.

THE <u>IDENTITY</u> OF THE HOLY SPIRIT IS CRUCIAL!

Romans 8 emphasizes the presence and power of the Holy Spirit in the life of the believer. The <u>IDENTITY</u> of the Holy Spirit is crucial to our understanding of His work in us. He is a real Person; He is not a "force" or an "it." Two things are very clear in the Bible about His Person and work:

He is GOD!

In Acts 5:3-4 we have clear evidence about the Holy Spirit being God. In verse 3, Peter says to Ananias: *"Why hath Satan filled thine heart to lie to the Holy Ghost?"* In verse 4, he continues: *"thou hast not lied unto men, but unto God."*

Hebrews 9:14 says that He is the *"eternal"* Spirit. I Corinthians 2:10-11 says that the Spirit knows what God alone knows. In Psalm 139:7-10, it is clear that we cannot escape His presence — He is omnipresent!

In Matthew 28:19 we are admonished to baptize those who are made disciples *"in the Name of the Father, and of the Son, and of the Holy Spirit."* The word *"Name"* is singular, not plural — in reference to God, it is never used in the plural, only in the singular.

He is a PERSON!

The fundamental marks of personality are attributed to the Holy Spirit in the teaching of the Bible.

(1)   He has a MIND!

Romans 8:27 says: *"And he that searcheth the hearts knoweth what is the <u>mind of the Spirit</u>, because He maketh intercession for the saints according to the will of God."*

(2)   He has EMOTIONS!

Ephesians 4:30 says: *"And <u>grieve not</u> the Holy Spirit of God, whereby ye are sealed unto the day of redemption."*

(3)   He has a WILL!

We read in I Corinthians 12:11: *"But all these worketh that one and the selfsame Spirit, dividing to every man severally <u>as He will</u>."*

HIS <u>INFLUENCE</u> UPON THE UNBELIEVER IS CLEAR!

In John 16:8-11, the Holy Spirit *"convicts"* the unbeliever of *"sin, righteousness,* and *judgment."* In Acts 7:51 we learn that unbelievers can *"resist"* the Holy Spirit, and in Hebrews 10:26-29 we read that they can *"insult"* the Holy Spirit!

HIS <u>INDWELLING</u> OF THE BELIEVER IS ESSENTIAL!

Believers are *"regenerated"* or *"born again"* by the Holy Spirit. John 3:5-8 teaches:

"Jesus answered, Verily, verily, I say unto thee, Except a man be born of water and of the Spirit, he cannot enter into the kingdom of God. That which is born of the flesh is flesh; and that which

is born of the Spirit is spirit. Marvel not that I said unto thee, Ye must be born again. The wind bloweth where it lusteth, and thou hearest the sound thereof, but canst not tell whence it cometh, and whither it goeth: so is every one that is born of the Spirit." Also, in Titus 3:5 we read: *"Not by works of righteousness which we have done, but according to His mercy He saved us by the washing of regeneration, and renewing of the Holy Ghost."*

Believers are also *"sealed"* by the Holy Spirit. In II Corinthians 1:20-22, it says: *"For all the promises of God in Him are yea, and in Him, Amen, unto the glory of God by us. Now He which stablisheth us with you in Christ, and hath anointed us, is God; Who hath also <u>sealed</u> us, and given the earnest of the Spirit in our hearts."*

Again, in Ephesians 1:13-14 we read: *"In Whom ye also trusted, after that ye heard the word of truth, the gospel of your salvation: in Whom also after that ye believed, ye were <u>sealed</u> with that Holy Spirit of promise, which is the earnest of our inheritance until the* *redemption of the purchased possession, unto the praise of His glory."*

The Bible also teaches that all believers are *"baptized"* into the body of Jesus Christ. In I Corinthians 12:13 we read: *"For by one Spirit are we all <u>baptized</u> into one body, whether we be Jews or Gentiles, whether we be bond or free; and have been all made to drink into one Spirit."*

HIS <u>IMPACT</u> UPON THE BELIEVERS IS GREATLY NEEDED!

For wisdom and understanding
Acts 6:3; I Corinthians 2:10-16

For comfort and encouragement
John 14:16; Romans 8:16, 26

For the use of spiritual gifts
I Corinthians 12:4-11

For spiritual power and witness
Acts 1:8; 4:31-33; Ephesians 3:14-16, 20

For spiritual responses
Ephesians 5:18-21

For control of sinful desires
Galatians 5:16

In Romans 8:9-11, we learn three important truths about the Person and work of the Holy Spirit:

> (1)   The <u>PRESENCE</u> of the Holy Spirit in the life of the believer is crucial to our *"confidence"* – v. 9

"But ye are not in the flesh, but in the Spirit, if so be that the Spirit of God dwell in you. Now if any man have not the Spirit of Christ, he is none of His."

The words *"if so be"* should be clearly translated as "if and it is so."

> (2)   The <u>PRINCIPLE</u> of righteousness is essential as well – v. 10

"And if Christ be in you, the body is dead because of sin; but the Spirit is life because of righteousness."

The point of the above verse is simple in one sense – sin brings death, but righteousness brings life. John 6:63 adds: *"It is the Spirit that quickeneth; the flesh profiteth nothing: the words that I speak unto you, they are spirit, and they are life."*

    (3)   The <u>POWER</u> of the Spirit brings us great confidence concerning the future – v. 11

"But if the Spirit of Him that raised up Jesus from the dead dwell in you, He that raised up Christ from the dead shall also quicken your mortal bodies by His Spirit that dwelleth in you."

The <u>CONCLUSIONS</u> we draw – vv. 12-13

"Therefore, brethren, we are debtors, not to the flesh, to live after the flesh. For if ye live after the flesh, ye shall die: but if ye through the Spirit do mortify the deeds of the body, ye shall live."

1. The <u>REASON</u> we are *"debtors"* is the presence and power of the Holy Spirit! – v. 12

2. The <u>RESULTS</u> we can expect –
   v. 13

If we live *"after the flesh"* – <u>DEATH</u>!
If we mortify the deeds of the body –
<u>LIFE</u>!

The meaning of *"mortify"* (put to death)
is the argument of the Apostle Paul
through chapters 6-8 – he uses this
thought 11 times.

OUR SECURITY IS <u>GIVEN</u> BY THE PRESENCE AND POWER OF THE HOLY SPIRIT!
Romans 8:1-17

1. As to the <u>RIGHTEOUSNESS</u> of the
   law – 8:1-4

2. As to the <u>REALITY</u> of the flesh –
   8:5-13

3. As to our <u>RELATIONASHIP</u> with
   God – 8:14-17

*"For as many as are led by the Spirit of
God, they are the sons of God. For ye
have not received the spirit of bondage
again to fear; but ye have received the
Spirit of adoption, whereby we cry,*

Abba, Father. The Spirit itself beareth witness with our spirit, that we are the children of God: And if children, then heirs; heirs of God, and joint-heirs with Christ, if so be that we suffer with Him, that we may be also glorified together."

The term *"sons of God"* in the Jewish Bible (Old Testament) is used of "angels." (cf. Genesis 6:2, 4; Job 1:6; 2:1; 38:7) The New Testament uses two different Greek words, often used interchangeably in the same passage.

tekna – little born one – refers to BIRTH

huios – refers to ADOPTION and inheritance

In Romans 8:14 – it is *huios*
In Romans 8:15 – it is *tekna*
In Romans 8:19 – it is *huios*
In Romans 8:21 – it is *tekna*

Notice three things about the work of the Holy Spirit in our personal RELATIONSHIP to God and the security we have because of it!

(1) The Holy Spirit <u>GUIDES</u> us – v. 14 – *"led by the Spirit of God"*

There is no "if" to begin verse 14; it should be "as many as."

HOW DOES THE HOLY SPIRIT GUIDE US?

To <u>PEACE</u> – Psalm 23:2 – *"He maketh me to lie down in green pastures; He <u>leadeth</u> me beside the still waters."*

Isaiah 5:23 – *"ye shall go out with joy, and be <u>led</u> forth with peace."*

To <u>RIGHTEOUSNESS</u> – Psalm 23:3 – *"He restoreth my soul: He <u>leadeth</u> me in the paths of righteousness for His Name's sake."*

Isaiah 48:17 – *"which <u>leadeth</u> thee by the way that thou shouldest go"*

Psalm 107:6-7 – *"Then they cried unto the LORD in their trouble, and He delivered them out of their distresses, and He <u>led</u> them forth by the right way."*

To <u>FREEDOM</u> – Galatians 5:1 – *"Stand fast in the liberty wherewith Christ hath made us free, and be not entangled again with the yoke of bondage."* 5:18 – *"But if ye be <u>led</u> of the spirit, ye are not under the law."*

To <u>REPENTANCE</u> – Romans 2:4 – *"the goodness of God <u>leadeth</u> thee to repentance."*

To <u>SAFETY</u> – Psalm 106:9 – *"He rebuked the Red sea also, and it was dried up: so He <u>led</u> them through the depths, and through the wilderness."*

Deuteronomy 8:2 – *"And thou shalt remember all the way which the LORD thy God <u>led</u> thee these forty years in the wilderness..."* 8:15 – *"Who <u>led</u> thee through the great and terrible wilderness."*

In John 10:3 we read that the good Shepherd *"<u>leadeth</u> them out."*

To <u>TRUTH</u> – John 16:13 – *"Howbeit when He, the Spirit of truth, is come, He will <u>guide</u> you into all truth..."*

A WONDERFUL SONG

This well-known song expresses this truth beautifully!

"He <u>leadeth</u> me! O blessed thought! O words with heavenly comfort fraught! Whate'er I do, where'er I be, still 'tis God's hand that <u>leadeth</u> me. He <u>leadeth</u> me, He <u>leadeth</u> me! By His own hand He <u>leadeth</u> me. His faithful follower I will be, for by His hand He <u>leadeth</u> me.

(2)   The Holy Spirit <u>GUARANTEES</u> our access to the Father — v. 15

"For we have not received the spirit of bondage again to fear; but ye have received the Spirit of adoption, whereby we cry, Abba, Father."

The Spirit <u>ELIMINATES</u> fear!
"ye have not received the spirit of bondage again to fear"

The Spirit <u>ENCOURAGES</u> prayer!
"whereby we cry…"

Used in the Psalms over 40 times, emphasizing urgent prayer!

The word *"Abba"* is used today in Israel when Jewish children refer to their own Father. It is a term of deep affection and intimate relationship.

> **(3) The Holy Spirit <u>GIVES</u> assurance to us that we belong to God!**
> **vv. 16-17**

He <u>CONFIRMS</u> the truthfulness of God's Word – *"beareth witness"*

He <u>CONVINCES</u> us that we have a real inheritance coming because of our faith in Jesus Christ – *"And if children, then heirs; heirs of God, and joint-heirs with Christ..."*

He <u>COMFORTS</u> us in our trials, knowing that one day it will be worth it all! – *"if so be that we suffer with Him, that we may be also glorified together."*

ANOTHER WONDERFUL SONG!

"When all my labors and trials are o'er; and I am safe on that beautiful shore; Just to be near the dear Lord I adore, will through the ages be glory for me! O that will be glory for me; glory for me, glory for me! When by His grace I shall look on His face – that will be glory – be glory for me!"

Yes. the Holy Spirit is the key to our **SECURITY**! But, in addition to His **PRESENCE** and **POWER** (Romans 8:1-17), our **SECURITY** is **GROUNDED IN HOPE**! (Romans 8:18-25)

Romans 8:18 speaks of future glory as the great expectation and hope of believers!

1. The **REVELATION** of future glory!

"For I reckon that the sufferings of this present time are not worthy to be compared with the glory which shall be revealed in us." The future glory which God has promised to the believer is obviously much greater that any of our

sufferings. The word *"worthy"* (Greek: *axios*) refers to "balance." Our sufferings cannot possibly match the glory we shall one day experience!

I Peter 4:12-13 says: *"Beloved, think it not strange concerning the fiery trial which is to try you, as though some strange thing happened unto you: But rejoice, inasmuch as ye are partakers of Christ's sufferings; that, when His glory shall be revealed, ye may be glad also with exceeding joy."*

The late Lutheran commentator (Lenski) wrote about the above: *"When we are going through difficult times, we often give them too much consideration, fail to look at the coming glory, and lose our balance, and sense of proportion."* How true that is!

There are many types of suffering in this life in addition to physical aches and pains, illness, disease and disability; There is also the matter of mental anguish and stress, loneliness and isolation, misunderstandings, and strained relationships. Also, the loss of loved ones can be devastating, as well as the concern for the spiritual condition of others, especially family; There is also the pain of guilt feelings, bad self-esteem, and even physical deprivation and hunger. Many have lost their jobs, and are experiencing the difficulties of financial loss.

Verse 18 begins *"I reckon"* – the Greek word, *logizomai*, means "to reason" or "to calculate" or "use logic."

2. The <u>REALIZATION</u> of future deliverance! Romans 8:19-23

"For the earnest expectation of the creature waiteth for the manifestation of the sons of God. For the creature was made subject to vanity, not willingly, but by reason of Him Who hath subjected the same in hope, because the creature itself also shall be delivered from the bondage of corruption into the glorious liberty of the children of God. For we know that the whole creation groaneth and travaileth in pain together unto now. And not only then, but ourselves also, which have the firstfruits of the Spirit, even we ourselves groan within ourselves,

waiting for the adoption, to wit, the redemption of our body."

Notice carefully the following five things about these verses:

    (1)   The <u>RETURN</u> of Jesus Christ v. 18 – *"the glory which shall be revealed"*

Colossians 3:4 says: *"When Christ, Who is our life, shall appear, then shall ye also appear with Him in glory."*

    (2)   The <u>REVEALING</u> of the sons of God – v. 19 – *"earnest expectation"*

The word refers to an intense watching and waiting – stretching the head from the body!

Matthew 24:42 – *"Watch therefore: for ye know not what hour your Lord doth come."*

Matthew 24:44 – *"Therefore be ye also ready: for in such an hour as ye think not the Son of man cometh."*

Matthew 25:13 – *"Watch therefore, for ye know neither the day nor the hour wherein the Son of man cometh."*

    (3)   The <u>RELEASE</u> of all creation from bondage – vv. 22-23 *"the creature was made subject to vanity"*

    (4)   The <u>REUNION</u> of all believers – I Thessalonians 4:17 – *"Then we which are alive and remain shall be caught up together with them in the clouds, to meet the Lord in the air: and so shall we ever be with the Lord."*

    (5)   The <u>REDEMPTION</u> of our bodies – v. 23

"And not only they, but ourselves also, which have the firstfruits of the Spirit, even we ourselves groan within ourselves, waiting for the adoption, to wit, the redemption of our body."

Philippians 3:20-21 – *"For our conversation is in heaven; from whence also we look for the Savior, the Lord*

Jesus Christ: Who shall change our vile body, that it may be fashioned like unto His glorious body, according to the working whereby He is able even to subdue all things unto Himself."

I John 3:1-3 – "Behold, what manner of love the Father hath bestowed upon us, that we should be called the sons of God: therefore the world knoweth us not, because it knew Him not. Beloved, now are we the sons of God, and it doth not yet appear what we shall be: but we know that, when He shall appear, we shall be like Him; for we shall see Him as He is. And every man that hath this hope in Him purifieth himself, even as He is pure."

3. The <u>REALITY</u> of our present hope – 8:24-25

"For we are saved by hope: but hope that is seen is not hope: for what a man seeth, why doth he yet hope for? But if we hope for that we see not, then do we with patience wait for it."

(1)   It brings us to <u>SALVATION</u> – v. 24

"we are saved by hope"

Hebrews 6:17-19 – *"Wherein God, willing more abundantly to shew unto the heirs of promise the immutability of His counsel, confirmed it by an oath: That by two immutable things, in which it was impossible for God to lie, we might have a strong consolation, who have fled for refuge to lay hold upon the hope set before us: Which hope we have as an anchor of the soul, both sure and stedfast, and which entereth into that within the veil."*

> (2) It helps us in our present <u>SUFFERING</u> – v. 25 – *"with patience wait for it"*

Our SECURITY is...

<u>GIVEN</u> by the presence and power of the Holy Spirit!

<u>GROUNDED</u> in our hope!

And now...

<u>GUARANTEED</u> by the facts
Romans 8:26-39

1. The <u>PRAYER</u> of the Spirit
8:26-27

"Likewise the Spirit also helpeth our infirmities: for we know not what we should pray for as we ought: but the Spirit itself maketh intercession for us with groanings which cannot be uttered. And He that searcheth the hearts knoweth what is the mind of the Spirit, because He maketh intercession for the saints according to the will of God."

(1)   The <u>CONTEXT</u> of this prayer – *"likewise"*

Two possibilities of interpretation here: One is that it refers to the trials and sufferings – the Spirit helps us like hope does! Secondly, some believe that it refers to the work of the Holy Spirit to which he has been referring throughout the chapter!

Paul was talking about the *"Spirit of adoption"* when he brought up the issue of suffering (v. 17). The digression of verses 18-25 is not drawing us away from his discussion, but in verse 26, Paul returns to the main arguments of our security that deal with the presence and power of the Holy Spirit in our lives. The real issue of the chapter is security or the assurance of our salvation.

The phrase in v. 26 – *"the Spirit also"* in addition to the other things about the Spirit that Paul has mentioned, forms a clear connection with the words *"the Spirit beareth witness"* and *"the Spirit also helpeth..."*

> (2)   The <u>CONDITION</u> which necessitates this prayer – *"infirmities"*

Several manuscripts contain the singular word *"infirmity"* including one of the earliest papyrus manuscripts.

The Greek word is *astheneia* and refers to "no strength" – so that the way it is phrased in this verse is not referring to the sufferings of the previous context but rather the common condition of us all – "weak." We are all "weak" – utterly helpless without the Lord's strength and help. Our infirmities may lead us to sin, but our infirmities in and of themselves are not sinful.

In Matthew 26:41, Yeshua said to His sleepy disciples: *"Watch and pray, that ye enter not into temptation: the spirit indeed is willing, but the flesh is <u>weak</u>."*

> (3)   The <u>CAUSE</u> which makes the prayer of the Spirit so essential – *"for we know not what we should pray for as we ought"*

It is not that we don't know how to pray (although that can be a problem, for in Luke 11:1 the disciples asked Yeshua – *"Lord, teach us to pray"*) – the problem is that we don't know <u>WHAT</u> to pray when we are going through trials and great difficulties.

The primary effect of our "weakness" is that we don't know <u>what</u> to pray in difficult situations. The possibilities are much broader than we are willing to admit or acknowledge. It is the Spirit and the sovereignty of God that will bring the final answer!

For example, when going through difficult trials and afflictions, here are the ways we often deal with them:

"Lord, please take this away from me!"

This is how Paul was praying in the context of II Corinthians 12:7-10.

"Lord, please give me what I want!"

According to Deuteronomy 3:23-28, this was the prayer of Moses, and God did not answer it the way Moses desired!

"Lord, why are you doing this to me?"

It is easy to pray this kind of prayer – it was the situation in the life of Job. Read Job 1:20-11 and 2:9-10.

(4) The <u>CONSEQUENCES</u> of our lack of knowledge about the <u>what</u> and <u>why</u> of our trials – *"groanings which cannot be uttered"*

Some people teach that these are the *"groanings"* of the Holy Spirit! But, that

is impossible – He is God! They belong
to us – *"cannot be uttered."* This
passage is not referring to heavenly
language or speaking in tongues; it
simply means "wordless." We have
nothing to say because we don't know
why these things are happening to us.
These "groanings" within us are the
proof that we belong to the Lord, and
that the Spirit is working in us!

(5)   The <u>CHARACTER</u> of
the Spirit's work in us
– *"helpeth"* and
"maketh intercession"

The word *"helpeth"* combines three
words in Greek: *sunantilambanomai*
sun – "together"
anti – "in the stead of"
lambano – "to receive"

The basic idea is that of one person
helping another. The Spirit leads us to
cry *"Abba, Father"* but the cry is uttered
by us, not Him, for He is not the Son of
the Father!

The words *"The Spirit maketh
intercession"* is like that of a lawyer who
intercedes in behalf of his client.

However, there is a slight difference when comparing the intercessory work of our Lord Yeshua. Both are "advocates" or "comforters" – called alongside of to help. When a lawyer addresses the court in behalf of his client, he illustrates the work of our Lord Yeshua (Romans 8:34; Hebrews 7:25; I John 2:1-2), but when the lawyer instructs the client as to what to say, he illustrates the work of the Holy Spirit.

(6) The <u>CONFIDENCE</u> that we have – *"He that searcheth the hearts knoweth what is the mind of the Spirit"*

We cannot read another's heart or even our own! God not only hears our groans, He understands them when we do not! He knows <u>why</u> it is all happening to us!

(7) The <u>CONCLUSION</u> we can draw – *"He maketh intercession for the saints according to the will of God"*

Prayer is the training camp that prepares us to face all of life with total confidence in the sovereignty and purposes of our blessed Lord – to Him be all the glory!

2. The <u>PURPOSE</u> of God
Romans 8:28-30

"And we know that all things work together for good to them that love God, to them who are the called according to His purpose. For whom He did foreknow, He also did predestinate to be conformed to the image of His Son, that He might be the firstborn among many brethren. Moreover whom He did predestinate, them He also called: and whom He called, them He also justified: and whom He justified, them He also glorified."

WHAT WONDERFUL WORDS!

(1) Our <u>CONFIDENCE</u> if based on it – v. 28 – *"we know"*

Knowledge based on facts about God is found at least 44 times in the Bible.

(2) Our CIRCUMSTANCES are controlled by it – *"all things work together for good"*

Notice that everything is <u>INCLUDED</u> – *"all things."* Romans 11:36 says: *"For of (out of – ek) Him, and through (dia) Him, and to (eis) Him, are all things: to Whom be glory forever. Amen!"*

Ephesians 1:11 – *"In Whom also we have obtained an inheritance, being predestinated according to the purpose of Him Who worketh all things after the counsel of His own will."*

In addition, notice that everything is <u>INTENDED</u> to result in *"good."* Psalm 119:68 says of the LORD GOD: *"Thou art good, and doest good."*

II Corinthians 4:15 says: *"For all things are for your sakes, that the abundant grace might through the thanksgiving of many redound to the glory of God."*

(3) Our <u>CALLING</u> is at the heart of it – *"who are called according to His purpose"*

I Corinthians 1:9 says: *"God is faithful, by Whom ye were <u>called</u> unto the fellowship of His Son Jesus Christ our Lord."*

II Timothy 1:9 adds: *"Who have saved us, and <u>called</u> us with an holy <u>calling</u>, not according to our works, but according to His own purpose and grace, which was given us in Christ Jesus before the world began."*

Romans 1:7 told the believers in Rome that they were *"<u>called</u> to be saints."*

(4) Our <u>CONFORMITY</u> to His Son is behind it – *"to be conformed to the image of His Son"*

Although every *"image"* is a *"likeness"* not every *"likeness"* is an *"image."*

In Colossians 1:15 we read about our Lord Yeshua: *"For it pleased the Father that in Him should all fullness dwell."* Literally, the Greek text reads that *"all the fullness was pleased to dwell in Him."* Hebrews 1:3 says: *"Who being the brightness of His glory, and the express image of His Person, and upholding all things by the word of His power, when He had by Himself purged our sins, sat down on the right hand of the Majesty on high."*

OUR <u>CONFORMITY</u> TO CHRIST INVOLVES THREE BASIC THINGS:

> **(1)** It is a <u>PLAN</u> based on God's foreknowledge!

Romans 8:29 says *"whom He did <u>foreknow</u>, He also did predestinate."*

Acts 2:23 reads: *"Him, being delivered by the determinate counsel and <u>foreknowledge</u> of God, ye have taken and by wicked hands have crucified and slain."*

I Peter 1:2 adds: *"Elect according to the <u>foreknowledge</u> of God the Father,* *through sanctification of the Spirit, unto obedience and sprinkling of the blood of Jesus Christ..."*

> (2)   It is a <u>PURPOSE</u> that centers in the exaltation of His Son!

Romans 8:29 says *"that He might be the firstborn among many brethren."*

The Greek word for *"firstborn"* is *prototokos*. It does not merely speak of one who was born <u>first</u>, but it emphasizes preeminence.

Colossians 1:15 says of our Lord Yeshua: *"the firstborn of every creature."* Hebrews 1:6 adds: *"And again, when He bringeth in the first begotten into the world, He saith, And let all the angels of God worship Him."*

Philippians 2:9-11 speaks powerfully of the preeminence of our Lord when it says: *"Wherefore God also hath highly exalted Him, and given Him a Name which is above every name; That at the Name of Jesus every knee should bow, of things in heaven, and things in earth, and things under the earth; and that every tongue should confess that Jesus Christ is Lord, to the glory of God the Father."*

> **(3)** **It is a <u>PRINCIPLE</u> that affects us both physically and spiritually!**

PHYSICALLY – we will one day be *"conformed"*!

I Corinthians 15:49 – *"And as we have borne the image of the earthy, we shall also bear the image of the heavenly."*

Philippians 3:20-21 – *"For our conversation* (Greek word gives us our English word "politics") *is in heaven; from whence also we look for the Savior, the Lord Jesus Christ: Who shall change our vile body, that it may be fashioned like unto His glorious body, according to the working whereby He is able even to subdue all things unto Himself."*

I John 3:1-3 – *"Behold, what manner of love the Father hath bestowed upon us, that we should be called the sons of God: therefore the world knoweth us* *not, because it knew Him not. Beloved, now are we the sons of God, and it doth not yet appear what we shall be: but we know that, when He shall appear, we shall be like Him; for we shall see Him as He is. And every man that hath this hope in him purifieth himself, even as He is pure."*

SPIRITUALLY – we are continually being *"conformed"* by the work of the Holy Spirit within us!

II Corinthians 3:18 – *"But we all, with open face beholding as in a glass the glory of the Lord, are changed into the same image from glory to glory, even as by the Spirit of the Lord."*

(4) Our <u>CERTAINTY</u> of our salvation is totally dependent upon it – v. 30

"Moreover whom He did predestinate, them He also called: and whom He called, them He also justified: and whom He justified, them He also glorified."

It is <u>ROOTED</u> in His predestination!
"whom He did predestinate"

It means to "mark out an horizon ahead of time. Acts 4:27-28 presents just such an argument:

"For of a truth against Thy holy Child Jesus, Whom Thou hast anointed, both Herod, and Pontius Pilate, with the Gentiles, and the people of Israel, were gathered together, for to do whatsoever Thy hand and Thy counsel determined before to be done."

The above verses clearly show the plan of God was behind all the events of the crucifixion of our Lord!

Ephesians 1:4-6 also presents this wonderful truth:

"According as He hath chosen us in Him before the foundation of the world, that we should be holy and without blame before Him in love: Having predestinated us unto the adoption of children by Jesus Christ to Himself, according to the good pleasure of His will, to the praise of the glory of His

grace, wherein He hath made us accepted in the Beloved (One).*"*

It is <u>RECEIVED</u> in His called!
"them He also called"

Romans 11:29 says: *"For the gifts and calling of God are without repentance."* That means that God will not change His mind on this matter – praise the Lord!

It is <u>RELATED</u> to our justification!
"them He also justified"

Romans 3:24 says: *"Being justified freely by His grace through the redemption that is in Christ Jesus."*

It is <u>REVEALED</u> in our glorification!
"them He also glorified"

Back in Romans 8:18 we read: *"For I reckon that the sufferings of this present time are not worthy to be compared with the glory which shall be revealed in us."*

One of the most encouraging and marvelous passages on our future glorification is that of II Corinthians 4:16-18:

"For which cause we faint not; but though our outward man perish, yet the inward man is renewed day by day, For our light affliction, which is but for a moment, worketh for us a far more exceeding and eternal weight of glory; While we look not at the things which are seen, but at the things which are not seen: for the things which are seen are temporal; but the things which are not seen are eternal."

OUR SECURITY IS...

GIVEN BY THE PRESENCE AND POWER OF THE HOLY SPIRIT – Romans 8:1-7

GROUNDED IN OUR HOPE - Romans 8:18-25

GUARANTEED BY THE FACTS – Romans 8:26-39

Those four facts include:

The <u>PRAYER</u> of the Spirit Romans 8:26-27

The PURPOSE of the Father
Romans 8:28-30

The PROMISE of God
Romans 8:31-34

The POWER of love
Romans 8:35-39

The PROMISE of God
Romans 8:31-34

"What shall we then say to these things? If God be for us, who can be against us? He that spared not His own Son, but delivered Him up for us all, how shall He not with Him also freely give us all things? Who shall lay any thing to the charge of God's elect? It is God that justifieth."

The opening question – *"What shall we then say to these things?"* It is very Jewish in answer to a given question, to answer with more questions. Paul uses this quite often in his writings – for example:

Romans 3:5 – *"what shall we say?"*

Romans 4:1 – *"What shall we say then?"*

Romans 6:1 – *"What shall we say then?"*

Romans 7:7 – *"What shall we say then?"*

Romans 8:31 – *"What shall we then say to these things?"*

Romans 9:14 – *"What shall we say then?"*

Romans 9:30 – *"What shall we say then?"*

The immediate context of *"these things"* in Romans 8:31-34 deals with the facts about our assurance, such as the Person and work of the Holy Spirit.

   1. As to His <u>PROTECTION</u> – v. 31

QUESTION #1 – *"If God be for us, who can be against us?"*

The word *"If"* in Greek (*ei* with the indicative mood) should be translated "If and it is true" or "Since."

Psalm 27:1-3 says: *"The LORD is my light and my salvation; whom shall I fear? The LORD is the strength of my life; of whom shall I be afraid? When the wicked, even mine enemies and my foes, came upon me to eat up my flesh, they stumbled and fell. Though an host should encamp against me, my heart shall not fear: though war should rise against me, in this will I be confident."*

Psalm 46:1-2 adds: *"God is our refuge and strength, a very present help in trouble. Therefore will not we fear, though the earth be removed, and though the mountains be carried into the midst of the sea."* Verse 7 says: *"The LORD of hosts is with us; the God of Jacob is our refuge"* (repeated in verse 11 as well).

Psalm 56:4 states clearly: *"In God I will praise His word, in God I have put my trust; I will not fear what flesh can do unto me."*

The Bible is filled with assurances from the Lord – if our trust is in Him, we have no need to be afraid.

2. As to His <u>PROVISION</u> – V. 32

QUESTION #2 – *"How shall He not with Him also freely give us all things?"*

The premise is clear – *"He that spared not His own Son, but delivered him up for us all..."*

Ephesians 1:3 reminds us all: *"Blessed be the God and Father of our Lord Jesus Christ, Who hath blessed us with all spiritual blessings in heavenly places in Christ."*

3. As to His <u>PARDON</u> – v. 33

QUESTION #3 – *"Who shall lay any thing to the charge of God's elect?"*

The simple premise behind this question is: *"It is God that justifieth."*

Paul wrote in Titus 3:5: *"Not by works of righteousness which we have done, but according to His mercy He saved us, by the washing of regeneration, and renewing of the Holy Ghost."*

4. As to His <u>PRAYER</u> – v. 34

QUESTION #4 – *"Who is he that condemneth?"*

The premise here brings great joy to the heart of all believers: *"It is Christ that died, yea rather, that is risen again, Who is even at the right hand of God. Who also maketh intercession for us."*

Our blessed Lord is our "advocate." Hebrews 7:25 – *"Wherefore He is able to save them to the uttermost that come unto God by Him, seeing He ever liveth to make intercession for them."* In I John 3:1-2 we read: *"My little children, these things write unto you, that ye sin not. And if any man sin, we have an advocate with the Father, Jesus Christ the righteous: And He is the propitiation for our sins: and not for ours only, but also for the sins of the whole world."*

This intercession work of our blessed Lord Yeshua is going on right now – He is at *"the right hand of God the Father."* What wonderful encouragement to know that our Lord is praying for us!

The **POWER** of love
Romans 8:35-39

"Who shall separate us from the love of Christ? Shall tribulation, or distress, or

persecution, or famine, or nakedness, or peril, or sword? As it is written, For Thy sake we are killed all the day long; we are accounted as sheep for the slaughter. Nay, in all these things we are more than conquerors through Him that loved us. For I am persuaded, that neither death, nor life, nor angels, nor principalities, nor powers, nor things present, nor things to come, nor height, nor depth, nor any other creature, shall be able to separate us from the love of God, which is in Christ Jesus our Lord."

WHAT REMARKABLE WORDS OF ENCOURAGEMENT TO EVERY BELIEVER!

QUESTION #5 – *"Who shall separate us from the love of Christ?"*

The basic premise (v. 37) – *"in all these things we are more than conquerors through Him that loved us."* **The Greek word that translates the words** *"more than conquerors"* **is** *hupernikao.* **The last part of that word refers to victory or conquest. It is used as the name of certain tennis shoes – "Nike." The preposition** *huper* **means "above" or "more than." God's love conquers all!**

Romans 8:36 is a quotation from Psalm 44:20-26 that speaks of Israel's suffering – being cast off by God and scattered among the nations. Because of the resurrection and the promise of eternal life, we are *"more than conquerors"* as it relates to all that we suffer in this life. All that is listed in verse 35 cannot compare with what has been promised to the believer in eternal life!

John 6:37-39 gives us this encouragement: *"All that the Father giveth Me shall come to Me; and him that cometh to Me I will in no wise cast out. For I came down from heaven, not to do Mine own will, but the will of Him that sent Me. And this is the Father's will which hath sent Me, that of all which He hath given Me I should lose nothing, but should raise it up again at the last day."*

John 10:28-30 adds: *"And I give unto them eternal life; and they shall never perish, neither shall any man pluck them out of My hand. My Father, which gave them Me, is greater than all; and no man is able to pluck them out of My Father's hand. I and My Father are one."*

Lina Sandell Berg (1832-1903) wrote over 650 hymns, and was regarded as Sweden's greater songwriter. At her funeral, a choir and the congregation sang the words of her most well-known and beloved hymn – MORE SECURE IS NO ONE EVER. The hymn was based on the words of Romans 8:38-39.

In 1953, 10,000 people gathered to dedicate a bronze statute in her memory. Once again, they sang the words to her famous hymn:

More secure is no one ever than the loved ones of the Savior; Not yon star on high abiding, nor the bird in home next hiding.

God His own doth tend and nourish – in His holy courts they flourish; like a Father kind He spares them, in His loving arms He bears them.

Neither life nor death can ever, from the Lord His children sever; for His love and deep compassion, comforts them in tribulation.

Little flock, to joy then yield thee; Jacob's God will ever shield thee; Rest secure with this Defender, at His will all foes surrender.

What He takes or what He gives us – shows the Father's love so precious; We may trust His purpose wholly, 'tis His children's welfare solely!

Romans 8 began with these words: *"There is therefore now NO CONDEMNATION to them which are in Christ Jesus."*

Romans 8 ends with these words: *"Nor height, nor depth, nor any other creature, shall be able to separate us from the love of God, which is in Christ Jesus our Lord."* **Yes, in addition to "NO CONDEMNATION" we also have "NO SEPARATION" – Praise the Lord!**

THE PROBLEMS
OF THE
RIGHTEOUSNESS
OF GOD
Romans 9:1-11:36

Chapter 6
The REJECTION of Israel
Romans 9:1-33

How do we understand the rejection of
Israel in the light of Paul's teachings in
Romans 1-8? Does this mean that Israel
is no longer the recipient of God's
blessings? Has the Church replaced
Israel in God's prophetic plan (as so
many churches believe and teach!)? Did
God's judgment upon Israel in 70 AD
cancel His *"everlasting covenant"* with
Abraham, Isaac, and Jacob? These
questions (and more) will be answered
within the next three chapters of
Romans.

We start with the emotions of the
Apostle Paul himself. The "REJECTION"
is seen as we examine his sorrow over
that matter.

The REJECTION of Israel –
seen in the <u>SORROW</u> of Paul
Romans 9:1-5

1. As he <u>REVEALED</u> his personal feelings – 9:1-3

"I say the truth in Christ, I lie not, my conscience also bearing me witness in the Holy ghost, that I have great heaviness and continual sorrow in my heart. For I could wish that myself were accursed from Christ for my brethren, my kinsmen according to the flesh."

> **(1)   His feelings were <u>CONTROLLED</u> by the truth – v. 1a**

"I say the truth in Christ, I lie not."

> **(2)   His feelings were <u>CAUSED</u> by the Holy Spirit – v. 1b**

"my conscience also bearing me witness in the Holy Ghost"

Similar words were found in Romans 2:15: *"Which shew the work of the law written in their hearts, their conscience also bearing witness, and their thoughts the meanwhile accusing or else excusing one another."*

The Bible teaches that we are *"convicted"* by our conscience (John 8:9), and that the conscience can be *"seared"* (I Timothy 4:2) and *"defiled"* (I Corinthians 8:7; Titus 1:15), and be *"weak"* (I Corinthians 8:10, 12) and *"evil"* (Hebrews 10:22). Paul speaks of a *"good"* conscience (Hebrews 13:18) that desires to live honestly; He also speaks of a *"pure"* conscience (I Timothy 2:9) and the need to *"purge"* our conscience (Hebrews 9:14; 10:2).

In Acts 23:1 Paul said: *"I have lived in all <u>good conscience</u> before God until this day"* (II Corinthians 1:12; 4:2).

        (3)   His feelings were <u>CHARACTERIZED</u> by deep sorrow and grief – v. 2

"great heaviness and continual sorrow in my heart" – The Greek word translated as *"heaviness"* is *lupe* which is used 16 times in the New Testament.

Matthew 9:36 speaks of our Lord's compassion when we read: *"But when He saw the multitudes, He was moved with compassion on them, because they fainted, and were scattered abroad, as sheep having no shepherd."*

Luke 19:41 records: *"And when He was come near, He beheld the city, and wept over it."*

Jesus spoke of the reaction of the disciples to His announcement that He was going back to the Father – John 16:6: *"But because I have said these things unto you, sorrow hath filled your heart."* He continued in John 16:20-12 with these words:

"Verily, verily, I say unto you, that ye shall weep and lament, but the world shall rejoice: and ye shall be sorrowful, but your sorrow shall be turned into joy. A woman when she is in travail hath sorrow, because her hour is come: but as soon as she is delivered of the child, she remembereth no more the anguish, for joy that a man is born into the world. And ye now therefore have sorrow: but I will see you again, and your heart shall rejoice, and your joy no man taketh from you."

The Greek word that is translated as *"sorrow"* is *odune* and is used only twice in the New Testament. Here in Romans 9:2 it is used and also in I Timothy 6:10 where Paul warns about the *"love of money"* being the *"root of all evil."* He told Timothy that those who pursue the love of money *"have erred from the faith, and pierced themselves through with many <u>sorrows</u>."*

(4)   His feelings were <u>CENTERED</u> in his desire for their salvation – v. 3

"For I could wish that myself were accursed from Christ for my brethren, my kinsmen according to the flesh."

The strength of these feelings reminds us of Moses in Exodus 32:31-32:

"And Moses returned unto the LORD, and said, Oh, this people have sinned a great sin, and have made them gods of gold. Yet now, if Thou wilt forgive their sin – and if not, blot me, I pray Thee, out of Thy book which Thou hast written."

It seems these days that such burden and compassion for the Jewish people's salvation (like Moses and Paul) is rare indeed!

2. As He <u>REALIZED</u> the blessings of Israel – 9:4-5

"Who are Israelites; to whom pertaineth the adoption, and the glory, and the covenants, and the giving of the law, and the service of God, and the promises; Whose are the fathers, and of whom as concerning the flesh Christ came, Who is over all, God blessed forever. Amen."

Consider the blessings to which he was referring:

      (1)   God's <u>PEOPLE</u> – *"Israelites"*

      (2)   God's <u>PURPOSE</u> – *"adoption"*

      (3)   God's <u>PRESENCE</u> – *"the glory"*

      (4)   God's <u>PROMISES</u> – *"the covenants"*

      (5)   God's <u>PRINCIPLES</u> –

"the giving of the law"

(6)   God's <u>PLACE</u> –
"the service of God"

The Greek word for *"service"* is *latreia*
and is primarily referring to the worship
of the tabernacle and temple.

(7)   God's <u>PROPHECIES</u> –
"the promises"

(8)   God's <u>PATRIARCHS</u> –
"the fathers"

The word *"fathers"* refers to Abraham,
Isaac, and Jacob.

(9)   God's <u>PERSON</u> –
*"Messiah" – "Christ
came"*

His <u>INCARNATION</u> – *"as concerning the
flesh Christ* (Messiah) *came"*

His <u>INFLUENCE</u> – *"Who is over all"*

His true <u>IDENTITY</u> – *"God blessed
forever"* – I John 5:20 says: *"And we
know that the Son of God is come, and
hath given us an understanding, that*

we may know Him that is true, even in His Son Jesus Christ. This is the true God, and eternal life."

<u>NOTE</u>: The demonstrative pronoun *"This"* is a masculine singular pronoun and must grammatically agree with a masculine singular noun that is the closest antecedent – that would be the word *"Christ"* – and it cannot refer to the word *"life"* because it is a feminine noun in Greek! Here is a powerful and inescapable truth – JESUS IS CALLED "THE TRUE GOD" in I John 5:20!

The <u>REJECTION</u> of Israel is seen in the <u>sorrow</u> of Paul! Romans 9:1-5

The <u>REJECTION</u> of Israel is also seen in the <u>selection</u> of the seed! Romans 9:6-13

The case of ISAAC and ISHMAEL Romans 9:6-9

"Not as though the word of God hath taken none effect. For they are not all Israel, which are of Israel: neither, because they are the seed of Abraham, are they all children: but, in Isaac shall the seed be called. That is, They which are the children of the flesh, these are not the children of God: but the children of the promise are counted for the seed. For this is the word of promise, At this time will I come, and Sarah shall have a son."

Genesis 17:18-21 is the attempt of Abraham to have Ishmael (son of Egyptian handmaiden named Hagar) as the promised seed:

"And Abraham said unto God, O that Ishmael might live before Thee! And God said, Sarah thy wife shall bear thee a son indeed; and thou shalt call his name Isaac: and I will establish My covenant with him for an everlasting covenant, and with his seed after him. And as for Ishmael, I have heard thee: Behold, I have blessed him, and will make him fruitful, and will multiply him exceedingly; twelve princes shall he beget, and I will make him a great nation. But My covenant will I

establish with Isaac, which Sarah shall bear unto thee at this set time in the next year."

   1. The <u>PLAN</u> of God does NOT include all!

Romans 9:6b – *"For they are not all Israel, which are of Israel."*

God's <u>WORD</u> has not failed – *"not as though the word of God hath taken none effect"*

God's <u>WILL</u> was clearly revealed – *"in Isaac shall thy seed be called"*

   2. The <u>PROMISE</u> of God made it clear – vv. 8-9

   Physical <u>connection</u> is not enough! *"the children of the flesh – these are NOT the children of God"*

John 1:12-13 says: *"But as many as received Him, to them gave He power to become the sons of God, even to them that believe on His Name: Which were born, not of blood, nor of the will of the flesh, nor of the will of man, but of God."*

Spiritual <u>commitment</u> is
absolutely necessary!
*"children of the promise are
counted for the seed"* – we must
believe God's Word!

The case of JACOB and ESAU
Romans 9:10-13

*"And not only this; but when Rebecca
also had conceived by one, even by our
father Isaac; (For the children being not
yet born, neither having done any good
or evil, that the purpose of God
according to election might stand, not
of works, but of Him that calleth;) It
was said unto her, The elder shall serve
the younger. As it is written, Jacob
have I loved, but Esau have I hated."*

   1. The <u>CAUSE</u> behind it – vv. 10-11
      "the purpose of God"

The <u>POINT</u> at which the decision was
made – *"being not yet born"* – we are
chosen <u>before</u> we come into existence!

The <u>PRESENCE</u> of good or evil was not a
factor or influence on God's choice!
"neither having done any good or evil"

The **PERFORMANCE** of good deeds was not a factor either! *"not of works"*

Ephesians 2:8-9- *"For by grace are ye saved through faith; and that not of yourselves: it is the gift of God: Not of works, lest any man should boast."*

Galatians 2:16 – *"Knowing that a man is not justified by the works of the law, but by the faith of Jesus Christ, even we have believed in Jesus Christ, and not by the works of the law: for by the works of the law shall no flesh be justified."*

    2. The **CALL** of God is what fulfilled the promise of God – *"but of Him that calleth"*

I Corinthians 1:9 – *"God is faithful, by Whom ye were <u>called</u> unto the fellowship of His Son Jesus Christ our Lord."*

II Timothy 1:9 – *"Who hath saved us, and <u>called</u> us with an holy <u>calling</u>, not according to our works, but according to His own purpose and grace, which was given us in Christ Jesus before the world began."*

3. The <u>CHOICE</u> was God's alone!
    *"that the purpose of God
    according to election might
    stand"*

His <u>DECISION</u> was not what was
expected! *"the elder shall serve the
younger."*

In the case of Judah – he was NOT the
oldest son of Leah (Reuben).
(Genesis 49:3-4, 8-10)

In the case of David – he was NOT the
oldest son of Jesse (Eliab).
(I Samuel 16:6-7, 9-13)

The <u>DEEDS</u> of the two sons revealed
God's choice – *"Jacob have I loved, but
Esau have I hated"* - this was said after
they were born, lived, and died!
(Malachi 1:2-5 and Obadiah 1:3-4)

The <u>REJECTION</u> of Israel was seen in the <u>SORROW</u> of Paul Romans 9:1-5

The <u>REJECTION</u> of Israel was seen in the <u>SELECTION</u> of the seed – Romans 9:6-13

The <u>REJECTION</u> of Israel was seen in the <u>SOVEREIGNTY</u> of God – Romans 9:14-24

   1. The <u>REVELATION</u> of his mercy – vv. 14-18

"What shall we say then? Is there unrighteousness with God? God forbid! For He saith to Moses, I will have mercy on whom I will have mercy, and I will have compassion on whom I will have compassion. So then it is not of him willeth, nor of him that runneth, but of God that sheweth mercy. For the Scripture saith unto Pharaoh, Even for this same purpose have I raised thee up, that I might shew My power in thee, and that My Name might be declared throughout all the earth.

Therefore hath He mercy on whom He will have mercy, and whom He will He hardeneth."

Proverbs 28:13-14 says: *"He that covereth his sins shall not prosper: but whoso confesseth and forsaketh them shall have mercy."*

The case of MOSES
vv. 15-16 – *"For He saith to Moses..."*

The quotation is found in Exodus 33:19: *"And He said, I will make all My goodness pass before thee, and I will proclaim the Name of the LORD before thee; and will be gracious to whom I will be gracious, and will shew mercy on whom I will shew mercy."*

This passage in Romans 9 is NOT a discussion of whether people are believers or not, whether they are saved or not; It is concerned with their assurance of salvation; one can be saved without having assurance of it.

TWO REASONS FOR ACCUSING GOD OF BEING UNRIGHTEOUS:

(1)   It seems to us to be
       unrighteous on God's part to
       give mercy to some and not to
       others.

(2)   It also seems to be unrighteous
       on the part of God to hate and
       to condemn some before they
       are born – v. 13.

The issue here in Romans 9:15-16 is not
of righteousness or justice; it deals with
compassion and mercy. If God dealt
with any of us in justice and
righteousness, we would all be in Hell,
because that is what we deserve!
Remember the words of Romans 3:10:
"there is none righteous; no, not one!"

Let's make sure we are understanding
this passage.

(1)   God is NOT merciful to all!

That is the false teaching of so many –
universalism (taught by William Barclay
and C. H. Dodd).

(2)   God does NOT show mercy
       to any one on the basis of
       human worth or performance!

It is NOT by human <u>desire</u>!
"not of him that willeth"

It is NOT by human <u>deeds</u>!
"nor of him that runneth"

If God rewarded *"mercy"* to those who
wanted it or earned it, then no one
would accuse Him of being unrighteous
of unjust; The charge arises because God
chooses one and not the other – when
neither of them had done anything at all;
he has not desired, he has not willed, he
has not done anything at all! God
chooses before we are born!

The real mystery is NOT that everybody
is not saved, but anybody is saved at all!
God owes nothing to anybody!

Isaiah 55:8-9 says: *"For My thoughts
are not your thoughts, neither are your
ways My ways, saith the LORD. For as
the heavens are higher than the earth,
so are My ways higher than your ways,
and My thoughts than your thoughts."*

The case of PHARAOH
vv. 17-18 – *"For the scripture
saith unto Pharaoh..."*

DID GOD HARDEN PHARAOH'S HEART?

Exodus 4:21 – *"but I will harden his heart"*

Exodus 7:3-5 – *"And I will harden Pharoah's heart, and multiply My signs and My wonders in the land of Egypt, But Pharaoh shall not hearken unto you, that I may lay My hand upon Egypt, and bring forth Mine armies, and My people the children of Israel, our of the land of Egypt by great judgments. And the Egyptians shall know that I am the LORD, when I stretch forth Mine hand upon Egypt, and bring out the children of israel from among them."*

Exodus 7:13-14 – *"And He hardened Pharaoh's heart, that he hearkened not unto them; as the LORD had said. And the LORD said unto Moses, Pharaoh's heart is hardened, he refuseth to let the people go."*

Exodus 7:22 – *"And the magicians of Egypt did so with their enchantments; and Pharaoh's heart was hardened,* *neither did he hearken unto them; as the LORD had said."*

Exodus 8:19 – "Then the magicians said unto Pharaoh, This is the finger of God: and Pharaoh's heart was hardened, and he hearkened not unto them; as the LORD had said."

Exodus 9:7 – "And the heart of Pharaoh was hardened, and he did not let the people go."

Exodus 9:12 – "And the LORD hardened the heart of Pharaoh, and he hearkened not unto them; as the LORD had spoken unto Moses."

Exodus 10:1 – "And the LORD said unto Moses, Go in unto Pharaoh: for I have hardened his heart, and the heart of his servants, that I might shew these My signs before him..."

Exodus 10:20 – "But the LORD hardened Pharaoh's heart, so that he would not let the children of Israel go."

Exodus 10:27 – "But the LORD hardened Pharaoh's heart, and he would not lte them go."

Exodus 11;10 – *"and the LORD hardened Pharaoh's heart, so that he would not let the children of Israel go out of his land."*

Exodus 14:4 – *"And I will harden Pharaoh's heart, that he shall follow after them; and I will be honored upon Pharaoh, and upon all his host; that the Egyptians may know that I am the LORD."*

Exodus 14:17-18 – *"And I, behold, I will harden the hearts of the Egyptians, and they shall follow them: and I will get Me honor upon Pharaoh, and upon all his host, upon his chariots, and upon his horsemen. And the Egyptians shall know that I am the LORD, when I have gotten Me honor upon Pharaoh, upon his chariots, and upon his horsemen."*

The previous verses make it clear that the Lord *"hardened"* Pharaoh's heart.

DID PHARAOH HARDEN HIS OWN HEART?

However, we also read of Pharaoh's own responses:

Exodus 8:15 – *"But when Pharaoh saw that there was respite, he hardened his heart, and hearkened not unto them: as the LORD had said."*

Exodus 8:32 – *"And Pharaoh hardened his heart at this time also, neither would he let the people go."*

Exodus 9:34-35 – *"he sinned yet more, and hardened his heart, he and his servants. And the heart of Pharaoh was hardened, neither would he let the children of Israel go; as the LORD had spoken by Moses."*

1. His <u>DESIGN</u> was twofold:

   (1) To <u>DEMONSTRATE</u> His power! – *"that I might show My power in thee"*

   (2) To <u>DECLARE</u> His Name – *"that My Name might be declared throughout all the earth"*

2. His <u>DECISION</u> is therefore sovereign!

"There hath he mercy on whom he will have mercy, and whom He will He hardeneth"

2. The <u>RIGHT</u> to do whatever He wants! vv. 19-24

(1) The <u>PROBLEM</u> – v. 19

"Thou wilt say then unto Me, Why doth He yet find fault? For who hath resisted His will?

This objection proves the point of the passage that God alone determines the salvation of every person.

(2) The <u>ANSWER</u> – vv. 20-24

"Nay but, O man, who art thou that repliest against God? Shall the thing formed say to Him that formed it, Why hast Thou made me thus? Hath not the potter power over the clay, of the same lump to make one vessel unto honor, and another unto dishonor? What if God, willing to shew His wrath, and to make His power known, endured with much longsuffering the vessels of wrath

fitted to destruction: And that He might make known the riches of His glory on the vessels of mercy, which He had afore prepared unto glory, Even us, whom He hath called, not of the Jews only, but also of the Gentiles?"

FOUR PARTS TO THIS ANSWER:

As to our sinful <u>POSITION</u> – *"clay"*

II Corinthians 4:3-7 – *"But if our gospel be hid, it is hid to them that are lost: In whom the god of this world hath blinded the minds of them which believe not, lest the light of the glorious gospel of Christ, Who is the image of God, should shine unto them. For we preach not ourselves, but Christ Jesus the Lord; and ourselves your servants for Jesus' sake. For God Who commanded the light to shine out of darkness, hath shined in our hearts, to give the light of the knowledge of the glory of God in the face of Jesus Christ. But we have this treasure in <u>earthen vessels</u> (clay pots), that the excellency of the power may be of God, and not of us."*

The words *"the thing formed"* (v. 20) are from the Greek word *plasma* (our word "plastic" comes from it).

As to His sovereign <u>POWER</u> to choose –

v. 21 – *"Hath not the potter power over the clay, of the same lump to make one vessel unto honor, and another unto dishonor?"*

Isaiah 29:16 – *"Surely your turning of things upside down shall be esteemed as the potter's clay: for shall the work say of him that made it, He made me not? Or shall the things framed say of him that framed it, He had no understanding?"*

God did not create anything unto *"dishonor."* The *"clay"* refers to fallen humanity. Because of our sin, no one deserves mercy, not one! We not only do not deserve mercy, we have no claim upon God to give us mercy!

As to His specific <u>PLAN</u> – vv. 22-23

"What if God, willing to shew His wrath, and to make His power known,

endured with much longsuffering the vessels of wrath fitted to destruction: And that He might make known the riches of His glory on the vessels of mercy, which He had afore prepared unto glory..."

> **(1)** Toward the vessels of wrath – v. 22

It reveals His <u>POWER</u>!
It reveals His <u>PATIENCE</u>!

The words *"fitted to destruction"* are from a Greek word *katerismena* – meaning what they did to themselves!

> **(2)** Toward the vessels of mercy – v. 23 – *"to make the riches of His glory known"*

It reveals His <u>GLORY</u>!
It reveals the <u>GROUND</u> upon which that glory is seen – *"which He had afore prepared unto glory."*

As to His saved <u>PEOPLE</u> – v. 24
"whom He hath called"
cf. Romans 8:28-30

THE REJECTION OF ISRAEL – *Romans 9:1-33*

Seen in the **SORROW** of Paul
Romans 9:1-5

Seen in the **SELECTION** of the seed
Romans 9:6-13

Seen in the **SOVEREIGNTY** of God
Romans 9:14-24

Seen in the **SCRIPTURES** that prophesied it!
Romans 9:25-29

1. God's **PEOPLE** – vv. 25-26

"As He saith also in Hosea, I will call them My people, which were not My people; and her beloved, which was not beloved. And it shall come to pass, that in the place where it was said unto them, Ye are not My people; there shall they be called the children of the living God."

The context of the passage from Hosea that is quoted here in Romans 9 deals with the northern kingdom of Israel. In the graphic story Hosea takes an adulterous wife named Gomer from whom he has two children: a son named Jezreel, which speaks of God's judgment upon Israel; and a daughter named Loruhamah (which means *"no mercy"*) who has a son named Loammi, meaning *"no people."*

But, the Lord will again refer to them as *"My people"* and *"the children of the living God."* God's purposes are rooted in His character, and He will never cast away His people, even though He has and will judge them for their sin and idolatry.

Hosea 2:19-20 says three times *"I will betroth thee"* – and presents three issues:

> The issue of ETERNITY – *"forever"*
>
> The issue of God's CHARACTER – *"in righteousness, judgment, lovingkindness, and mercies"*

The issue of God's FAITHFULNESS
"in faithfulness"

2. God's <u>PROMISE</u> – v. 27

"Isaiah also crieth concerning Israel, Though the number of the children of Israel be as the sand of the sea, a remnant shall be saved"

Isaiah 10:20-22 – *"And it shall come to pass in that day, that the remnant of Israel, and such as are escaped of the house of Jacob, shall no more again stay upon him that smote them; but shall stay upon the LORD, the Holy One of Israel, in truth. The remnant shall return, even the remnant of Jacob, unto the mighty God. For though Thy people Israel be as the sand of the sea, yet a remnant of them shall return: the consumption decreed shall overflow with righteousness."*

Isaiah 11:11-12 – *"And it shall come to pass in that day, that the Lord shall set His hand again the second time to recover the remnant of His people, which shall be left, from Assyria, and from Egypt, and from Pathos, and from*

Cush, and from Elam, and from Shinar, and from Hamath, and the islands of the sea. And He shall set up an ensign for the nations, and shall assemble the outcasts of Israel, and gather together the dispersed of Judah from the four corners of the earth."

Zechariah 13:8-9 – *"And it shall come to pass, that in all the land, saith the LORD, two parts therein shall be cut off and die; but the third part shall be left therein. And I will bring the third part through the fire, and will refine them as silver is refined, and will try them as gold is tried: they shall call on My Name, and I will hear them: I will say, It is My people: and they shall say, The LORD is my God."*

3. God's <u>PLANS</u> – v. 28

"For He will finish the work, and cut it short in righteousness: because a short work will the Lord make upon the earth."

The word *"work"* is the Greek word *logos,* usually translated as *"word"* or God's revelation. He will finish His word – a short word indicates that it will come suddenly and rapidly. Paul is, no doubt, thinking of the original context of Hosea – that God's judgment would come exactly as He had prophesied, and it will come quickly.

This verse is a loose translation of the end of Isaiah 10:22-23. It is much like Isaiah 46:11 – *"I have spoken it, I will also bring it to pass; I have purposed it, I will also do it."*

4. God's <u>PROTECTION</u> – v. 29

"And as Isaiah said before, Except the Lord of Sabaoth had left us a seed, we had been as Sodom, and been made like unto Gomorrah."

Isaiah 1:9 – *"Except the LORD of hosts had left unto us a very small remnant, we should have been as Sodom, and we should have been like unto Gomorrah."*

We read in Genesis 19:24-25 these words about the destruction of Sodom and Gomorrah: *"Then the LORD rained upon Sodom and upon Gomorrah brimstone and fire from the LORD out of heaven; and He overthrew those cities, and all the plain, and all the inhabitants of the cities, and that which grew upon the ground."*

But. God spared Lot, his wife, and two daughter-in-laws. II Peter 2:6-9 says:

"And turning the cities of Sodom and Gomorrah into ashes condemned them with an overthrow, making them an example unto those that after should live ungodly; and delivered just Lot, vexed with the filthy conversation of the wicked: (For that righteous man dwelling among them, in seeing and hearing, vexed his righteous soul from day to day with their unlawful deeds;) The Lord knoweth how to deliver the godly out of temptations, and to reserve the unjust unto the day of judgment to be punished."

The <u>REJECTION</u> of Israel

Seen in the <u>SORROW</u> of Paul
Romans 9:1-5

Seen in the <u>SELECTION</u> of the seed
Romans 9:6-13

Seen in the <u>SOVEREIGNTY</u> of God
Romans 9:14-24

Seen in the <u>SCRIPTURES</u> that prophesied it
Romans 9:25-29

Seen in the <u>STUMBLING</u> of Israel
Romans 9:30-33

They <u>STUMBLED</u> over the <u>WAY</u> of God's righteousness – vv. 30-31

"What shall we say then? That the Gentiles, which followed not after righteousness, have attained to righteousness, even the righteousness which is of faith. But Israel, which followed after the law of righteousness, hath not attained to the law of righteousness."

The opening question – *"What shall we say then?"* reminds us of Romans 8:31 and 9:14. Interestingly, the definite article *"the"* is not used in the Greek text in front of the word *"Gentiles."* The subject was brought up back in verse 24 as it relates to God's sovereignty in showing mercy.

1. The <u>PRINCIPLE</u> is clear – *"even the righteousness which is of faith"* – all of Romans establishes this fact of the gospel!

2. The <u>PURSUIT</u> of righteousness does not guarantee God's righteousness – *"followed after"* (Gentiles did not pursue it at all!)

3. The <u>PROBLEM</u> with Israel's zeal is that it was rooted in human performance and religion tradition, NOT in the teaching of the Bible and/or the example of our father Abraham!

They <u>STUMBLED</u> over the <u>WORKS</u> of the law – v. 32

"Wherefore? Because they sought it not by faith, but as it were by the works of the law. For they stumbled at that stumbling-stone."

1. Human <u>PERFORMANCE</u> was the way they sought to be right with

God – *"as it were by the works of the law"*

Galatians 3:10-14 teaches:
"For as many as are of the works of the law are under the curse: for it is written, Cursed is every one that continueth not in all things which are written in the book of the law to do them. But that no man is justified by the law in the sight of God, it is evident: for, The just shall live by faith. And the law is not of faith: but, The man that doeth them shall live in them. Christ hath redeemed us from the curse of the law, being made a curse for us: for it is written, Cursed is every one that hangeth on a tree. That the blessing of Abraham might come on the Gentiles through Jesus Christ; that we might receive the promise of the Spirit through faith."

2. God's <u>PLAN</u> became a *"stumblingstone"*

I Corinthians 1:23 says: *"But we preach Christ crucified, unto the Jews a stumbling-block, and unto the Greeks foolishness."*

311

Galatians 3:21-29 presents the argument clearly:

"Is the law then against the promises of God? God forbid; for if there had been a law given which could have given life, verily righteousness should have been by the law. But the Scripture hath concluded all under sin, that the promise by faith of Jesus Christ might be given to them that believe. But before faith came, we were kept under the law, shut up unto the faith which should afterwards be revealed. Wherefore the law was our schoolmaster to bring us unto Christ, that we might be justified by faith. But after that faith is come, we are no longer under a schoolmaster. For ye are all the children of God by faith in Christ Jesus. For as many of you as have been baptized into Christ have put on Christ. There is neither Jew nor Greek, there is neither bond nor free, there is neither male nor female; for ye are all one in Christ Jesus. And if ye be Christ's, then are ye Abraham's seed, and heirs according to the promise."

They stumbled over the <u>WORD</u> of salvation – v. 33

"As it is written, Behold, I lay in Sion a stumblingstone and rock of offence: and whosoever believeth on Him shall not be ashamed."

1. The STONE was <u>ESTABLISHED</u> by God – *"Behold, I lay in Sion a stumblingstone and rock of offence"*

The sovereignty of God is declared once more!

2. The STONE was <u>ELIMINATED</u> by the religious leaders!

Psalm 118:22 prophesies: *"The stone which the builders refused is become the head stone of the corner."*

I Peter 2:6-8 – *"Wherefore also it is contained in the Scripture, Behold, I lay in Sion a chief corner stone, elect, precious: and he that believeth on Him shall not be confounded. Unto you therefore which believe He is precious: but unto them which be disobedient, the stone which the builders disallowed, the same is made the head of the corner, and a stone of stumbling, and a rock of offence, even to them which stumble at the word, being disobedient: whereunto also they were appointed."*

3. The STONE was <u>EXALTED</u> by God! *"<u>chief</u> corner stone"* and *"<u>head</u> of the corner"*

4. The STONE was <u>EXPLAINED</u> to be a Person – the Messiah of Israel! *"whosoever believeth on Him shall not be ashamed"*

5. The STONE will <u>EXIST</u> as a kingdom forever!

Daniel 2:44 – *"And in the days of these kings shall the God of heaven set up a kingdom, which shall never be destroyed: and the kingdom shall not be left to other people, but it shall break in pieces and consume all these kingdoms, and it shall stand forever!"*

Chapter 7
The <u>RECEPTION</u> of the Gentiles
Romans 10:1-21

The <u>NATURE</u> of God's righteousness – *Romans 10:1-13*

1. The <u>PRAYER</u> of Paul
Romans 10:1

"Brethren, my heart's desire and prayer to God for Israel is, that they might be saved."

The Bible reveals that Moses prayed for Israel (Numbers 21:7); Samuel prayed for them (I Samuel 7:3-5; 12:22-23); David prayed for them (I Chronicles 21:17); Solomon prayed for them (I Kings 8:38-39, 49-52) and so did Nehemiah (Nehemiah 1:5-6, 10).

> (1) It was an inward <u>DESIRE</u> – *"my heart's desire"*

The Greek word for *"desire"* is *eudokia* and is used 12 times in the New

Testament, usually referring to God's will.

> **(2)** It was a strong <u>DEPENDENCY</u> upon God – *"and prayer to God"*

The Greek word for *"prayer"* is *deesis*, found 19 times in the New Testament. (such as Ephesians 6:18 or Philippians 4:6)

> **(3)** It was their spiritual <u>DESTINY</u> for which he prayed – *"that they might be saved"* (cf. Romans 1:16 and Romans 9:1-3)

2. The <u>PROBLEM</u> of Israel
Romans 10:2-3

"For I bear them record that they have a zeal of God, but not according to knowledge. For they being ignorant of God's righteousness, and going about to establish their own righteousness, have not submitted themselves unto the righteousness of God."

His words *"I bear them record"* reveal that Paul was an eyewitness to it and experienced it himself.

> (1) Their <u>DEDICATION</u> to God was not controlled by biblical revelation – *"a zeal of God, but not according to knowledge"*

Acts 22:3-5 says of Paul: *"I am verily a man which am a Jew, born in Tarsus, a city in Cilicia, yet brought up in this city at the feet of Gamaliel, and taught according to the perfect manner of the law of the fathers, and was zealous toward God, as ye all are this day. And I persecuted this way unto the death, binding and delivering into prisons both men and women. As also the high priest doth bear me witness, and all the estate of the elders: from whom also I received letters unto the brethren, and went to Damascus, to bring them which were there bound unto Jerusalem."*

Paul understood personally what it was like to be dedicated to God and to have zeal, and yet be unaware of the truth of the gospel. He was indeed one who was *"zealous toward God."*

> (2)   Their <u>DEFICIENCY</u> in knowing God's righteousness was based on their own human efforts and traditions – v. 3

"For they being ignorant of God's righteousness, and going about to establish their own righteousness"

In Matthew 15:3-9, Yeshua said of the scribes and Pharisees:

"Why do ye also transgress the commandment of God by your tradition? God commanded, saying, Honor thy father and mother; and, He that curseth father or mother, let him die the death. But ye say, Whosoever shall say to his father or his mother, It is a gift, by whatsoever thou mightiest be profited by me; And honor not his father or his mother, he shall be free. Thus have ye made the commandment of God of none effect by your tradition. Ye hypocrites, well did Isaiah prophesy of you, saying, This people draweth

nigh unto Me with their mouth, and honoreth Me with their lips; but their heart is far from Me. But in vain they do worship Me, teaching for doctrines the commandments of men."

> (3)   Their <u>DISOBEDIENCE</u> to God's righteousness was rooted in a lack of submission – *v. 3b*

"have not submitted themselves unto the righteousness of God."

The <u>PURPOSE</u> of Jesus Christ
Romans 10:4

The law demands obedience in what you do; Christ demands faith in what He did!

<u>LEGALISM</u> is the belief that keeping the law and its requirements is essential for salvation and spiritual growth.

Galatians 3:1-3 adds: *"O foolish Galatians, who hath bewitched you, that ye should not obey the truth, before whose eyes Jesus Christ hath been evidently set forth, crucified among you? This only would I learn of you, Received ye the Spirit by the works of*

the law, or by the hearing of faith? Are ye so foolish? Having begun in the Spirit, are ye now made perfect by the flesh?

THE PROBLEM OF THE LAW:

> (1)   It cannot give life!

II Corinthians 3:6: *"Who also hath made us able ministers of the new testament; not of the letter, but of the spirit: for the letter killeth, but the spirit giveth life."*

Galatians 3:21: *"Is the law then against the promises of God? God forbid: for if there had been a law given which could have given life, verily righteousness should have been by the law."*

> (2)   It cannot make us righteous before God!

Romans 3:20: *"Therefore by the deeds of the law there shall no flesh be justified in His sight: for by the law is the knowledge of sin."*

Romans 3:28: *"Therefore we conclude that a man is justified by faith without the deeds of the law."*

(3)   It cannot take away our sin!

Hebrews 10:1-4: *"For the law having a shadow of good things to come, and not the very image of the things, can never with those sacrifices which they offered year by year continually make the comers thereunto perfect. For then would they not have ceased to be offered? Because that the worshippers once purged should have had no more conscience of sins. But in those sacrifices there is a remembrance again made of sins every year. For it is not possible that the blood of bulls and of goats should take away sins."*

(4)   It cannot cancel God's promise to Abraham!

Galatians 3:16-17: *"Now to Abraham and his seed were the promises made. He saith not, And to seeds, as of many; but as of one, and to thy seed, which is Christ. And this I say, that the covenant, that was confirmed before of God in Christ, the law, which was four hundred and thirty years after, cannot disannul, that it should make the promise of none effect."*

(5)   It cannot last forever!

Hebrews 8:6-13: *"For now hath He obtained a more excellent ministry, by how much also He is the Mediator of a better covenant, which was established upon better promises. For if that first covenant had been faultless, then should not place have been sought for the second. For finding fault with them, He saith, Behold, the days come, saith the Lord, when I will make a new covenant with the house of Israel and with the house of Judah: Not according to the covenant that I made with their fathers in the day when I took them by the hand to lead them out of the land of Egypt; because they continued not in My covenant, and I regarded them not, saith the Lord. For this is the covenant that I will make with the house of Israel after those days, saith the Lord; I will put My laws into their mind, and write them in their hearts, and I will be to them a God, and they shall be to Me a people. And they shall not teach every man his neighbor, and every man his brother, saying, Know the Lord: for all shall know Me from the least to the greatest. For I will be merciful to their unrighteousness, and their sins and* *their iniquities will I remember no more. In that He saith, A new covenant, He hath made the first old. Now that which decayeth and waxeth old is ready to vanish away."*

THE PURPOSE OF THE LAW:

(1) It <u>RELATES</u> primarily to Israel, not to Gentiles.

Romans 2:14 said: *"For what the Gentiles, which have not the law, do by nature the things contained in the law, these, having not the law, are a law unto themselves."*

(2) It <u>REMOVES</u> our ignorance of sin!

Romans 3:20: *"Therefore by the deeds of the law there shall no flesh be justified in His sight: for by the law is the knowledge of sin."*

Romans 7:7: *"What shall we say then? Is the law sin? God forbid. Nay, I had not known sin, but by the law; for I had not known lust, except the law said, Thou shalt not covet."*

(3)   It <u>RELECTS</u> the character of God Himself!

Romans 7:12: *"Wherefore the law is holy, and the commandment holy, and just, and good."* Paul calls it *"the law of God"* in Romans 7:22, 25; and 8:7

(4)   It <u>REGULATES</u> society and is made for unbelievers!

I Timothy 1:9-10: *"Knowing this, that the law is not made for a righteous man, but for the lawless and disobedient, for the ungodly and for sinners, for unholy and profane, for murderers of fathers and murderers of mothers, for manslayers, for whoremongers, for them that defile themselves with mankind, for menstealers, for liars, for perjured persons, and if there be any other thing that is contrary to sound doctrine."*

(5)   It <u>REVEALS</u> our carnality!

Romans 7:14: *"For we know that the law is spiritual: but I am carnal, sold under sin."*

(6) It <u>REINFORCES</u> our need of a Savior and that justification is by faith alone!

Galatians 2:19-21: *"For I through the law am dead to the law, that I might live unto God. I am crucified with Christ: nevertheless I live; yet not I, but Christ liveth in me: and the life which I now live in the flesh I live by the faith of the Son of God, Who loved me, and gave Himself for me. I do not frustrate the grace of God: for if righteousness come by the law, then Christ is dead in vain."*

The PRINCIPLE of faith
Romans 10:5-11

1. What Moses <u>DESCRIBES</u> – v. 5

"For Moses describeth the righteousness which is of the law, That the man which doeth those things shall live by them."

Leviticus 18:5 – *"Ye shall therefore keep My statutes, and My judgments: which is a man do, he shall live in them: I am the LORD."*

Ezekiel 20:11 – *"And I gave them My statutes, and shewed them My judgments, which if a man do, he shall even live in them."*

Ezekiel 20:13 – *"But the house of Israel rebelled against Me in the wilderness; they walked not in My statutes, and they despised My judgments, which if a man do, he shall even live in them; and My Sabbaths they greatly polluted: then I said, I would pour out My fury upon them in the wilderness, to consume them."*

Ezekiel 20:21 – *"Notwithstanding the children rebelled against Me: they walked not in My statutes, neither kept My judgments to do them, which is a man do, he shall even live in them; they polluted My Sabbaths: then I said, I would pour out My fury upon them, to accomplish My anger against them in the wilderness."*

The Greek word translated *"describeth"* is the word *graphei* which means *"writes."*

    2. What righteousness <u>DECLARES</u> – vv. 6-10

"But the righteousness which is of faith speaketh on this wise, Say not in thine heart, Who shall ascend into heaven? (that is, to bring Christ down from above:) Or, Who shall descend into the deep? (that is, to bring up Christ again from the dead.) But what saith it? The word is nigh thee, even in thy mouth, and in the heart: that is, the word of faith, which we preach; That if thou shalt confess with thy mouth the Lord Jesus, and shalt believe in thine heart that God hath raised Him from the dead, thou shalt be saved. For with the heart man believeth unto righteousness; and with the mouth confession is made unto salvation."

The word in verse 8 translated *"word"* is from the Greek word *rhema*. The Greek text has the definite article *"the"* in front of the word *"word"* and the word *"faith."*

      (1)   It <u>REFUSES</u> to accept any act of human effort or performance or personal worth - v. 6 *"Say NOT in thine heart..."*

The words *"the deep"* are from the Greek word *abussos* which is used 9 times and translated as *"the bottomless pit,"* the place of Satan and demons, and where the Antichrist comes from – *"the beast"* and where Satan will be bound for 1000 years (Revelation 20:1-3).

Ephesians 4:8-10 speaks of Christ descending into the *"lower parts of the earth."* I Peter 3:19 speaks of Christ going to preach to the *"spirits in prison"* which according to verse 20 is the place where those who died in the flood of Noah's day are found.

> (2)　It <u>REINFORCES</u> the necessity of personal faith in the word of God – v. 8

I Corinthians 1:18 says: *"For the preaching of the cross is to them that perish foolishness; but unto us which are saved it is the power of God."*

The point of this passage is that faith does not cause His incarnation or His resurrection! Faith is resting in the proclamation of what has already occurred – He came into this world and died for our sins, and He arose from the dead, and is now ascended to the right hand of the throne of God. Our responsibility is to put our faith in what has already occurred, not in our ability to believe, but in what He alone did for us!

> (3) It <u>REQUIRES</u> our response to the word vv. 9-10

Our response involves two basic things:
Outward <u>CONFESSION</u>
Inward <u>CONVICTION</u>

The resurrection is true whether we believe it or not, which only goes to prove beyond doubt that salvation is by faith alone – faith that rests solely upon the word of God!

> 3. What the Scripture <u>DEMANDS</u> – v. 11

"For the scripture saith, Whosoever believeth on Him shall not be <u>ashamed</u>."

Mark 8:38: *"Whosoever therefore shall be <u>ashamed</u> of Me and of My words in this adulterous and sinful generation;*

of him also shall the Son of man be <u>ashamed</u>, when He cometh in the glory of His Father with the holy angels."

Romans 1:16 – *"For I am not <u>ashamed</u> of the gospel of Christ: for it is the power of God unto salvation to every one that believeth; to the Jew first, and also to the Greek."*

Romans 5:5 – *"And hope maketh not <u>ashamed</u>; because the love of God is shed abroad in our hearts by the Holy Ghost which is given unto us."*

Romans 6:21 – *"What fruit had ye then in those things whereof ye are now <u>ashamed</u>? For the end of those things is death."*

Romans 9:33 – *"As it is written, Behold, I lay in Sion a stumblingstone and rock of offence: and whosoever believeth on Him shall not be <u>ashamed</u>."*

The PROMISE of salvation
Romans 10:12-13

1. The <u>RELATIONSHIP</u> of Jew and Gentile – v. 12a – *"there is no difference"*

2. The <u>RICHES</u> that will come from the Lord – v. 12b – *"the same Lord over all is rich unto all that call upon Him"*

3. The <u>RESPONSE</u> that is needed – v. 13 – *"whosoever shall call upon the Name of the Lord shall be saved"*

   (1) It is <u>AVAILABLE</u> to anyone – *"whosoever"*

Revelation 22:17 – *"And the Spirit and the bride say, Come. And let him that heareth say, Come. And let him that is athirst, Come. And <u>whosoever</u> will, let him take the water of life freely."*

   (2) It is <u>ACCEPTED</u> when we call upon the Name of the Lord!

   (3) It is <u>ABSOLUTE</u> in its promise – *"shall be saved"*

THE NECESSITY OF HEARING THE MESSAGE
Romans 10:14-21

1. The <u>OPPORTUNITY</u> must be given – vv. 14-15

"How then shall they call on Him in Whom they have not believed? And how shall the believe in Him of Whom they have not heard? And how shall they hear without a preacher? And how shall they preach, except they be sent? As it is written, How beautiful are the feet of them that preach the gospel of peace, and bring glad tidings of good things."

      (1)   It requires a <u>MAN</u> to be sent!

Nahum 1:15a – *"Behold upon the mountains the feet of him that bringeth good tidings, that publisheth peace!"*

The Greek word for *"preacher"* **is literally** *"one preaching."* **The emphasis is not on the man, but on the message!**

Isaiah 52:7 – *"How beautiful upon the mountains are the feet of him that bringeth good tidings, that publisheth peace; that bringeth good tidings of good, that publisheth salvation; that saith unto Zion, Thy God reigneth!*

In the above context, the captives see the beautiful feet coming to announce that they are now free!

Ephesians 6:15 – *"And your feet shod with the preparation of the gospel of peace."*

> **(2)** It requires a <u>MESSAGE</u> to be preached – v. 15b

"the gospel of peace....glad tidings of good things." **cf. Isaiah 61:1ff; Luke 2:10; 8:1; Acts 13:32-33; I Corinthians 1:17-21; 2:1-5.**

The Greek text uses the verb *euaggelizo* which is used 90 times in the New Testament; the noun *euagglion* is used 77 times. The word *"gospel"* is found 101 times and speaks of "good news." The phrase *"gospel of peace"* appears only here and in Ephesians 6:15.

> **(3)** It requires a <u>METHOD</u> to be given – v. 14 – *"call upon Him"*

The issue is Jesus Christ and what we believe about Him! The issue of "believing" seems to precede that of "calling." To *"call upon the Name of the Lord"* requires a person to know Who Jesus is and believe in what He has done for us!

2. Our <u>OBEDIENCE</u> is essential – vv. 16-17

"But they have not all obeyed the gospel. For Isaiah saith, Lord, who hath believed our report? So then faith cometh by hearing, and hearing by the word of God."

The opening word of verse 16 *"But"* is the Greek *alla*, a word of great contrast!

(1) The <u>PROOF</u> from the Bible – Isaiah 53:1

"Who hath believed our report? And to whom is the arm of the LORD revealed?"

In John 12:37 we read *"But though He had done so many miracles before them, yet they believed not on Him."*

The root reason for their failure to believe is stated in John 12:43: *"For they loved the praise of men more than the praise of God."*

> (2) The <u>PRINCIPLE</u> being taught – v. 17

"So then faith cometh by hearing, and hearing by the word of God."

The source from which saving faith comes *"hearing...the word of God."* Hebrews 11:3 says: *"Though faith we understand that the worlds were framed by the word of God, so that things which are seen were not made of things which do appear."*

3. The <u>OBJECTIONS</u> are not valid – vv. 18-21

There are two basic objects or questions: v. 18 – *"Have they not heard?"* v. 19 – *"Did not Israel know?"*

> (1) The <u>PROCLAIMING</u> of God's message was accomplished!

v. 18 – *"But I say, Have they not heard? Yes verily, their sound went into all the*

earth, and their words unto the ends of the world."

Psalm 19:1-4a – *"The heavens declare the glory of God; and the firmament sheweth His handiwork. Day unto day uttereth speech, and night unto night sheweth knowledge. There is no speech nor language, where their voice is not hear. Their line is gone out through all the earth, and their words to the end of the world."*

Romans 1:20 taught us: *"For the invisible things from the creation of the world are clearly seen, being understood by the things that are made, even His eternal power and Godhead; so that they are without excuse."*

> **(2)** The <u>PURPOSE</u> of God for the Gentiles was achieved – vv. 19-20

"But I say, Did not Israel know? First Moses saith, I will provoke you to jealousy by them that are no people, and by a foolish nation I will anger you. But Isaiah is very bold, and saith, I was found of them that sought Me not; I was

made manifest unto them that asked not after Me."

The passage referring to what Moses said is found in Deuteronomy 32:15-21, and the passage from Isaiah is Isaiah 65:1.

        (3)   The <u>PROBLEM</u> of Israel was not the lack of opportunity!

v. 21 – *"But to Israel He saith, All day long I have stretched forth My hands unto a disobedient and gainsaying people."*

We read in Acts 7:51-53: *"Ye stiffnecked and uncircumcised in heart and ears, ye do always resist the Holy Ghost: as your fathers did, so do ye. Which of the prophets have not your fathers persecuted? And they have slain them which shewed before of the coming of the Just One; of Whom ye have been now the betrayers and murderers: Who have received the law by the disposition of angels, and have not kept it."*

Chapter 8
The RESTORATION of Israel
Romans 11:1-36

The <u>RESTORATION</u> of Israel is a clearly
revealed prophecy throughout the Bible.
It is amazing how many Christians think
that it is not a future event, and that the
Church has replaced Israel in God's
prophetic program.

THE <u>REMNANT</u> IS PROOF!
Romans 11:1-6

The great question: *"Hath God cast
away His people which He foreknew?"*
GOD FORBID! It is unthinkable –
impossible – may it never be!

Romans 8:29 says: *"For whom He did
<u>foreknow</u>, He also did predestinate to
be conformed to the image of His Son,
that He might be the firstborn among
many brethren."*

I Peter 1:2 adds: *"Elect according to the
<u>foreknowledge</u> of God the Father,
through sanctification of the Spirit,
unto obedience and sprinkling of the
blood of Jesus Christ."*

1. The <u>EXAMPLES</u> – vv. 1-5

There are three examples given in these opening verses of chapter 11: the Apostle Paul, Elijah, and *"a remnant according to the election of grace."*

(1) The Apostle Paul himself

"For I am an Israelite, of the seed of Abraham, of the tribe of Benjamin." Paul wrote in I Corinthians 15:10: *"But by the grace of God I am what I am: and His grace which was bestowed upon me was not in vain; but I labored more abundantly than they all: yet not I, but the grace of God which was with me."*

In Paul's wonderful testimony in I Timothy 1:12-17 he wrote in v. 14: *"And the grace of our Lord was exceeding abundant with faith and love which is in Christ Jesus."*

(2) The Prophet Elijah

Romans 11:2b-4 speaks clearly of a *"remnant"* at the time of Elijah: *"Wot ye not what the scripture saith of Elijah? How he maketh intercession to God against Israel, saying, Lord, they have killed Thy prophets, and digged down Thine altars; and I am left alone, and they seek my life. But what saith the answer of God unto him? I have reserved to Myself seven thousand men, who have not bowed the knee to the image of Baal."*

His <u>APPEAL</u> – v. 2b
"maketh intercession to God against Israel"

Apparently Elijah believes that God has cast them away for what they have done!

His <u>ATTITUDE</u> – v. 3

He <u>enumerates</u> all that they had done!
"killed Thy prophets, and digged down Thine altars"

He <u>emphasizes</u> that he is the only one left! *"I am left alone"*

He <u>explains</u> that his own life is in danger and then God will have no one upon which to depend!
"they seek my life"

God's <u>ANSWER</u> – v. 4

"I have reserved to Myself 7000 men, who have not bowed the knee to the image of Baal." This is the only mention of the pagan god Baal in the New Testament; The name appears 62 times in the Old Testament.

(3)   The present time – v. 5

"Even so then at this present time also there is a remnant according to the election of grace."

The Greek word for *"election"* appears 7 times in the Greek New Testament – *ekloge.* The word *elektos* is used 23 times in the New Testament.

II Timothy 1;9 says: *"not according to our works, but according to His own purpose and grace, which was given us in Christ Jesus before the world began."*

2. The <u>EXPLANATION</u> – v. 6

"And if by grace, then is it no more of works: otherwise grace is no more grace. But if it be of works, then is it no more grace: otherwise work is no more work."

The word *"grace"* appears 131 times in the New Testament; the *"grace of God"* is used 24 times.

"Grace" and *"works"* are mutually exclusive! Consider the following teachings of the Bible about grace:

Grace came by Jesus Christ - John 1:17

We are saved by grace – Ephesians 2:8-9

We are justified by grace – Romans 3:24

Our salvation is a gift of God's grace – Romans 5:15

Grace is greater than our sin – Romans 5:20

All believers are under grace, not law - Romans 6:14

God is the *"God of all grace"* – I Peter 5:10

God's grace is sufficient and capable of sustaining us under trials and infirmities – II Corinthians 12:9-10

God's grace has appeared to all men – Titus 2:11

Grace characterizes God's throne and grace will be given to help us – Hebrews 4:16

Grace is needed to serve God – Hebrews 12:28

Grace is given to the humble – James 4:6

Spiritual gifts come from the *"manifold grace of God"* – I Peter 4:10

Believers are exhorted to *"grow in grace"* - II Peter 3:18

Believers were chosen before the world was created so that we would be *"to the praise of the glory of His grace"* – Ephesians 1:6

The Lord will continue to show us in the ages to come *"the exceeding riches of His grace"* – Ephesians 2:7

FOUR DANGEROUS RESPONSES TO THE GRACE OF GOD

Rejection of the *"once-for-all"* sacrifice of Jesus Christ is described as an insult to the *"Spirit of grace"* – Hebrews 10:29

Refusing to repent is described as coming short of the *"grace of "God"* – Hebrews 12:15-17

Resisting God's standards of sexual purity is called *"turning the grace of our God into lasciviousness"* – Jude 4

Returning to the law in order to be declared righteous is called *"frustrating the grace of God"* – Galatians 2:21 – and is also called *"fallen from grace"* – Galatians 5:4

The REJECTION was prophesied!
Romans 11:6-10

> 1. The **SUMMARY** of Paul's argument about the remnant
>   v. 7 – *"What then?"*

Israel was blocked from achieving what they wanted!

Romans 9:31 – *"But Israel, which followed after the law of righteousness, hath not attained to the law of righteousness."*

Romans 10:3 – *"For they being ignorant of God's righteousness, and going about to establish their own righteousness, have not submitted themselves unto the righteousness of God."*

A few were <u>blessed</u> with righteousness by faith, apart from the works of the law!

Romans 10:4 – *"For Christ is the end of the law for righteousness to every one that believeth."*

Many were <u>blinded</u> by the Lord!

Isaiah 6:10 – *"Make the heart of this people fat, and make their ears heavy, and shut their eyes; lest they see with their eyes, and hear with their ears, and understand with their heart, and convert, and be healed."*

2. The <u>SCRIPTURES</u> that reveal Israel's rejection – vv. 8-10

345

"according as it is written"

Isaiah 29:10-19 – the reason was "hypocrisy" (v. 13) – when they are restored it will be the *"meek"* and the *"poor"* who shall *"rejoice in the Holy One of Israel."*

Psalm 69:20-28 – the reason was rejection of the Messiah Himself!

The <u>RESULT</u> of their fall
Romans 11:11-12 – *"I say then"*

   1. The <u>MOTIVE</u> behind Israel's rejection – v. 11

"I say then, Have they stumbled that they should fall? God forbid! But rather through their fall salvation is come unto the Gentiles, for to provoke them to jealousy."

It was not to <u>BANISH</u> them forever!
Hosea 1:6-10

It was to <u>BRING</u> salvation to the Gentiles!

The salvation of the Gentiles was always a part of God's prophetic plan.
cf. Genesis 12:3b; Isaiah 42:6; 49:1-6; 60:1-3; 66:23; Micah 4:1-3; Zechariah 14:16-19; Romans 15:9-12

2. The <u>METHOD</u> that was used – *"to provoke them to jealousy"*
cf. Romans 10:19

3. The <u>MESSAGE</u> we should learn from this – v. 12

"Now if the fall of them be the riches of the world, and the diminishing of them the riches of the Gentiles, how much more their fullness?"

The <u>FAILURE</u> of Israel does not mean that God is finished with them!

The <u>FALL</u> of Israel has resulted in great blessings for the Gentiles!

The <u>FUTURE</u> of the world will be greater in blessing when the day comes that Israel as a nation will be saved!
"how much more their fullness"

The <u>RESPONSE</u> they will have Romans 11:13-16

"For I speak to you Gentiles; inasmuch as I am the apostle of the Gentiles, I magnify mine office: If by any means, I may provoke to emulation them which are my flesh, and might save some of them. For if the casting away of them be the reconciling of the world, what shall the receiving of them be, but life from the dead? For if the firstfruit be holy, the lump is also holy: and if the root be holy, so are the branches."

1. The **<u>AUTHORITY</u>** of the apostle Paul is crucial to the argument – v. 13 – *"the apostle of the Gentiles"*

2. The **<u>AIM</u>** of the apostle was rooted in the salvation of His people, the Jews – v. 14

Romans 1:16 – *"For I am not ashamed of the gospel of Christ: for it is the power of God unto salvation to every one that believeth; to the Jew first, and also to the Greek."*

Romans 9:1-3 – *"I say the truth in Christ, I lie not, my conscience also bearing me witness in the Holy Ghost, that I have great heaviness and continual sorrow in my heart. For I could wish that myself were accursed from Christ for my brethren, my kinsmen according to the flesh."*

Romans 10:1- *"Brethren, my heart's desire and prayer to God for Israel is, that they might be saved."*

I Corinthians 9:19-22 – *"For though I be free from all men, yet have I made myself servant unto all, that I might gain the more. And unto the Jews I became as a Jew, that I might gain the Jews; to them that are under the law, as under the law, that I might gain them that are under the law; To them that are without law, as without law, (being not without law to God, but under the law to Christ,) that I might gain them that are without law. To the weak became I as weak, that I might gain the weak: I am made all things to all men, that I might by all means save some."*

3. The future <u>ACCEPTANCE</u> of Israel by God will be an amazing miracle! v. 15
"what shall the receiving of them be, but life from the dead?"

4. Their __ATTACHMENT__ to God's promises and covenant is obvious – v. 16

(1)　Illustrated by BREAD
"If the firstfruit be holy, the lump is also holy" – cf. Numbers 15:17-21 – *"the heave offering"*

(2)　Illustrated by the OLIVE TREE
"and if the root be holy, so are the branches"

The *"firstfruit"* and the *"root"* refer to the fathers – Abraham, Isaac, and Jacob, and specifically to God's covenant with them (land, nation, and descendant Who will bless the world).

The *"lump"* and the *"branches"* refer to the nation of Israel.

The __REACTION__ the Gentiles should have!
Romans 11:17-24

1. There should be no __PRIDE__! vv. 17-20

"And if some of the branches be broken off, and thou, being a wild olive tree, wert grafted in among them, and with them partakest of the root and fatness of the olive tree: Boast not against the branches, but if thou boast, thou bearest not the root, but the root thee. Thou wilt say then, The branches were broken off, that I might be grafted in. Well; because of unbelief they were broken off, and thou standest by faith. Be not highminded, but fear."

There should be no <u>pride</u> because of the <u>ROOT</u> – vv. 17-18
"Boast not against the branches"

2. There should be no <u>PRESUMPTION</u> – vv. 21-24

"For if God spared not the natural branches, take heed lest He also spare not thee. Behold therefore the goodness and severity of God: on them which fell,

severity; but toward thee, goodness, if thou continue in His goodness: otherwise thou also shalt be cut off. And they also, if they abide not still in unbelief, shall be grafted in: for God is able to graft them in again. For if thou wert cut out of the olive tree which is wild by nature, and wert grafted contrary to nature into a good olive tree: how much more shall these, which be the natural branches, be grafted into their own olive tree?"

"PRESUMPTION" is a dangerous fact that is condemned in Psalm 19:13 – *"Keep back Thy servant from presumptuous sins; let them not have dominion over me."*

    (1)   The <u>ATTITUDE</u> that the opportunity for salvation will always be there is a very dangerous belief!

    (2)   The <u>ACCEPTANCE</u> of His goodness does not mean that His severity is impossible!

(3)   The <u>ABILITY</u> of God to restore Israel is not only possible – it is part of His prophetic plan!

Jeremiah 23:3-8 makes this very clear! *"And I will gather the remnant of My flock out of all countries whither I have driven them, and will bring them again to their folds; and they shall be fruitful and increase. And I will set up shepherds over them which shall feed them: and they shall fear no more, nor be dismayed, neither shall they be lacking, saith the LORD. Behold, the days come, saith the LORD, that I will raise unto David a righteous BRANCH, and a King shall reign and prosper, and shall execute judgment and justice in the earth. In His days Judah shall be saved, and Israel shall dwell safely: and this is His Name whereby He shall be called, THE LORD OUR RIGHTEOUSNESS. Therefore, behold, the days come, saith the LORD, that they shall no more say, The LORD liveth, which brought up the children of Israel out of the land of Egypt; But, The LORD liveth, which brought up and which led the seed of the house of Israel out of the north country, and from all countries whither I had driven them; and they shall dwell in their own land."*

     (4)   The <u>ACCOMPLISHMENT</u> of God's purposes toward Israel would be much easier than the salvation of the Gentiles!

The <u>REVELATION</u> of a mystery – Romans 11:25-32

The word *"mystery"* is used 22 times in the English Bible; the Greek word is *musterion* and is used 27 times in Greek.

1. The <u>CONCERN</u> of Paul about spiritual and prophetic ignorance – v. 25a

"For I would not, brethren, that ye should be ignorant of this mystery, lest ye should be wise in your own conceits."

The word *"ignorant"* is a common concern in the New Testament. It is used in at least seven ways:

(1)   Ignorant of Messianic prophecies – Acts 3:17-18

(2)   Ignorant of God's purpose in changing circumstances – Romans 1:13

(3)   Ignorant about believers who have died – I Thessalonians 4:13-18

(4)   Ignorant about the delay in the Second Coming of Jesus Christ – II Peter 3:8-9

(5)   Ignorant about spiritual gifts – I Corinthians 12:1

(6)   Ignorant about sufferings in the life of a believer – II Corinthians 1:8-9

(7)   Ignorant about God's plan for Israel – Romans 11:25

2. The <u>CHARACTER</u> of a Biblical mystery

A *"mystery"* refers to that which was not known in the past, but is now being revealed. Here are some "mysteries" in the Bible:

(1)   **The Kingdom**
       Matthew 13:11

(2)   **The Rapture**
       I Corinthians 15:51

(3)   **His Will**
       Ephesians 1:9-10

(4)   **Christ**
       Ephesians 3:3-11; Colossians 4:3

(5)   **Marriage**
       Ephesians 5:32

(6)   **The Gospel**
       Ephesians 6:19

(7)   **Christ in you**
       Colossians 1:26-27

(8)   **God**
       Colossians 2:2-3;
       Revelation 10:7

(9)   Iniquity
II Thessalonians 2:7

(10) The Faith
I Timothy 3:9

(11) Godliness
I Timothy 3:16

(12) Seven Stars & Candlesticks
Revelation 1:20

(13) The Harlot and the Beast
Revelation 17:5, 7

In I Corinthians 4:1 Paul spoke about being *"stewards of the mysteries of God."*

3. The <u>CONDITION</u> of Israel *"blindness in part"*

(1)   It is <u>PARTIAL</u> – *"in part"*

(2)   It is <u>PRESENT</u> until the fullness of the Gentiles cf. Romans 11:11-12; Revelation 7:9ff

(3)   It is <u>PROPHETIC</u> that it would occur – *"until the*

fullness of the Gentiles be come in"

4. The <u>COMING</u> of salvation *"and so all Israel shall be saved: as it is written, There shall come out of Sion the Deliverer..."*

(1)   The <u>PROMISE</u> – *"all Israel"*

Zechariah 13:8-9 indicates that only one-third of the Nation will repent and turn to the Messiah for salvation!

(2)   The <u>PERSON</u> – *"the Deliverer"*

Isaiah 59:20-21 – *"And the Redeemer shall come to Zion, and unto them that turn from transgression in Jacob, saith the LORD. As for Me, this is My covenant with them, saith the LORD; My Spirit that is upon thee, and My words which I have put in thy mouth, shall not depart out of thy mouth, nor out of the mouth of thy seed's seed, saith the LORD, from henceforth and forever."*

Zechariah 12:10 – *"And I will pour upon the house of David, and upon the inhabitants of Jerusalem, the Spirit of grace and of supplications: and they shall look upon Me Whom they have pierced, and they shall mourn for Him, as one mourneth for his only son, and shall be in bitterness for Him, as one that is in bitterness for his firstborn."*

> (3)   The <u>PURPOSE</u> – *"and shall turn away ungodliness from Jacob"*

Zechariah 13:1 – *"In that day there shall be a fountain opened to the house of David and to the inhabitants of Jerusalem for sin and for uncleanness."*

5. The <u>COVENANT</u> of God – *"For this is My covenant unto them, when I shall take away their sins"* – v. 27

We read in Isaiah 43:25 – *"I, even I, am He that blotteth out thy transgressions for Mine own sake, and will not remember thy sins."*

Isaiah 44:21-22 – *"Remember these, O Jacob and Israel; for thou art My servant: I have formed thee; thou art My servant: O Israel, thou shalt not be forgotten of Me. I have blotted out, as a thick cloud, thy transgressions, and, as a cloud, thy sins: return unto Me; for I have redeemed thee."*

Isaiah 45:22 – *"Look unto Me, and be ye saved, all the ends of the earth: for I am God, and there is none else."*

Jeremiah 31:33-34 – *"But this shall be the covenant that I will make with the house of Israel; After those days, saith the LORD, I will put My law in their inward parts, and write it in their hearts; and will be their God, and they shall be My people. And they shall teach no more every man his neighbor, and every man his brother, saying, Know the LORD: for they shall all know Me, from the least of them unto the greatest of them, saith the LORD: for I will forgive their iniquity, and I will remember their sin no more."*

6. The <u>CHOICE</u> of God – v. 28

(1) They are the <u>ENEMIES</u> of the gospel – v. 28a – *"for your sakes"*

(2) They are the <u>ELECTION</u> of God – v. 28b – *"but as touching the election, they are beloved for the fathers' sakes"*

The word *"fathers"* refers to Abraham, Isaac, and Jacob.

7. The <u>CALLING</u> of God – v. 29

"For the gifts and calling of God are without repentance."

(1) It is God's <u>DECISION</u> – *"the gifts and calling of God"*

Romans 1:7 refers to the believers in Rome: *"To all that be in Rome, beloved of God, <u>called</u> to be saints..."*

Romans 8:28 speaks of those who *"love God"* and says *"to them who are the <u>called</u> according to His purpose."*

Romans 10:13 says: *"For whosoever shall <u>call</u> upon the Name of the Lord shall be saved."*

I Corinthians 1:9: *"God is faithful, by Whom ye were <u>called</u> unto the fellowship of His Son Jesus Christ our Lord."*

II Timothy 1:9 says: *"Who hath saved us, and <u>called</u> us with an holy <u>calling</u>..."*

> (2)   It is God's <u>DETERMINATION</u> to keep His Word - *"without repentance"*

This is not referring to our repentance, but to God's. It is not the Greek word for "impenitent" that is used in Romans 2:5 – *ametanoeton*. The Greek word here in verse 29 is the word *ametameleta*, the root word refers to being sorry afterwards – God is not this way! He does not change His mind and actions regarding His calling!

8. The <u>CONCLUSION</u> to which Paul brings us - vv. 30-32

(1) God's mercy is <u>ACCESSIBLE</u> to the Gentiles through the unbelief of Israel – v. 30

"For as ye in times past have not believed God, yet have now obtained mercy through their unbelief."

(2) God's mercy will be <u>ACCEPTED</u> by the Jews through the mercy of the Gentiles – v. 31

"Even so have these also now not believed, that through your mercy they also may obtain mercy."

(3) God's mercy is <u>AVAILABLE</u> to all in spite of their unbelief – v. 32

"For God hath concluded them all in unbelief, that He might have mercy upon all."

The <u>REALIZATION</u> of God's plan – Romans 11:33-36

"O the depth of the riches both of the wisdom and knowledge of God! How unsearchable are His judgments, and

His ways past finding out! For who hath known the mind of the Lord? or who hath been His counselor? For of Him, and through Him, and to Him, are all things: to Whom be glory forever. Amen."

These verses form one of the greatest passages in the Bible describing the majesty and superiority of our God above all!

Our COMPREHENSION of the plan and purposes of God!
vv. 33-35

Notice five things said about God in these verses:

1. His riches are UNFATHOMABLE!

"O the depth of the riches both of the wisdom and knowledge of God!"

The word *"depth"* (Greek: *bathos*) was also used in Romans 8:39 in describing the love of God: *"Nor height, nor depth, nor any other creature, shall be able to separate us from the love of God, which is in Christ Jesus our Lord."*

Ephesians 2:7 – *"That in the ages to come He might show the exceeding <u>riches</u> of His grace in His kindness toward us through Christ Jesus."*

Colossians 2:3 adds: *"In Whom are hid all the treasures of wisdom and knowledge."*

2. His judgments are <u>UNSEARCHABLE</u>!

"How unsearchable are His judgments"

In the Greek text, a double compound is used – meaning, it is totally impossible for us to discover!

3. His ways are <u>UNKNOWABLE</u>!

"and His ways past finding out"

The Greek word, *anexichniastoi*, is again a double compound and means - It is totally impossible for us to discover! The translation of this word means "to trace out by tracks."

Ephesians 3:8 speaks of *"the unsearchable riches of Christ."*

4. His understanding is UNOBTAINABLE!

"For who hath known the mind of the Lord? or who hath been His counselor?

This is a direct quotation from Isaiah 40:12-14:

"Who hath measured the waters in the hollow of His hand, and meted out heaven with the span, and comprehended the dust of the earth in a measure, and weighed the mountains in scales and the hills in a balance? Who hath directed the Spirit of the Lord, or being His counselor hath taught Him? With whom took he counsel, and who instructed Him, and taught Him in the path of judgment, and shewed to Him the way of understanding?"

Obviously – NO ONE!

5. His needs are UNMEETABLE!

"Or who hath first given to Him, and it shall be recompensed unto Him again?"

Job 41:11 says: *"Who hath prevented Me, that I should repay him? Whatsoever is under the whole heaven is Mine."*

Romans 12;19 says: *"Dearly beloved, avenge not yourselves, but rather give place unto wrath: for it is written, Vengeance is Mine; I will repay, saith the Lord."*

I Thessalonians 3:9 adds: *"For what thanks can we render to God again for you, for all the joy wherewith we joy for your sakes before our God...?"*

His <u>CONTROL</u> of His plan and purposes – v. 36

"For of Him, and through Him, and to Him, are all things: to Whom be glory forever. Amen"

This letter to the Romans is not over yet! But after speaking of the majesty and abilities of our God, it was time to say **AMEN!**

1. The <u>ORIGIN</u> of His plan –
   "For of Him"

The Greek preposition translated *"of"* is the word *ek,* meaning "out of" by way of source. All comes from Him! John 1:3 says of our Messiah: *"All things were made by Him, and without Him was not anything made that was made."*

2. The <u>OPERATION</u> of His plan -
"through Him"

The preposition *"through"* is the Greek word *dia* which speaks of the channel through which His plan is accomplished!

3. The <u>OBJECT</u> of His plan –
"and to Him"

The Greek preposition is *eis* which speaks of the result of that plan and purpose – It is intended to give Him glory and praise!

4. The <u>OBJECTIVE</u> He will accomplish through His plan
– "to Whom be glory forever"

AMEN!

THE
PRACTICES
OF THE
RIGHTEOUSNESS
OF GOD

Romans 12:1-16:27

Chapter 9
LIVING FOR CHRIST
Romans 12:1-8

When God's righteousness has brought you salvation and now controls your life, it will affect how you live!

1. The <u>MOTIVATION</u> – *"by the mercies of God"*

Undoubtedly these *"mercies"* are referring to the first 11 chapters. His *"mercies"* are everlasting!

2. The <u>MANNER</u> in which it begins – *"that ye present your bodies a living sacrifice, holy, acceptable unto God, which is your reasonable service."*

The word *"present"* is the same word as in Romans 6:13 – *"yield."* The issue here is referring to the dedication of our bodies to the Lord to use as He sees fit and as He desires. It is our *"reasonable service"* or the logical result of our worship and praise.

3. The <u>MEANS</u> by which it is fulfilled in your life – *"and be not conformed to this world, but be ye transformed by the renewing of your mind."*

It is our decision – either *"conform"* to the world, or *"be transformed"* by the *"renewing of your mind."*

The word *"conformed"* is from the Greek word *suschematidzesthe.* The word *"world"* is the Greek word *aioni,* which refers to the age or culture in which we all live and move from day to day. We either adapt to the world around us, and adopt their ways, beliefs, lifestyles, attitudes, and ungodly responses, or we renew our minds in the ways of the Lord and the principles of His Word – this renewal results in mental transformation.

The word *"but"* is the Greek word *alla* which reveals a great contrast. No wonder so many believers are confused and discouraged. The Greek word for *"transformed"* is the compound word *metamorphousthe.* It refers to our spiritual DNA as *"new creatures in*

Christ." The same Greek word appears in II Corinthians 3:18:

"But we all, with open face beholding as in a glass the glory of the Lord, are <u>changed</u> into the same image from glory to glory, even as by the Spirit of the Lord."

The *"glass"* (or "mirror") into which we look – reveals the *"glory of the Lord"* - and as our minds are *"renewed"* by what we see and understand, we are being changed, through the power of the Holy Spirit (using the Word of God) into the *"same image"* – in other words, we begin to reflect the Person and lifestyle of our Lord and Savior Jesus Christ!

4. The <u>MOTIVE</u> for doing it – *"that ye may prove what is that good, and acceptable, and prefect, will of God."*

Most believers speak of doing the will of God as their most important priority in life. But, when there is an absence of "renewal" in the way we think, understand, and perceive what God wants of us, the result is conformity to this age and culture in which we live, instead of a transformation that makes us more and more Christlike in all we do and say!

5. The <u>MINDSET</u> that is needed
– "not to think of himself more highly than he ought to think; but to think soberly..."

This "mindset" is both negative and positive in its effect upon our lives.

NEGATIVELY – *"not to think of himself more highly than he ought to think"*

The Greek word *huperphronein* means "to think above" and is used only here in the New Testament. A similar idea is found in Romans 12:16: *"Be of the same mind one toward another. Mind not high things, but condescend to men of low estate. Be not wise in your own conceits."*

POSITIVELY – *"but to think soberly"* – the Greek word *sophroneo* is used six times in the New Testament. Its root verb *phroneo* is found some 30 times.

It is used in Mark 5:15 of the man who was healed of demon possession and was now *"in his right mind."* It is also used in II Corinthians 5:13 of the opposite of being insane – it is connected with prayer and watching in I Peter 4:7 and it is used in Philippians 2:5-8 emphasizing an attitude of humility.

6. The <u>MEASURE</u> of faith we need – *"according as God hath dealt to every man the measure of faith"*

The word *"dealt"* is the Greek word *emerise* meaning "to divide" or "distribute." It is found in Hebrew 2:4 where we read: *"God also bearing them witness, both with signs and wonders, and with divers miracles, and gifts of the Holy Ghost, according to His own will."*

In I Corinthians 12:6 we read: *"And there are diversities of operations, but it is the same "God which worketh all in all."* In I Corinthians 12: 7 we realize that the Apostle Paul is speaking about the distribution and use of spiritual gifts. He says: *"But the manifestation of the Spirit is given to every man to profit withal."* Also, in I Corinthians 12:11 we read: *"But all these worketh that one and the selfsame Spirit, dividing to every man severally as He will."*

I Peter 4:10-11 adds this amazing fact:
"As every man hath received the gift, even so minister the same one to another, as good stewards of the manifold grace of God. If any man speak, let him speak as the oracles of God; if any man minister (serve), let him do it as of the ability which God giveth that God in all things may be glorified through Jesus Christ, to Whom be praise and dominion forever and ever. Amen."

Looking carefully at the opening three verses of Romans 12, we see four issues:

(1)   DEDICATION – *verse 1*
(2)   TRANSFORMATION – *verse 2*
(3)   HUMILITY – *verse 3a*
(4)   FAITH – *verse 3b*

The truth is we need faith in God and in the existence of spiritual gifts which He has given to every believer through the power of the Holy Spirit Who controls the use of our gifts. We need to trust the Lord for the purpose and use of our gifts which Ephesians 4:11-12 says it is for the edification of the body of Christ – which means we are to "build up" other believers by the use of our gifts.

7. The <u>MINISTRY</u> of spiritual gifts that reveals it

Romans 12:4-8 lays out the ministry of spiritual gifts:

"For as we have many members in one body, and all members have not the same office: So we, being many, are one body in Christ, and every one members one of another. Having then gifts differing according to the grace that is given to us, whether prophecy, let us prophesy according to the proportion of faith; Or ministry, let us wait on our ministering: or he that teacheth, on teaching; Or he that exhorteth, on exhortation: he that giveth, let him do it with simplicity; he that ruleth, with diligence; he that sheweth mercy, with cheerfulness."

1. It involves our <u>RELATIONSHIP</u> with one another – vv. 4-5

There is one body, but many members, and we all have different gifts and ministries to use for the glory of the Lord and the edification of other believers.

I Corinthians 12:12-17 tells us a similar story about gifts:

"For as the body is one, and hath many members, and all the members of that one body, being many, are one body: so also is Christ. For by one Spirit are we all baptized into one body, whether we be Jews or Gentiles, whether we be bond or free; and have been all made to drink into one Spirit. For the body is not one member, but many. If the foot shall say, Because I am not the hand, I am not of the body; is it therefore not of the body? And if the ear shall say, because I am not the eye, I am not of the body; is it therefore not of the body? If the whole body were an eye, where were the hearing? If the whole were hearing, where were ther smelling?"

DIFFERENCES – *"all members have not the same office."* The Greek word *praxin* is found 6 times. Its root verb is *prasso* and is used 36 times – it refers to what we do or practice – in other words, our deeds.

DEPENDENCY – *"every one members of one of another"* – we need each other and the exercise of their spiritual gifts.
I Corinthians 12:7 says: *"But the manifestation of the Spirit is given to every man to profit withal.*

    2. It involves our <u>RECEIVING</u> of God's grace – v. 6 – *"Having then gifts differing according to the grace that is given to us..."*

Grace gives us what we do not deserve nor can earn or achieve by our own efforts.

    3. It involves our <u>RESPECT</u> for the differences in the gifts – I Corinthians 12:4-6 reveals the *"differences."*

"Now there are diversities of gifts, but the same Spirit. And there are differences in administrations, but the same Lord. And there are diversities of operations, but it is the same God which worketh all in all."

(1) There are differences in the NUMBER of gifts but the *"same Spirit"* Who gives them.

(2) There are differences in the WAY the gifts are used, but the *"same Lord"* that we all seek to glorify.

(3) There are differences in the EXTENT to which the gifts affect the lives of others, but the *"same God."*

4. It involves our <u>RECOGNITION</u> of the true nature of these gifts.

There are seven gifts listed here in Romans 12. Since there are more listed in the New Testament, the question might be – WHY THE SEVEN?

(1) This might be just a <u>SAMPLING</u> – more gifts could have been listed!

(2) This might be a <u>SUMMARY</u> of all the gifts – perhaps the rest of them fit into these

seven or are supportive of them.

(3) This might simply be a **SELECTION** of the gifts that illustrate the point of the passage!

(4) These gifts could be a **STANDARD** of church ministry after the New Testament was completed.

SOME INTERESTING FACTS:

(1) The Greek preposition *en* is used with all except *"prophecy."*

(2) The word *"If"* (Greek: *eite*) is used with the first four, but not with the last three.

(3) The definite article *"the"* is used with ministry, teaching, and exhortation, but not with the other four.

BRIEF DEFINITIONS OF THE SEVEN SPIRITUAL GIFTS:

PROPHESYING – meets the spiritual needs of the body

I Corinthians 14:3-4 – *"But he that prophesieth speaketh unto men to edification, and exhortation, and comfort. He that speaketh in an unknown tongue edifieth himself; but he that prophesieth edifieth the church."*

MINISTERING – meets the practical needs of the body

I Peter 4:11 – *"If any man minister, let him do it as of the ability which God giveth; that God in all things may be glorified through Jesus Christ, to Whom be praise and dominion forever and ever."*

TEACHING – meets the intellectual needs of the body

Titus 2:12-15 – *"Teaching us that, denying ungodliness and worldly lusts, we should live soberly, righteously, and godly, in this present world; Looking for that blessed hope, and the glorious appearing of the great God and our Savior Jesus Christ; Who gave Himself for us, that He might redeem us from all iniquity, and purify unto Himself a peculiar people, zealous of good works. These things speak, and exhort, and rebuke with all authority. Let no man despise thee."*

EXHORTING – meets the emotional needs of the body

II Corinthians 1:3-4 – *"Blessed be God, even the Father of our Lord Jesus Christ, the Father of mercies, and the God of all comfort; Who comforteth us in all our tribulation, that we may be able to comfort them which are in any trouble, by the comfort wherewith we ourselves are comforted of God."*

GIVING – meets the financial needs of the body

II Corinthians 9:6-7 – *"But this I say, He which soweth sparingly shall reap also sparingly; and he which soweth bountifully shall reap also bountifully. Every man according as He purposeth in his heart, so let him give, not grudgingly, or of necessity: for God loveth a cheerful giver."*

RULING – meets the organizational needs of the body

Hebrews 13:17 – *"Obey them that have the rule over you, and submit yourselves for they watch for your souls, as they that must give account, that they may do it with joy, and not with grief: for that is unprofitable for you."*

SHEWING MERCY – meets the physical needs of the body

Romans 9:15-16 – *"For He saith to Moses, I will have mercy on whom I will have mercy, and I will have compassion on whom I will have compassion. So then it is not of him that willeth, nor of him that runneth, but of God that sheweth mercy."*

5. It involves our <u>RELIANCE</u> upon the way in which the gifts are to be used.

There is a <u>principle</u> in the use of gifts that refers to the control of the Word of God – *"according to the proportion* (Greek: *analogia*) *of <u>the faith</u>."* There is also an issue dealing with the <u>practice</u> of spiritual gifts. We read *"let us wait on."* The Greek preposition <u>en</u> is used with the last six gifts – whatever gift you have, exercise that on a regular basis.

The last three gifts in this list of seven reveal a <u>pattern</u> to follow in using our gifts.

<u>GIVING</u> – do it with *"simplicity"*

The Greek word translated *"simplicity"* is the word *haplotes* – it is used seven times and is the opposite of the word "double." It refers to being single-minded, not doing it for any ulterior motives.

<u>RULING</u> – do it with *"diligence"*

The Greek word *proistamenos* means "to lead" or "to stand in front of people" and motivate them for the Lord – a leadership gift. The word for *"diligence"* is the Greek word *spoude* which is used 14 times – it means you are quick to respond to the needs of the people over whom you are to rule.

<u>SHOWING MERCY</u> – do it with *"cheerfulness"*

The Greek word *hilaroteti* gives us our English word "hilarious." It refers to the bright color of gold when it is cast into a furnace. II Corinthians 9:7 says: *"for God loveth a <u>cheerful</u> giver."*

Chapter 10
LOVE OF GOD
Romans 12:9-21

The <u>CHARACTERISTICS</u> of LOVE
Romans 12:9-13

"Let love be without dissimulation. Abhor that which is evil; cleave to that which is good. Be kindly affectioned one to another with brotherly love; in honor preferring one another; Not slothful in business; fervent in spirit; serving the Lord; Rejoicing in hope; patient in tribulation; continuing instant in prayer."

The key statement of this wonderful passage on God's love is the one that begins verse 9 – *"Let love be without dissimulation."* The Greek word used in this statement is *ahupokritos* which is found six times, and literally means "no hypocrisy."

II Corinthians 6:6 – *"love unfeigned"*
I Timothy 1:5 – *"faith unfeigned"*
II Timothy 1:5 – *"unfeigned faith"*
James 3:17 – *"without hypocrisy"*
I Peter 1:22 – *"unfeigned love"*

LOVE is <u>CONTROLLED</u> by God's standards – v. 9

"Abhor that which is evil; cleave to that which is good."

    1. It includes <u>DESPISING</u> what is evil.

The Greek word that is translated *"abhor"* is *apostugountes* and is only found here. A similar idea is found in I Thessalonians 5:22 where we read: *"Abstain from all appearance of evil."*

    2. It includes <u>DOING</u> what is good.

The word *"cleave"* is the Greek word *kollomenoi* and is found 10 times in the New Testament. Galatians 6:10 says: *"As we have therefore opportunity, let us do good unto all men, especially unto them who are of the household of faith."*

LOVE is <u>CAREFUL</u> about the feelings of others – v. 10

"Be kindly affectioned one to another with brotherly love; in honor preferring one another."

1. It <u>TREATS</u> others like family.

The words *"kindly affectioned"* come from the Greek word *philostorgoi* and is only used here. It is a compound word putting the Greek word for "friend" with the word for "family love."

2. It <u>TREASURES</u> others with great respect.

The Greek word used here (and only here) is *proegoumenoi* and refers to someone taking the lead or setting the example.

LOVE is <u>COMMITTED</u> to the service of the Lord – v. 11

"Not slothful in business; fervent in spirit; serving the Lord"

1. It involves <u>ENERGY</u> – *"not slothful in business"*

2. It involves <u>ENTHUSIASM</u> – *"fervent in spirit"*

3. It involves <u>EXALTATION</u> – *"serving the Lord"*

Ephesians 6:5-8 – *"Servants, be obedient to them that are your masters according to the flesh, with fear and trembling, in singleness of your heart, as unto Christ; Not with eye-service, as men-pleasers; but as the servants of Christ, doing the will of God from the heart; With good will doing service, as to the Lord, and not to men: Knowing that whatsoever good thing any man doeth, the same shall he receive of the Lord, whether he be bond or free."*

Colossians 3:22-24 – *"Servants, obey in all things your masters according to the flesh; not with eye-service, as men-pleasers; but in singleness of heart, fearing God: and whatsoever ye do, do it heartily, as to the Lord, and not unto men; Knowing that of the Lord ye shall receive the reward of the inheritance: for ye serve the Lord Christ."*

LOVE is <u>CONFIDENT</u> in God's power and plan – v. 12

"Rejoicing in hope; patient in tribulation; continuing instant in prayer."

1. It involves <u>PROMISE</u> – *"rejoicing in hope"*

Romans 5:2 says: *"rejoice in hope of the glory of God."* Romans 15:13 adds: *"Now the God of hope fill you with all joy and peace in believing, that ye may abound in hope, through the power of the Holy Ghost."*

2. It involves <u>PATIENCE</u> – *"patient in tribulation"*

The Greek word *hupomenontes* refers to one who "bears up under a load." Life can certainly be a "load" to handle.

Romans 8:24-25 connects our *"hope"* with our *"patience"*:

"For we are saved by hope: but hope that is seen is not hope; for what a man seeth, why doth he yet hope for? But if we hope for that we see not, then do we with patience wait for it."

3. It involves <u>PRAYER</u> – *"continuing instant in prayer"*

Colossians 4:2-4 – *"Continue in prayer, and watch in the same with thanksgiving; Withal praying also for us, that God would open unto us a door of utterance, to speak the mystery of Christ, for which I am also in bonds: That I may make it manifest, as I ought to speak."*

I Thessalonians 5:16-18 adds: *"Rejoice evermore. Pray without ceasing. In every thing give thanks: for this is the will of God in Christ Jesus concerning you."*

LOVE is <u>CONCERNED</u> about the needs of others – v. 13

"Distributing to the necessity of saints; given to hospitality."

1. In involves <u>HELPING</u> when there are material and financial needs.

Ephesians 4:28 – *"Let him that stole steal no more: but rather let him labor, working with his hands the thing which is good, that he may have to give to him that needeth."*

James 2:15-16 – *"If a brother or sister be naked and destitute of daily food, and one of you say unto them, Depart in peace, be ye warmed and filled; notwithstanding ye give them not those things which are needful to the body; what doth it profit?"*

I John 3:17-18 – *"But whoso hath this world's good, and seeth his brother have need, and shutteth up his bowels of compassion from him, how dwelleth the love of God in him? My little children, let us not love in word, neither in tongue; but in deed and truth."*

    2. It involves <u>HOSPITALITY</u> – *"given to hospitality"*

The Greek word for *"hospitality"* means to *"show friendship to strangers."* Hebrews 13:1-2 says: *"Let brotherly love continue. Be not forgetful to entertain strangers: for thereby some have entertained angels unawares."*

I Peter 4:9-11: *"Use hospitality one to another without grudging. As every men hath received the gift, even so minister the same one to another, as good stewards of the manifold grace of God. If any man speak, let him speak as the oracles of God; if any man minister, let him do it as of the ability which God giveth: that God in all things may be glorified through Jesus Christ, to whom be praise and dominion forever and ever. Amen."*

The <u>COMMANDS</u> of LOVE
Romans 12:14-21

"Bless them with persecute you; bless, and curse not. Rejoice with them that do rejoice, and weep with them that weep. Be of the same mind one toward another. Mind not high things, but condescend to men of low estate. Be not wise in your own conceits. Recompense to no man evil for evil. Provide things honest in the sight of all men. If it be possible, as much as lieth in you, live peaceably with all men. Dearly beloved, avenge not yourselves, but rather give place unto wrath: for it is written, Vengeance is Mine; I will repay, saith the Lord. Therefore if thine enemy hunger, feed him; if he thirst, give him drink: for in so doing thou shalt heap coals of fire on his head. Be not overcome of evil, but overcome evil with good."

God's LOVE is <u>COMPLIMENTARY</u> toward those who persecute you – v. 14

"Bless them which persecute you: bless, and curse not."

Matthew 5:10-12 – *"Blessed are they which are persecuted for righteousness' sake: for theirs is the kingdom of heaven. Blessed are ye, when men shall revile you, and persecute you, and shall say all manner of evil against you falsely, for My sake. Rejoice, and be exceeding glad: for great is your reward in heaven: for so persecuted they the prophets which were before you."*

Two important questions to ask:

1. <u>WHY</u> are you being persecuted?

Is it *"for righteousness' sake"*?
(Matthew 5:10; I Peter 3:17b – *"for well-doing"*?)

Is it *"for My sake"*? (Matthew 5:11)

2. <u>HOW</u> should you respond to the persecution?

Matthew 5:12 - *"Rejoice and be exceeding glad"*

I Peter 2:20 – *"take it patiently"*

I Peter 3:14 – *"be not afraid of their terror, neither be troubled"*

I Peter 3:15 – *"But sanctify the Lord God in your hearts; and be ready always to give an answer to every man that asketh you a reason of the hope that is in you with meekness and fear."*

I Peter 4:16 – *"let him not be ashamed; but let him glorify God on this behalf"*

LOVE is <u>COMPASSIONATE</u> toward the experiences of others
Romans 12:15

"Rejoice with them that do rejoice, and weep with them that weep."

Compassion does two things in relating to the difficulties and trials of others:

1. It <u>REJOICES</u> with them!

When Elisabeth delivered a baby boy (John the Baptist), her neighbors and cousins realized the Lord had *"great mercy"* upon her, so they *"<u>rejoiced</u> with her."* (Luke 1:57-58)

In the parables that Yeshua taught, He spoke of a shepherd who had 100 sheep, and when he is missing just one, he will go after it until he finds it. In Luke 15:5-6 we read: *"And when he hath found it, he layeth it on his shoulders, rejoicing, And when he cometh home, he calleth together his friends and neighbors, saying unto them, Rejoice with me; for I have found my sheep which was lost."*

Our Lord then said: *"I say unto you, that likewise joy shall be in heaven over one sinner that repenteth, more than over ninety and nine just persons, which need no repentance."*

Similar words were said about a woman who found a lost piece of silver (Luke 15:8-10).

2. It <u>REACTS</u> with sorrow!

Life is filled with many "sorrows." But, compassionate friends are "few and far-between."

When Yeshua wept at the grave of Lazarus, it was because he saw Mary weeping along with other Jews who came with her. When they saw Yeshua weeping, they responded: *"Behold how He loved him!"*

In I Corinthians 12:25-26 we read: *"That there should be no schism in the body; but that the members should have the same care for one another. And whether one member suffer, all the members suffer with it; or one member be honored, all the members rejoice with it."* That is the response of Biblical compassion!

LOVE is <u>CONSIDERATE</u> of the opinions of others – v. 16

"Be of the same mind one toward another. Mind not high things, but condescend to men of low estate. Be not wise in your own conceits."

There are four responses mentioned in the above verse:

1. As to <u>ACCEPTANCE</u> of others – *"be of the same mind one toward another"*

Romans 15:5-7 – *"Now the God of patience and consolation grant you to be likeminded one toward another according to Christ Jesus: That ye may with one mind and one mouth glorify God, even the Father of our Lord Jesus Christ. Wherefore receive ye one another, as Christ also received us to the glory of God."*

II Corinthians 13:11 – *"Finally, brethren, farewell. Be perfect, be of good comfort, be of one mind, live in peace; and the God of love and peace shall be with you."*

Philippians 2:2 – *"Fulfill ye my joy, that ye be like-minded, having the same love, being of one accord, of one mind."*

Philippians 4:2 – *"I beseech Euodias, and beseech Syntyche, that they be of the same mind in the Lord."*

2. As to <u>AMBITION</u> toward others – *"mind not high things"*

If you translate the grammatical construction of the Greek language here, it is literally "Stop doing it!"

Consider the words of Mark 10:43-45: *"But so shall it not be among you: but whosoever will be great among you, shall be your minister (servant): And whosoever of you will be the chiefest, shall be servant of all. For even the Son of man came not to be ministered unto, but to minister, and to give His life a ransom for many."*

It is quite natural to have an ambitious attitude toward others. An example of this attitude is found in III John 9 where we read: *"I wrote unto the church: but Diotrephes, who loveth to have the preeminence among them, receiveth us not."*

   3. As to our <u>ASSOCIATIONS</u> with others – *"but condescend to men of low estate"*

Matthew 18:1-4 – *"At the same time came the disciples unto Jesus, saying, Who is the greatest in the kingdom of heaven? And Jesus called a little child unto Him, and set him in the midst of them, and said, Verily I say unto you, Except ye be converted, and become as little children, ye shall not enter into the kingdom of heaven. Whosoever therefore shall humble himself as this little child, the same is greatest in the kingdom of heaven."*

In James 2:1-10 there is a detailed story about the *"respect of persons"* and our attitudes toward them when they come into *"your assembly"* (Greek word is the word *"synagogue."*) The passage rebukes those who cater to the rich and show them preference over the poor. The passage even says that if you show such *"respect of persons"* – *"ye commit sin"* (verse 9).

4. As to our <u>ATTITUDES</u> toward others – *"Be not wise in your own conceits"* (same phrase found in Romans 11:25)

This verse appears to be a direct quote from Proverbs 3:7 – *"Be not wise in thine own eyes: fear the LORD, and depart from evil."*

If you think you are wiser and smarter than others, it is an *"evil"* attitude!

400

LOVE is <u>CONSTRAINED</u> in its reaction to evil – vv. 17-21

"Recompense to no man evil for evil. Provide things honest in the sight of all men. If it be possible, as much as lieth in you, live peaceably with all men. Dearly beloved, avenge not yourselves, but rather give place unto wrath: for it is written, "Vengeance is Mine: I will repay, saith the Lord. Therefore if thine enemy hunger, feed him; if he thirst, give him drink: for in so doing thou shalt heap coals of fire on his head. Be not overcome of evil, but overcome evil with good."

In this passage we find four critical issues about the love of God.

    1. It <u>REPAYS</u> no one with evil – v. 17

"Recompense to no man evil for evil. Provide things honest in the sight of all men."

In Matthew 5:38-42 we find this critical teaching of our Lord:

"Ye have heard that it hath been said, An eye for an eye, and a tooth for a

tooth: But I say unto you, That ye resist not evil: but whosoever shall smite thee on thy right cheek, turn to him the other also. And if any man will sue thee at the law, and take away thy coat, let him have thy cloak also. And whosoever shall compel thee to go a mile, go with him twain. Give to him that asketh thee, and from him that would borrow of thee turn not thou away."

I Peter 2:22-23 – *"Who did no sin, neither was guile found in His mouth: Who, when He was reviled, reviled not again; when He suffered, He threatened not, but committed Himself to Him that judgeth righteously."*

Our Lord's example is powerful for us!

I Peter 3:9-12 adds: *"Not rendering evil for evil, or railing for railing: but contrariwise blessing; knowing that ye are thereunto called, that ye should inherit a blessing. For he that will love life, and see good days, let him refrain his tongue from evil, and his lips that they speak no guile: Let him eschew evil, and do good; let him seek peace, and ensue it. For the eyes of the Lord are over the righteous, and his ears are open unto their prayers: but the face of the Lord is against them that do evil."*

    2. It <u>REFLECTS</u> a desire for peace – v. 18 – *"If it be possible, as much as lieth in you, live peaceably with all men"*

Matthew 5:9 tells us: *"Blessed are the peacemakers: for they shall be called the children of God."*

Romans 14:16-19 says: *"Let not then your good be evil spoken of: For the kingdom of God is not meat and drink; but righteousness, and peace, and joy in the Holy Ghost. For he that in these things serveth Christ is acceptable to God, and approved of men. Let us therefore follow after the things which make for peace, and things wherewith one may edify another."*

Colossians 3:15 – *"And let the peace of God rule in your hearts, to the which also ye are called in one body; and be ye thankful."*

Hebrews 12:14 – *"Follow peace with all men, and holiness, without which no man shall see the Lord."*

3. It <u>REFUSES</u> to seek revenge – v. 19
   "Dearly beloved, avenge not yourselves, but rather give place unto wrath: for it is written, Vengeance is Mine; I will repay, saith the Lord."

This quotation comes from Deuteronomy 32:35: *"To Me belongeth vengeance, and recompence."*

Leviticus 19:18 – *"Thou shalt not avenge, nor bear any grudge against the children of thy people, but thou shalt love thy neighbor as thyself: I am the LORD."*

Proverbs 20:22 – *"Say not thou, I will recompense evil; but wait on the LORD, and He shall save thee."*

Hebrews 10:30-31 – *"For we know Him that hath said, Vengeance belongeth unto Me, I will recompense, saith the Lord. And again, The Lord shall judge His people. It is a fearful thing to fall into the hands of the living God."*

4. It <u>RESPONDS</u> with good – vv. 20-21 – *"Therefore if thine enemy hunger, feed him; if he thirst, give*

him drink: for in so doing thou shalt heap coals of fire on his head. Be not overcome of evil, but overcome evil with good."

The above passage in Romans 12:20-21 is a direct quotation from Proverbs 25:21-22.

Galatians 6:10 – *"As we have therefore opportunity, let us do good unto all men, especially unto them which are of the household of faith."*

Chapter 11
LAW OF GOD
Romans 13:1-14

Our <u>SUBJECTION</u> to the law
Romans 13:1-5

"Let every soul be subject unto the higher powers. For there is no power but of God: the powers that be are ordained of God. Whosoever therefore resisteth the power, resisteth the ordinance of God: and they that resist shall receive to themselves damnation. For rulers are not a terror to good works, but to the evil. Wilt thou then not be afraid of the power? Do that which is good, and thou shalt have praise of the same: For he is the minister of God to thee for good. But if thou do that which is evil, be afraid; for he beareth not the sword in vain: for he is the minister of God, a revenger to execute wrath upon him that doeth evil. Wherefore ye must needs be subject, not only for wrath, but also for conscience sake."

1. Our <u>RESPONSIBILITY</u> – *"Let every soul be subject unto the higher powers"* – v. 1a

The Greek word translated as *"subject"* is *hupotasso* which means "to arrange under" and deals with rank (military term). It is used 49 times in the New Testament.

Titus 3:1 – *"Put them in mind to be <u>subject</u> to principalities and power, to obey magistrates, to be ready to every good work."*

I Peter 2:13-16 – *"<u>Submit</u> yourselves to every ordinance of man for the Lord's sake: whether it be to the king, as supreme; or unto governors, as unto them that are sent by him for the punishment of evildoers, and for the praise of them that do well. For so is the will of God, that with well-doing ye may put to silence the ignorance of foolish men: As free, and not using ;your liberty for a cloak of maliciousness, but as the servants of God."*

The word *"submit"* is also used of Jesus Christ in I Corinthians 15:28 – *"And when all things shall be subdued unto Him, then shall the Son also Himself be subject unto Him that put all things under Him, that God may be all in all."*

In a negative sense, the word is used of the *"carnal mind"* which Romans 8:7 says is *"not subject to the law of God."* Romans 10:3 adds that there are some who *"have not submitted themselves unto the righteousness of God."*

POSITIVE USAGES OF "SUBJECT"

Used of servants to masters – Titus 2:9
Used of young to old – I Peter 5:5
Used of angels to Christ – I Peter 3:22
Used of wives to husbands – Ephesians 5:22; Colossians 3:18; Titus 2:5; I Peter 3:1, 5
Used of believers to one another – Ephesians 5:21
Used of believers to God – James 4:7

2. The REASONS for this subjection to authority – vv. 1b-5

(1) Because of the COMMAND of God – v. 1b – *"For there is no power but of God: the*

powers that be are ordained of God"

The word *"powers"* is from the Greek word *exousia* – meaning "authority."

I Peter 2:15 calls it *"the will of God."*
Psalm 62:11 – *"God hath spoken once; twice have I heard this; that power belongeth unto God."*

GOD'S PURPOSE FOR AUTHORITY

(1)   To protect human life – Genesis 9:6; Exodus 19:11-13; 20:13

(2)   To protect personal and property rights – Exodus 20:14-17

(3)   To handle disputes between people over their rights – Deuteronomy 1:12-17; 16:18-20; 17:8-13; 19:15-21

(4)   To punish those who do evil – Deuteronomy 17:2-7; Romans 13:4

Civil disobedience is only permissible for the believer when the human authority demands that the believer violates the law of God.

In Acts 5:29 we read: *"Then Peter and the other apostles answered and said, We ought to obey God rather than men."*

    2.Because of the <u>CONSEQUENCES</u> we face if we don't submit to authority – vv. 2-4

"Whosoever therefore resisteth the power, resisteth the ordinance of God: and they that resist shall receive to themselves damnation. For rulers are not a terror to good works, but to the evil. Wilt thou then not be afraid of the power? Do that which is good, and thou shalt have praise of the same: For he is the minister of God to thee for good. But if thou do that which is evil, be afraid; for he beareth not the sword in vain: for he is the minister of God, a revenger to execute wrath upon him that doeth evil."

I Timothy 1:9-10 – *"Knowing this, that the law is not made for a righteous man, but for the lawless and disobedient, for the ungodly and for sinners, for unholy and profane, for murderers of fathers, and murderers of mothers, for manslayers, for whoremongers, for them that defile themselves with mankind, for menstealers, for liars, for perjured persons, and if there be any other thing that is contrary to sound doctrine"*

3. Because of our <u>CONSCIENCE</u> before God – v. 5 – *"Wherefore ye must needs be subject, not only for wrath, but also for conscience sake."*

The Greek word translated as *"conscience"* is *suneidesis* and is used 32 times in the New Testament of which 18 usages refer to an awareness of what is right and wrong. The other 14 times use adjectives with the word, such as:

A <u>weak</u> conscience – I Corinthians 8:10
A <u>seared</u> conscience – I Timothy 4:1
A <u>defiled</u> conscience – Titus 1:15
An <u>evil</u> conscience – Hebrews 10:22
A <u>good</u> conscience – I Timothy 1:5
A <u>pure</u> conscience – I Timothy 3:9

Unbelievers have a conscience according to Romans 2:14-15 which causes them to do what is in God's law without realizing it. Romans 9:1 speaks of a believer's conscience when Paul said: *"my conscience also bearing me witness in the Holy Ghost."*

In the context of Romans 13:5, the conscience submits to authority because it knows that it is the right thing to do.

Our <u>SUPPORT</u> of the law – vv. 6-7
"For for this cause pay ye tribute also: for they are God's ministers, attending continually upon this very thing. Render therefore to all their dues: tribute to whom tribute is due; custom to whom custom; fear to whom fear; honor to whom honor."

    1. The <u>REASON</u> – *"for this cause"* – the need to be subject to the governing authorities.

    2. The <u>RESPONSIBILITY</u> we have – *"pay ye tribute also"* (Pay your taxes!)

Matthew 22:15-22 is a key passage in describing the believer's responsibility to the government:

"Then went the Pharisees, and took counsel how they might entangle Him in His talk. And they sent out unto Him their disciples with the Herodians, saying, Master, we know that Thou art true, and teachest the way of God in truth, neither carest Thou for any man: for Thou regardest not the person of men. Tell us therefore, What thinkest Thou? Is it lawful to give tribute unto Caesar, or not? But Jesus perceives their wickedness, and said, Why tempt ye me, ye hypocrites? Show Me the tribute money, And they brought unto him a penny. And He saith unto them, Whose is this image and superscription? They say unto Him, Caesar's. Then saith He unto them, Render therefore unto Caesar the things which are Caesar's; and unto God the things that are God's. When they had heard these words, they marveled, and left Him, and went their way."

The teaching of the separation of church and state in American history is based on what Yeshua said in the above verses.

"Render to Caesar the things which are Caesar's; and unto God the things that are God's."

On 25 decisions of the United States Supreme Court they have used the phrase "separation of church and state" that was a part of a letter by Thomas Jefferson to the Danbury Baptists in 1802. Here's what the letter actually said:

> *"Believing with you that religion is a matter which lies solely between man and his God, that he owes account to none other for his faith or his worship, that the legitimate powers of government reach actions only, and not opinions, I contemplate with sovereign reverence that act of the whole American people which declared that their legislature should 'make no law respecting an establishment of religion, or prohibiting the free exercise thereof,' thus building a wall of separation between Church & State."*

The purpose of this article was NOT to renounce Christianity or give countenance to infidelity or any pagan religion, but to exclude all rivalry among Christian denominations and prevent any national ecclesiastical establishment which should give to a hierarchy the exclusive patronage of the national government.

The constitution of the United States says in its first amendment:

"Congress shall make no law respecting an establishment of religion, or prohibiting the free exercise thereof; or abridging the freedom of speech, or of the press; or the right of the people peaceably to assemble, and to petition the government for a redress of grievance."

3. The <u>RECOGNITION</u> of the duties of governing authorities – *"for they are God's ministers, attending continually upon this very thing."*

The words *"God's ministers"* use the Greek word *leitourgos* (which is used 5 times in the New Testament, and related words another 10 times.

Used of Paul's ministry
Romans 15:16

Used of angels – Hebrews 1:7

Used of our Lord Yeshua as our High Priest – Hebrews 8:2, 6

Used of the public ministry of priests, such as Luke 1:23.

Used of our financial support in II Corinthians 9:12

4. The <u>RENDERING</u> of what is due.

    Taxes – *tribute*
    Tolls - *custom*
    Trust – *fear*
    Thankfulness – *honor*

5. Our <u>RELATIONSHIP</u> to the governments of this world

(1)   <u>CITIZENSHIP</u>

Philippians 3:20-21 – *"For our conversation is in heaven; from whence also we look for the Savior, the Lord Jesus Christ: Who shall change our vile body, that it may be fashioned like unto His glorious body, according to the working whereby He is able even to subdue all things unto Himself."*

The word *"conversation"* in the King James Bible is based on a Greek word from which we get the word "politics." Our real "politics" are in heaven!

In John 17:16 we read: *"They are not of the world, even as I am not of the world."* And, in John 18:36, Yeshua said: *"My kingdom is not of this world."*

(2)   COMMITMENT

We read in Acts 4:18-20 these words: *"And they called them, and commanded them not to speak at all nor teach in the Name of Jesus."* Again, in Acts 5:27-29 we read: *"And when they had brought them, they set them before the council: and the high priest asked them, saying, Did not we straitly command you that ye should not teach in this Name? and, behold, ye have filled Jerusalem with your doctrine, and intend to bring this man's blood upon us. Then Peter and the other apostles answered and said, We ought to obey God rather than men."*

The result is also a lesson to all of us today – Acts 5:40-42: *"And to him they agreed: and when they had called the apostles, and beaten them, they commanded that they should not speak in the Name of Jesus, and let them go. And they departed from the presence of the council, rejoicing that they were counted worthy to suffer shame for His Name. And daily in the temple, and in every house, they ceased not to teach and preach Jesus Christ."*

(3)   <u>CONDUCT</u>

Matthew 5:13-16 – *"Ye are the salt of the earth: but if the salt have lost his savor, wherewith shall it be salted?   It is thenceforth good for nothing, but to be cast out, and to be trodden under foot of men.   Ye are the light of the world.   A city that is set on an hill cannot be hid. Neither do men light a candle, and put it under a bushel, but on a candlestick; and it gives light unto all that are in the house.   Let your light so shine before men, that they may see you good works, and glorify your Father which is in heaven."*

(4)   Prayerful <u>CONCERN</u>

Out of all that which can be described as the responsibilities of the believer, this needs to be one of the main priorities – prayer for the human authorities.

I Timothy 2:1-4 – *"I exhort therefore, that, first of all, supplications, prayers, intercessions, and giving of thanks, be made for all men; For kings, and for all that are in authority; that we may lead a quiet and peaceable life in all godliness and honesty. For this is good and acceptable in the sight of God our Savior; Who will have all men to be saved, and to come unto the knowledge of the truth."*

The SATISFACTION of the law Romans 13:8-10

"Owe no man any thing, but to love one another: for he that loveth another hath fulfilled the law. For this, Thou shalt not commit adultery, Thou shalt not kill, Thou shalt not steal, Thou shalt not bear false witness, Thou shalt not covet; and if there be any other commandment, it is briefly comprehended in this saying, namely, Thou shalt love thy neighbor as thyself. Love worketh no ill to his neighbor: therefore, love is the fulfilling of the law."

The simple phrase *"love one another"* is used 16 times in the New Testament.

1. Love <u>REALIZES</u> its obligation to others – v. 8 – *"Owe no man any thing, but to love one another"*

This is not a condemnation of borrowing money. Matthew 5:42 makes that clear: *"Give to him that asketh thee, and from him that would borrow of thee turn not thou away."*

2. Love <u>RESPECTS</u> the rights of others – v. 9

The right of marriage – *"thou shalt not commit adultery"*

The right to life – *"Thou shalt not kill"*

The right of property – *"Thou shalt not steal"*

The right of truth – *"Thou shalt not bear false witness"*

The right of ownership – *"Thou shalt not covet"* (desiring what does not belong to you)

3. Love <u>REFUSES</u> to do harm to a neighbor or friend – v. 10 – *"love is the fulfilling of the law"*

Matthew 5:43-48 – *"Ye have heard that it hath been said, Thou shalt love thy neighbor, and hate thine enemy. But I say unto you, Love your enemies, bless them that curse you, do good to them that hate you, and pray for them which despitefully use you, and persecute you; That ye may be the children of your Father which is in heave; for He maketh His sun to rise on the evil and on the good, and sendeth rain on the just and on the unjust. For if ye love them which love you, what reward have ye? Do not even the publicans the same? And if ye salute your brethren only, what do ye more than others? Do not even the publicans so? Be ye therefore pefect, even as your Father which is in heaven is perfect."*

Galatians 5:14 – *"For all the law is fulfilled in one word, even in this; Thou shalt love thy neighbor as thyself."*

Galatians 6:2 – *"Bear ye one another's burdens, and so fulfill the law of Christ."*

James 2:8 – *"If ye fulfill the royal law according to the scripture, Thou shalt love thy neighbor as thyself, ye do well."*

Our SALVATION in Jesus Christ should make a difference!
Romans 13:11-14

"And that, knowing the time, that now it is high time to awake out of sleep: for now is our salvation nearer than when we believed. The night is far spent, the day is at hand: let us therefore cast off the works of darkness, and let us put on the armor of light. Let us walk honestly, as in the day; not in rioting and drunkenness, not in chambering and wantonness, not in strife and envying. But put ye on the Lord Jesus Christ, and make not provision for the flesh, to fulfill the lusts thereof."

    1. The **NEARNESS** of it – vv. 11-12a

"And that, knowing the time, that now it is high time to awake out of sleep: for now is our salvation nearer than when we believed. The night is far spent, the day is at hand"

I Thessalonians 5:4-8: *"But ye, brethren, are not in darkness, that that day should overtake you as a thief. Ye are all children of light, and the children of the day: we are not of the night, nor of darkness. Therefore let us not sleep, as do others; but let us watch and be sober. For they that sleep, sleep in the night; and they that be drunken are drunken in the night. But let us, who are of the day, be sober, putting on the breastplate of faith and love; and for an helmet, the hope of salvation."*

I Peter 4:7: *"But the end of all things is at hand: be ye therefore sober, and watch unto prayer."*

> 2. The <u>NECESSITY</u> of applying what we have come to believe – vv. 12b-13

Notice that the words *"let us"* appear three times.

>> (1) <u>RESIST</u> the devil's <u>pressures</u> – v. 12b

"let us cast off the works of (<u>the</u>) darkness"

Ephesians 5:11-14 – *"And have no fellowship with the unfruitful works of darkness, but rather reprove them. For it is a shame even to speak of those things which are done of them in secret. But all things that are reproved are made manifest by the light: for whatsoever doth make manifest is light. Wherefore he saith, Awake thou that sleepest, and arise from the dead, and Christ shall give thee light."*

(2) <u>RELY UPON</u> the Lord's <u>protection</u> – v. 12c

"let us put on the armor of light"

Ephesians 6:11-13 – *"Put on the whole armor of God, that ye may be able to stand against the wiles of the devil. For we wrestle not against flesh and blood, but against principalities, against powers, against the rulers of the darkness of this world, against spiritual wickedness in high places. Wherefore take unto you the whole armor of God, that ye may be able to withstand in the evil day, and having done all, to stand."*

(3) **REFUSE** to live like non-believers <u>practice</u> v. 13 – *"let us walk honestly"*

I Thessalonians 4:12 – *"That ye may walk honestly toward them that are without, and that ye may have lack of nothing."*

THREE SETS OF SINFUL PRACTICES
Romans 13:13

(1) <u>INTEMPERANCE</u> – a lack of control – *"not in rioting and drunkenness"*

(2) <u>IMPURITY</u> – *"not in chambering and wantonness"* (Greek words for sexual sins)

(3) <u>INTOLERANCE</u> – hostility and tension in relationships – *"not in strife and envying"*

3. The <u>NEED</u> we constantly have – v. 13 – *"But put ye on the Lord Jesus Christ, and make not provision for the flesh, to fulfill the lusts thereof"*

The word *"But"* that opens verse 14 is the Greek *alla* – a word of great contrast!

The need we constantly have as believers is twofold:

> (1) To <u>CLOTHE</u> ourselves with the life and example of our Lord Jesus Christ – *"put ye on the Lord Jesus Christ"*

> (2) To <u>CONTROL</u> our sinful desires – *"make not provision for the flesh, to fulfill the lusts thereof"*

The Greek word that translates as *"make not provision"* is *pronoian* which simply means "to think ahead" or "to plan." That's the problem we all face. Our sin nature will not be removed until the Lord comes again (I John 3:1-3). I Peter 2:11 tells us: *"Dearly beloved, I beseech you as strangers and pilgrims, abstain from fleshly lusts, which war against the soul."*

I John 2:15-17 says: *"Love not the world, neither the things that are in the world. If any man love the world, the love of the Father is not in him. For all that is in the world, the lust of the flesh, and the lust of the eyes, and the pride of life, is not of the Father, but is of the world. And the world passeth away, and the lust thereof: but he that doeth the will of God abideth forever."*

Chapter 12
LIBERTY IN CHRIST
Romans 14:1-23

It <u>EXCLUDES</u> judgment of others!
Romans 14:1-12

"Him that is weak in the faith receive ye, but not to doubtful disputations. For one believeth that he may eat all things: another, who is weak, eateth herbs. Let not him that eateth despise him that eateth not; and let not him which eateth not judge him that eateth: for God hath received him. Who are thou that judgest another man's servant? To his own master he standeth or falleth. Yea, he shall be holden up: for God is able to make him stand. One man esteemeth one day above another: another esteemeth every day alike. Let every man be fully persuaded in his own mind. He that regardeth the day, regardeth it unto the Lord; and he that regardeth not the day, to the Lord he doth not regard it. He that eateth, eateth to the Lord, for he giveth God thanks; and he that eateth not, to the Lord he eateth not, and giveth God thanks. For none of us liveth to himself,

and no man dieth to himself. For whether we live, we live unto the Lord; and whether we die, we die unto the Lord: whether we live therefore, or die, we are the Lord's. For to this end Christ both died, and rose, and revived, that He might be Lord both of the dead and living. But why does thou judge thy brother? or why dost thou set at nought thy brother? for we shall all stand before the judgment seat of Christ. For it is written, As I live, saith the Lord, every knee shall bow to Me, and every tongue shall confess to God. So then every one of us shall give account of himself to God."

This passage is a powerful teaching that forbids "judging" among believers. There are three Greek words that are translated as *"judge"* or *"judgment."*

Krino – it means to decide, conclude, pass sentence, determine, etc. – it is used over 160 times as a noun and a verb.

Anakrino – to ask questions, examine, evaluate, etc. – used 17 times as a noun.

Diakrino – to discern, make a distinction, etc. – used 22 times, three of which as a noun.

The opening example concerns one who is described as *"weak in the faith."* It does not say *"weak in faith"* or *"weak in morals"* – the phrase *"in THE faith"* is referring to doctrines of salvation and our freedom in Jesus Christ.

The following characteristics describe this person who is *"weak in the faith"*:

Romans 14:2 – *"eateth herbs"*
Romans 14:15 – *"grieved"*
Romans 14:21 – *"stumbleth*
Romans 14:21 – *"offended"*
Romans 14:21 – *"made weak"*
Romans 14:23 – *"doubteth"*
Romans 15:1 – *"infirmities"*

WHEN IS IT RIGHT TO JUDGE?

1. We are to judge (*anakrino*) all things!

I Corinthians 2:15 – *"But he that is spiritual judgeth all things, yet he himself is judged of no man."*

2. We are to judge the spirits! (*anakrino*)

I John 4:1 – *"Beloved, believe not every spirit, but <u>try</u> the spirits whether they are of God: because many false prophets are gone out into the world."*

3. We are to judge (*diakrino*) between fellow believes who have a dispute!

I Corinthians 6:5 – *"I speak to your shame. Is it that there is not a wise men among you? no, not one that shall be able to <u>judge</u> between his brethren?"*

4. We are to judge those living in sin who refuse to repent! (*krino*)

I Corinthians 5:12-13 – *"For what have I to do to <u>judge</u> them also that are without? Do not ye <u>judge</u> them that are within? But them that are without God judgeth. Therefore put away from among yourselves that wicked person."*

5. We are to judge with righteous judgment! (*krino*)

John 7:24 – *"Judge not according the appearance, but judge righteous judgment."*

6. We are to judge ourselves! (*diakrino*)

I Corinthians 11:31 – *"For if we would judge ourselves, we should not be judged."*

WHEN IS IT WRONG TO JUDGE?

1. When our disagreements with other believers are over *"doubtful disputations"* (no proof of sin) – Romans 14:1

The Greek *diakriseis dialogismon* is referring to dialogue or argument about what is right or wrong about that which the Bible does not all it "sin."

2. When we think we are better than others or our position is the only correct one to consider – v. 3 – *"despiseth"*

The Greek word is *exoutheneito*. The discussion of Matthew 7:1-5 reveals that we usually do not see our own faults.

"Judge not, that ye be not judged. For with what judgment ye judge, ye shall be judged: and with what measure ye mete, it shall be measured to you again. And why beholdest thou the mote that is in thy brother's eye, but considerest not the beam that is in thine own eye? Or how wilt thou say to thy brother, Let me pull out the mote out of thine eye; and, behold, a beam is in thine own eye? Thou hypocrite, first cast out the beam out of thine own eye; and then shalt thou see clearly to cast out the mote out of thy brother's eye."

    3. When we try to play God – v. 4 - *"Who art thou that judgest another man's servant? To his own master he standeth or falleth."*

James 4:11-12 – *"Speak not evil one of another, brethren. He that speaketh evil of his brother, and judgeth his brother, speaketh evil of the law, and judgeth the law: but if thou judge the law, thou art not a doer of the law, but a judge. There is one lawgiver, who is able to save and to destroy: who art thou that judgest another?"*

4. When we don't respect the opinions and convictions of others – v. 5 – *"One man esteemeth one day above another: another esteemeth every day alike. Let every men be fully persuaded in his own mind."*

Galatians 4:10-11 – *"Ye observe days, and months, and times, and years. I am afraid of you, lest I have bestowed upon you labor in vain."*

Colossians 2:16-17 – *"Let no man therefore judge you in meat, or in drink, or in respect of an holyday, or of the new moon, or of the sabbath days: which are a shadow of things to come; but the body is of Christ."*

5. When we question the motives of others – v. 6 – *"He that regardeth the day, regardeth it unto the Lord; and he that regardeth not the day, to the Lord he doth not regard it."*

I Corinthians 4:3-5 – *"But with me it is a very small thing that I should be judged of you, or of man's judgment: yea, I judge not mine own self. For I know* *nothing by myself, ye am I not hereby justified: but he that judgeth me is the Lord. Therefore judge nothing before the time, until the Lord come, who both will bring to light the hidden things of darkness, and will make manifest the counsels of the hearts: and then shall every man have praise of God."*

6. When we doubt a person's relationship to the Lord – vv. 7-8 - *"For none of us liveth to himself, and no man dieth to himself, For whether we live, we live unto the Lord; and whether we die, we die unto the Lord: whether we live therefore, or die, we are the Lord's."*

7. When we forget our personal accountability to God – vv. 10-12

   (1) The <u>COMING</u> of judgment for all believers – v. 10

"But why dost thou judge thy brother? or why dost thou set at nought thy brother? for we shall all stand before the judgment seat of Christ."

II Corinthians 5:10 – *"For we must all appear before the judgment seat of Christ; that every one may receive the things done in his body, according to that he hath done, whether it be good of bad."*

> (2) The biblical <u>CONTEXT</u> for this judgment – v. 11

"For it is written, As I live, saith the Lord, every knee shall bow to Me, and every tongues shall confess to God."

Isaiah 45:23 – *"I have sworn by Myself, the word is gone out of My mouth in righteousness, and shall not return, That unto Me every knee shall bow, every tongue shall swear."*

> (3) The <u>CONCLUSION</u> we draw – v. 12

"So then every one of us shall give account of himself to God."

For 11 chapters in this wonderful Book of Romans we saw the theme of the "RIGHTEOUSNESS OF GOD" being developed. We learned that it is "BY FAITH" not by any works that we have done. And yet, it is clear from Romans 12, 13, and the early 12 verses of chapter 14 that the true "righteousness of God" will definitely manifest itself in the lives of those who claim to have it.

In the midst of the discussions of chapters 12, 13, and 14, we see the power and strength of God's love in the life of the believer. Chapter 12 emphasized the fact that this love of God needs to be *"without hypocrisy."* We now have come to see that our very liberty in Jesus Christ, that excludes judging others, must also exercise God's love to them.

OUR LIBERTY IN CHRIST
Romans 14:1-23

<u>EXCLUDES</u> the judgment of others
Romans 14:1-12

<u>EXERCISES</u> love to others
Romans 14:13-21

    1. Our primary <u>RESPONSIBILITY</u>
      v. 13

"Let us not therefore judge one another any more: but judge this rather, that no

man put a stumblingblock or an occasion to fall in his brother's way.

I Corinthians 8:1b – *"Knowledge puffeth up, but charity (love) edifieth."*

2. Our <u>RECOGNITION</u> of what is unclean – v. 14

"I know, and am persuaded by the Lord Jesus, that there is nothing unclean of itself: but to him that esteemeth any thing to be unclean, to him it is unclean."

(1) When we disobey God's standards!

I John 3:4 – *"Whosoever committeth sin transgresseth also the law: for sin is the transgression of the law."*

(2) When we fail to do what is right when we know what we should do!

James 4:17 – *"Therefore to him that knoweth to do good, and doeth it not, to him it is sin."*

> (3) When we violate our conscience!

Romans 14:20 – *"For meat destroy not the work of God. All things indeed are pure; but it is evil for that man who eateth with offence."*

Romans 14:23 – *"And he that doubteth is damned if he eat, because he eateth not of faith: for whatsoever is not of faith is sin."*

> (4) When we encourage others to go against their conscience!

I Corinthians 8:12 – *"But when ye sin so against the brethren, and wound their weak conscience, ye sin against Christ."*

3. Our <u>RESPONSE</u> to the brother who is hurt by what we are doing – v. 15 – *"But if thy brother be grieved with thy meat, now walketh thou not charitably. Destroy not him with they meat, for whom Christ died."*

4. Our <u>REALIZATION</u> of what is really important – vv. 16-17 – *"Let*

not then your good be evil spoken of: For the kingdom of God is not meat and drink; but righteousness and peace, and joy in the Holy Ghost."

5. Our <u>RELATIONSHIP</u> to Jesus Christ – v. 18 – *"For he that is these things serveth Christ is acceptable to God, and approved of men."*

6. Our <u>RESOLVE</u> to live in peace with one another – v. 19 – *"Let us therefore follow after the things which make for peace, and things wherewith one may edify another."*

    (1) It takes <u>EFFORT</u> – *"follow after the things which make for peace"*

Ephesians 4:3 – *"Endeavouring to keep the unity of the Spirit in the bond of peace."*

Hebrews 12:14 – *"Follow peace with all men, and holiness, without which no man shall see the Lord."*

(2)   It takes <u>EDIFICATION</u>
*"things wherewith one
may edify another"*

I Corinthians 8:1 – *"Now as touching
things offered unto idols, we know that
we all have knowledge.   Knowledge
puffeth up, but charity edifieth."*

I Corinthians 10:23 – *"All things are
lawful for me, but all things are not
expedient: all things are lawful for me,
but all things edify not."*

Ephesians 4:16 – *"From Whom the
whole body fitly joined together and
compacted by that which every joint
supplieth, according to the effectual
working in the measure of every part,
maketh increase of the body unto the
edifying of itself in love."*

I Thessalonians 5:11 – *"Wherefore
comfort yourselves together, and edify
one another, even as also ye do."*

7. Our <u>RESPECT</u> for the conscience
of others – v. 20- *"For meat
destroy not the work of God. All
things indeed are pure; but it is*

evil for that man who eateth with offence."

      (1)   The <u>ISSUE</u> is not the food itself – *"for meat destroy not the work of God"*

I Corinthians 8:8 – *"But meat commandeth us not to God; for neither, if we eat, are we the better; neither, if we eat not, are we the worse."*

      (2)   The <u>IMPACT</u> upon the individual is what is important – *"it is evil for that man who eateth with offense"*

8. Our <u>REFUSAL</u> to do anything that will hurt our brother – v. 21 – *"It is good neither to eat flesh, nor to drink wine, nor any thing whereby thy brother stumbleth, or is offended, or is made weak."*

I Corinthians 8:13 – *"Wherefore , if meat make my brother to offend, I will eat no flesh while the world standeth, lest I make my brother to offend."*

I Corinthians 10:24-33 — *"Let no man seek his own, but every man another's wealth. Whatsoever is sold in the shambles, that eat, asking no question for conscience sake; For the earth is the Lord's and the fullness thereof. If any of them that believe not bid you to a feast, and ye had disposed to go; whatsoever is set before you, eat, asking no question for conscience sake. But if any man say unto you, This is offered in sacrifice unto idols, eat not for his sake that shewed it, and for conscience sake: for the earth is the Lord's, and the fullness thereof: Conscience, I say, not thine own, but of the other: for why is my liberty judged of another man's conscience? For if I by grace be a partaker, why am I evil spoken of for that for which I give thanks? Wherefore therefore ye eat, or drink, or whatsoever ye do, do all to the glory of God. Give none offence, neither to the Jews, not to the Gentiles, nor to the church of God: Even as I please all men in all things, not seeking mine own profit, but the profit of many, that they may be saved."*

SUMMARY:

In the first paragraph of Romans 14:1-12, the emphasis is on our <u>attitudes</u> toward other believers who differ with us over *"doubtful disputations."*

In the next paragraph, the emphasis is on our <u>actions</u> in terms of the effect we have on other believers. The first paragraph dealt with <u>LEGALISM</u>, while the second paragraph deals with <u>LIBERTY</u>.

The answer to <u>LEGALISM</u> is our personal <u>ACCOUNTABILITY TO GOD</u>: the answer to <u>LIBERTY</u> (that becomes a license to do whatever you want regardless of how it affects other believers) is <u>LOVE</u>! It is only <u>LOVE</u> that edifies ("builds up") others!

OUR LIBERTY IN CHRIST
Romans 14:1-23

1. <u>EXCLUDES</u> judgment of others – *Romans 14:1-12*

2. <u>EXERCISES</u> love for others – Romans 14:13-21

3. <u>**EXPERIENCES**</u> **discernment for yourself** – Romans 14:22-23 – *"Hast thou faith? Have it to thyself before God. Happy is he that condemneth not himself in that thing which he alloweth. And he that doubteth is damned if he eat, because he eateth not of faith: for whatsoever is not of faith is sin."*

This discernment affects what you <u>believe</u> is right, and it also affects how you <u>behave</u> when you question the rightness of something.

Chapter 13
LIKEMINDEDNESS
Romans 15:1-33

In chapters 14 and 15 of Romans, the context reveals three principles and three issues relating to them – all helping us to get along with each other in the body of Jesus Christ.

DON'T JUDGE ONE ANOTHER!
Romans 14:1-12

Issue? ACCOUNTABILITY to God!

DON'T CAUSE ANOTHER BELIEVER TO STUMBLE!
Romans 14:13-23

Issue? LOVE for one another!

DON'T' PLEASE YOURSELF!
Romans 15:1-13

Issue? UNITY for the glory of God!

Being "likeminded" with other believers is not easy – to say the least!

Our <u>ATTITUDES</u> toward others – Romans 15:1-6

"We then that are strong ought to bear the infirmities of the weak, and not to please ourselves. Let every one of us please his neighbor for his good to edification. For even Christ pleased not Himself; but, as it is written, The reproaches of them that reproached thee fell on Me. For whatsoever things were written aforetime were written for our learning, that we through patience and comfort of the scriptures might have hope. Now the God of patience and consolation grant you to be LIKEMINDED one toward another according to Christ Jesus: That ye may with one mind and one mouth glorify God, even the Father of our Lord Jesus Christ."

1. Our <u>RESPONSIBILITY</u> –
vv. 1-4 - *"to bear the infirmities of the weak"*

Galatians 6:1-2 – *"Brethren, if a man be overtaken in a fault, ye which are spiritual, restore such an one in the spirit of meekness; considering thyself, lest thou also be tempted. Bear ye one another's burdens, and so fulfill the law of Christ."*

   (1) The <u>EXCEPTION</u> - v. 1
     "not to please ourselves"

II Timothy 3:2-4 speaks of a coming period of time known as *"perilous times"* in which people will be *"lovers of their own selves"* and *"lovers of pleasures more than lovers of God."*

Romans 8:8 says: *"So then they that are in the flesh cannot please God."* That's the heart of the problem. To be *"likeminded"* with other believers requires a lifestyle of not pleasing ourselves, and that involves being filled with the Holy Spirit, and not yourself!

Psalm 69:30-31 says: *"I will praise the Name of God with a song, and will magnify Him with thanksgiving. This also shall please the LORD better than an ox or bullock that hath horns and hoofs.*

   (2) The <u>EDIFICATION</u> of others
     v. 2 – *"Let every one of us please his neighbor for his good to <u>edification</u>"*

In Romans 14:19 we read: *"Let us therefore follow after the things which make for peace, and things wherewith one may edify another."*

One of the classic passages on *"edifying"* others is found in Ephesians 4:12-16:

"For the perfecting of the saints, for the work of the ministry, for the edifying of the body of Christ: Till we all come in the unity of the faith, and of the knowledge of the Son of God, unto a perfect man, unto the measure of the stature of the fullness of Christ; That we henceforth be no more children, tossed to and fro, and carried about with every wind of doctrine, by the sleight of men, and cunning craftiness, whereby they lie in wait to deceive; But speaking the truth in love, may grow up into Him in all things, which is the Head, even Christ: From Whom the whole body fitly joined together and compacted by that which every joint supplieth, according to the effectual working in the measure of every part, maketh increase of the body unto the edifying of itself in love."

Edification means "to build up" – the opposite of "tearing down." The sphere in which it happens is love – we need to *"love one another."*

      (3)   The <u>EXAMPLE</u> to follow – v. 3 – *"For even Christ pleased not Himself"*

In John 8:29 we read: *"And He that sent Me is with Me: the Father hath not left Me alone; for I do always those things that please Him."*

      (4)   The <u>ENCOURAGEMENT</u> of the Scriptures – v. 4

Romans 15:4 – *"For whatsoever things were written aforetime were written for our learning, that we through patience and comfort of the scriptures might have hope."*

The <u>PURPOSE</u> behind what was written – *"for our learning"*

The <u>PATIENCE</u> we need in applying what the Scriptures teach – *"through patience"*

The **PLACE** which the Scriptures have in helping us – *"through the comfort of the Scriptures"*

The **PROSPECT** that will result – *"might have hope"*

2. A spiritual <u>REASON</u> – vv. 5-6

"Now the God of patience and consolation grant you to be likeminded one toward another according to Christ Jesus: That ye may with one mind and one mouth glorify God, even the Father of our Lord Jesus Christ."

Yes, the real reason behind our attitude of like-mindedness is to *"glorify God."*

(1) The **NECESSITY** of God's help – *"Now the God of patience and consolation"*

(2) The <u>NEED</u> in order to achieve this spiritual reason

"to be likeminded one toward another according to Christ Jesus"

That simply means "what He wants" or "in obedience to Him" or "according to His example"

(3) The <u>NATURE</u> of this like-mindedness

"that ye may with one mind and one mouth glorify God, even the Father of our Lord Jesus Christ."

Philippians 2:1-4 is a powerful example of what we mean by *"like-mindedness."*

"If there be therefore any consolation in Christ, if any comfort of love, of any fellowship of the Spirit, if any bowels and mercies, Fulfill ye may joy, that ye be like-minded, having the same love, being of one accord, of one mind. Let nothing be done through strife or vainglory; but in lowliness of mind let each esteem other better than themselves. Look not every man on his own things, but every man also on the things of others."

Our <u>RESOURCES</u> – Philippians 2:1
    CONSOLATION in Christ
    COMFORT of love
    COMMUNION of the Spirit

COMPASSION

Our <u>RESPONSE</u> involves two basic
things – Philippians 2:3-4

Our AMBITION – *"Let nothing be
done through strife or vain glory"*

Our ATTITUDES toward others –
"in lowliness of mind"

If these traits are being manifested in us,
then our response toward others will
involve their <u>importance</u> and their
<u>interests</u>.

Our <u>ACCEPTANCE</u> of all believers
Romans 15:7-13

*"Wherefore receive ye one another, as
Christ also received us to the glory of
God. Now I say that Jesus Christ was a
minister of circumcision for the truth of
God, to confirm the promises made unto
the fathers: and that the Gentiles might
glorify God for His mercy; as it is
written, For this cause I will confess to
Thee among the Gentiles, and sing unto
Thy name. And again He saith, Rejoice,
ye Gentiles, with his people. And again,
Praise the Lord, all ye Gentiles; and*

laud Him, all ye people. And again, Esaias saith, There shall be a root of Jesse, and he that shall rise to reign over the Gentiles; in Him shall the Gentiles trust. Now the God of hope fill you with all joy and peace in believing, that ye may abound in hope, through the power of the Holy Ghost."

The command to *"receive on another"* is based on three things:

> 1. The <u>PRINCIPLE</u> behind it – v. 7 – *"as Christ also received us to the glory of God"*

This principle is not based on our performance or our response to Him or on our worthiness. It was the Person and work of our blessed Lord Yeshua that accepted us!

> 2. The <u>PROMISES</u> of God that prove it – vv. 8-12 (concerning Jews and Gentiles)

>> (1) <u>CONFIRMED</u> by Jesus Christ – v. 8

The promises that were confirmed by Him are those that speak of the coming

Messiah – when the *"fathers"* were told that the world would be blessed through one of their descendants.

> (2)   <u>CENTERED</u> in giving glory to God – v. 9a

In addition to confirming those promises, Jesus Christ also desired that the Gentiles would glorify Him for His *"mercy"* to the circumcision.

The words *"For this cause"* clearly point to Deuteronomy 32:43, the song of Moses and emphasize giving glory to God for His mercy to the Jewish people: *"Rejoice, O ye nations* (Gentiles – Hebrew: *goyim), with His people: for He will avenge the blood of His servants, and will render vengeance to His adversaries, and will be merciful unto His land, and to His people."*

> (3)   <u>CONCERNED</u> with the Gentiles praising God!

In Psalm 18:46-50 we read of this concern expressed by King David:

"The LORD liveth; and blessed be my Rock; and let the God of my salvation be

exalted. It is God that avengeth me, and subdueth the people under me. He delivereth me from mine enemies: yea, Thou liftest me up above those that rise up against me: Thou hast delivered me from the violent man. Therefore will I give thanks unto thee, O LORD, among the heathen (Gentiles), *and sing praises unto Thy Name. Great deliverance giveth He to His king, and sheweth mercy to His anointed, to David, and to His seed evermore."*

In Psalm 117:1-2 we read: *"O praise the LORD, all ye nations* (Gentiles): *praise Him, all ye people. For His merciful kindness if great toward us: and the truth of the LORD endureth forever. Praise ye the LORD."*

> (4) <u>CHARACTERIZED</u> by the coming of the Messiah – v. 12

The quotation comes from Isaiah 11:1: *"And there shall come forth a rod out of the stem of Jesse, and a Branch shall grow out of his roots"* – and, in Isaiah 11:10: *"And in that day there shall be a root of Jesse, which shall stand for an ensign of the people; to it shall the*

Gentiles seek: and His rest shall be glorious."

The title of the Messiah – *"the Branch"* is also found in Jeremiah 23:5-6: *"Behold, the days come, saith the LORD, that I will raise unto David a righteous Branch, and a King shall reign and prosper, and shall execute judgment and justice in the earth. In His days Judah shall be saved, and Israel shall dwell safely: and this is His Name whereby He shall be called, THE LORD, OUR RIGHTEOUSNESS."*

3. The <u>POWER</u> of the Holy Spirit that accomplishes it – v. 13

"Now the God of hope fill you with all joy and peace in believing, that ye may abound in hope, through the power of the Holy Ghost."

(1)   The <u>FATHER</u> is the source of this power – *"the God of hope"*

(2)   The <u>FULLNESS</u> of joy and peace comes through believing!

(3) The <u>FRUIT</u> that results is an abundance of hope!

Our <u>ADMONISHING</u> one another – Romans 15:14-21

"And I myself also am persuaded of you, my brethren, that ye also are full of goodness, filled with all knowledge, able also to admonish one another. Nevertheless, brethren, I have written the more boldly unto you in some sort, as putting you in mind, because of the grace that is given to me of God, That I should be the minister of Jesus Christ to the Gentiles, ministering the gospel of God, that the offering up of the Gentiles might be acceptable, being sanctified by the Holy Ghost. I have therefore whereof I may glory through Jesus Christ in those things which pertain to God. For I will not dare to speak of any of those things which Christ hath not wrought by me, to make the Gentiles obedient, by word and deed, through mighty signs and wonders, by the power of the Spirit of God; so that from Jerusalem, and round about unto Illyricum, I have fully preached the gospel of Christ. Yea, so have I strive to

preach the gospel, not where Christ was named, lest I should build upon another mans' foundation: But as it is written, To who he was not spoken of, they shall see; and they that have not heard shall understand."

1. The <u>PERSUASION</u> of Paul – v. 14

    (1)   Concerning their spiritual <u>MATURITY</u> – *"full of goodness and all knowledge"*

The Greek word translated *"goodness"* is *agathosune* which is used four times in the New Testament. It is listed as a part of the *"fruit of the Holy Spirit"* in Galatians 5:22. In Ephesians 5:9 it agrees with the passage in Galatians 5 and says *"For the fruit of the Spirit is in all goodness..."* II Thessalonians 1:11 we read: *"Wherefore also we pray always for you, that our God would count you worthy of this calling, and fulfill all the good pleasure of His <u>goodness</u>, and the work of faith with power."*

Colossians 1:9-10 speaks of the importance of His knowledge: *"For this cause we also, since the day we heard it,* *do not cease to pray for you, and to desire that ye might be filled with the <u>knowledge</u> of His will in all wisdom and spiritual understanding; That ye might walk worthy of the Lord unto all pleasing, being fruitful in every good work, and increasing in the <u>knowledge</u> of God."*

(2) Concerning their spiritual <u>MINISTRY</u> – *"able also to admonish one another"*

The word *"admonish"* is a word of counsel (Greek: *nouthetein*) and means "to place in the mind." The verb appears 8 times in the New Testament, and the noun 3 times. It is translated *"to warn"* as well. The following six times reveal its broad applications:

EMOTIONAL – Acts 20:31
PARENTAL – I Corinthians 4:14-16; Ephesians 6:4
HISTORICAL – I Corinthians 10:11
SPIRITUAL – Colossians 1:28
BIBLICAL – Colossians 3:16
CONFRONTATIONAL –

I Thessalonians 5:14; II
Thessalonians 3:15; Titus
3:10

2. The <u>PURPOSE</u> of Paul – vv. 15-21

In verse 16 – *"ministering the gospel of God"* and in verse 20 – *"to preach the gospel."*

(1) As to God's <u>GRACE</u> –
v. 15b – *"because of the grace that is given to me of God"*

(2) As to the <u>GENTILES</u> –
v. 16a – *"that I should be the minister of Jesus Christ to the Gentiles"*

(3) As to the <u>GOSPEL</u> of God – v. 16b – *"ministering the gospel of God"*

(4) As to the <u>GOAL</u> he had – v. 16c – *"that the offering up of the Gentiles might be acceptable, being*

sanctified by the Holy
Ghost"

(5)   As to the <u>GLORY</u>
involved – vv. 17-19 –
"*whereof I may glory
through Jesus Christ
in those things which
pertain to God*"

The <u>PERSON</u> of this glory – v. 17 –
"*through Jesus christ in those things
that pertain to God*"

The <u>PRINCIPLE</u> of this glory – v. 18 – "*I
will not dare to speak of any of those
things which christ hath not wrought
by me*"

The <u>POWER</u> that made it possible – v.
19a – "*by the power of the Spirit of God*"

The <u>PREACHING</u> that was involved – v.
19b – "*I have fully preached the gospel
of Christ (Messiah)*"

(6)   As to the <u>GUIDELINES</u>
he followed – v. 20 –
"*not where Christ was
named*"

The <u>ANTICIPATION</u> of Paul's visit
Romans 15:22-29

"For which cause also I have been much hindered from coming to you. But now having no more place in these parts, and having a great desire these many years to come unto you; Whensoever I take my journey into Spain, I will come to you: for I trust to see you in my journey, and to be brought on my way thitherward by you, if first I be somewhat filled with your company. But now I go unto Jerusalem to minister to the saints. For it have pleased them of Macedonia and Achaia to make a certain contribution for the poor saints which are at Jerusalem. It have pleased them verily; and their debtors they are. For if the Gentiles have been made partakers of their spiritual things, their duty is also to minister unto them in carnal things. When therefore I have performed this, and have sealed to them this fruit, I will come by you into Spain. And I am sure that, when I come unto you, I shall come in the fullness of the blessing of the gospel of Christ."

1. The <u>REASON</u> he had not been able to come – v. 22 – *"For this cause...much hindered"*

Acts 16:6-7 explains how he was *"hindered"* at times: *"Now when they had gone throughout Phrygia and the region of Galatia, and were forbidden of the Holy Ghost to preach the word in Asia, After they were come to Mysia, they assayed to go into Bithynia: but the Spirit suffered them not."*

I Thessalonians 2:14-18 adds: *"For ye, brethren, became followers of the churches of God which in Judea are in Christ Jesus: for ye also have suffered like things of your own countrymen, even as they have of the Jews: Who both killed the Lord Jesus, and their own prophets, and have persecuted us; and they please not God, and are contrary to all men: Forbidding us to speak to the Gentiles that they might be saved, to fill up their sins always: for the wrath is come upon them to the uttermost. But we, brethren, being taken from you for a short time in presence, not in heart, endeavored the more abundantly to see your face with great desire. Wherefore we would have come unto you, even I Paul, once and again; but Satan hindered us."*

2. The <u>REALIZATION</u> of how his desire could be fulfilled – vv. 23-24

"But now having no more place in these parts, and having a great desire these many years to come unto you; Whensoever I take my journey into Spain, I will come to you: for I trust to see you in my journey, and to be brought on my way thitherward by you, if first I be somewhat filled with your company."

The nature of the Book of Romans is very doctrinal and theological until we arrive at chapter 15 – Paul becomes quite personal.

3. The <u>RESPONSIBILITY</u> he had in going to Jerusalem first – vv. 25-28

   (1) His <u>CONCERN</u> – *"to minister unto the saints"*

   (2) The <u>CONTRIBUTION</u> that had been made – *"a certain contribution for the poor*

saints which are at
Jerusalem"

(3) The <u>CONCLUSION</u> he had
drawn – v. 27 – *"their duty is
also to minister unto them
in carnal things"*

(4) His <u>COMING</u> to see them
must follow this
responsibility – v. 28 –
*"have sealed to them this
fruit"*

4. The <u>RESPONSE</u> he was
anticipating – v. 29 – *"come in the
fullness of the blessing of the
gospel of Christ"*

The <u>ASSURANCE</u> of prayer
Romans 15:30-33

*"Now I beseech you, brethren, for the
Lord Jesus Christ's sake, and for the
love of the Spirit, that ye strive together
with me in your prayers to God for me;
That I may be delivered from them that
do not believe in Judea; and that my
service which I have for Jerusalem may
be accepted of the saints; That I may
come unto you with joy by the will of*

God, and may with you be refreshed. Now the God of peace be with you all. AMEN!"

1. His <u>REASONS</u> – v. 30

   (1) For the <u>LORD</u> – *"For the Lord Jesus Christ's sake"*

   (2) For the <u>LOVE</u> of the Spirit

2. His <u>REQUESTS</u> – vv. 31-32

The English word *"that"* is a word of purpose in Greek – *hina* and means "in order that." It is used three times here.

   (1) For personal <u>DELIVERANCE</u> *"that I may be delivered from them that do not believe in Judea"*

   (2) For emotional <u>ACCEPTANCE</u> *"that my service which I have for Jerusalem may be accepted of the saints"*

   (3) For spiritual <u>REFRESHING</u> *"that I may come unto you with joy by the will of God,*

and may with you be refreshed"

3. His closing <u>REMARKS</u> – v. 33
   "Now the God of peace be with you all – AMEN!"

Chapter 14
CONCLUSION
Romans 16:1-27

There are five powerful things that this final concluding chapter presents to us:

> We need to <u>ACCEPT</u> the ministry of others – vv. 1-2

> We need to <u>APPRECIATE</u> the ministry of others – vv. 3-16

> We need to <u>AVOID</u> those who cause divisions and offenses – vv. 17-20

> We need to <u>ACKNOWLEDGE</u> the blessing which others bring to our lives – vv. 21-24

> We need to <u>APPLY</u> what we have learned and thus give glory to God – vv. 25-27

We need to <u>ACCEPT</u> the ministry of others – vv. 1-2

"I commend unto you Phoebe our sister, which is a servant of the church which

is at Cenchrea: That ye receive her in the Lord, as becometh saints, and that ye assist her in whatsoever business she hath need of you: for she hath been a succourer of many, and of myself also."

1. Paul's <u>RECOMMENDATION</u> of Phoebe – v. 1

   (1) She is a "SISTER"
   (2) She is a "SERVANT"

The words *"servant of the church"* could suggest that she had an official ministry of being a "female deacon." It is possible that I Timothy 3:11 is referring to that ministry as well: *"Even so must their wives be grave, not slanderers, sober, faithful in all things."*

The words *"Even so"* connect with I Timothy 3:2 – *"a bishop"* and with I Timothy 3:8 – *"Likewise"* referring to *"the deacons"* - connecting the context would imply not a "wife" but rather a female deacon (deaconess).

2. Their <u>RESPONSIBILITY</u> to her – v. 2

     (1)   Involves their <u>ATTITUDE</u> – *"that ye receive her in the Lord, as becometh saints"*

     (2)   Involves their <u>ASSISTANCE</u> *"that ye assist her in whatever business she hath need of you"*

   3. Paul's <u>REASON</u> – *"for she hath been a succourer* (helper) *of many and of myself also"*

We need to <u>APPRECIATE</u> the ministry of others – vv. 3-16

   1. By <u>**REMEMBERING**</u> to give thanks for them – vv. 3-5a

"Greet Priscilla and Aquila my helpers in Christ Jesus: Who have for my life laid down their own necks: unto whom not only I give thanks, but also all the churches of the Gentiles. Likewise greet the church that is in their house."

     (1)   For their <u>COMING</u> into Paul's life – Acts 18:1-3

"After these things Paul departed from Athens, and came to Corinth; And found a certain Jew named Aquila, born in Pontus, lately come from Italy, with his wife Priscilla; (because that Claudius had commanded all Jews to depart from Rome:) and came unto them. And because he was of the same craft, he abode with them, and wrought: for by their occupation they were tentmakers."

      (2)   For their <u>COUNSEL</u> to Apollos – Acts 18:24-26

"And a certain Jew named Apollos, born at Alexandria, an eloquent man, and mighty in the scriptures, came to Ephesus. This man was instructed in the way of the Lord; and being fervent in the spirit, he spake and taught diligently the things of the Lord, knowing only the baptism of John. And he began to speak boldly in the synagogue: whom when Aquila and Priscilla had heard, they took him unto them, and expounded unto him the way of God more perfectly."

(3) For their <u>COMFORT</u> to Paul – *"my helpers in Christ Jesus"*

(4) For their <u>COURAGE</u> – *"who have for my life laid down their own necks"*

(5) For the <u>CHURCH</u> in their house – *"greet the church that is in their house"*

In I Corinthians 16:19 we read: *"The churches of Asia salute you. Aquila and Priscilla salute you much in the Lord, with the church that is in their house."*

II Timothy 4:19 says: *"Salute Prisca and Aquila, and the household of Onesiphorus."*

2. By **REFERRING** to your relationship to them!

(1) In terms of <u>AFFECTION</u>

EPAENETUS: *"well-beloved firstfruits of Asia unto Christ"*

AMPLIATUS – *"my beloved"*

STACHUS – *"my beloved"*

(2)   In terms of <u>APOSTLESHIP</u> *"who are of note among the apostles, who also were in Christ before me"*

(3)   In terms of <u>ACTIVITY</u> for the Lord

MARY – *"who bestowed much labor on us"*

URBANUS – *"our helper in Christ"*

TRYPHAENA & TRYPHOSA *"who labor in the Lord"*

PERSIS – *"who labored much in the Lord"*

(4)   In terms of <u>ACCEPTANCE</u> of all believers

APELLES – *"approved in Christ"*

ARISTOBULUS – *"salute them who are of his household"*

HERODIAN – *"my kinsman"*

NARCISSUS – *"household of...which are in the Lord"*

RUFUS – *"chosen in the Lord, and his mother and mine"*

In Mark 15:21 – *"And they compel one Simon a Cyrenian, who passed by, coming out of the country, the father of Alexander and Rufus, to bear His cross"*

ASYNERITUS, PHLEGON, HERMES, PATROBAS, HERMAS – *"and the brethren with them"*

PHILOLOGUS, JULIA, NEREUS, AND HIS SISTER, AND OLYMPAS – *"and all the saints which are with them"*

3. By **RESPONDING** to them with love and affection – v. 16

"Salute one another with an holy kiss. The churches of Christ salute you."

Some commentators on Romans believe that this greeting is similar to "shaking hands" as many do in the Western culture today. However, the use of the adjective *"holy"* with the word *"kiss"* would seem to eliminate the idea of simply shaking a person's hand. That would be done with strangers and non-believers. To argue that this is a "holy handshake" seems a bit much to believe!

I Corinthians 16:20 says: *"All the brethren greet you. Greet one another with an holy kiss."* It does not say, "greet every person you meet with a kiss." A *"kiss"* is certainly an act of deep affection. The command that appears 16 times in the Bible – *"love one another"* applies only to believers with each other, not to non-believers or strangers.

Once again in II Corinthians 13:12 we read: *"Greet one another with an holy kiss."* The same words are found in II Thessalonians 5:26 with one simple addition – *"Greet all the brethren with an holy kiss."*

I Peter 5:14 says: *"Greet ye one another with a kiss of charity (love)."*

Taking a look at this issue, we would do well to examine the following details:

(1)   It is a *"kiss"* that is to be given.

(2)   It is a *"kiss"* among believers only.

(3)   It is a *"kiss"* that can be given to *"all"* the believers.

(4)   It is a symbol of our *"love"* for one another.

(5)   It is a custom among the *"churches"* – Romans 16:16b

(6)   It is to be a *"holy kiss."*

The word *"holy"* implies that there is no sensuality or sexual desire involved in this show of physical affection.

4. We need to <u>AVOID</u> those who cause divisions and offenses! Romans 16:17-20

"Now I beseech you, brethren, mark them which cause divisions and offences contrary to the doctrine which ye have learned; and avoid them. For they that are such serve not our Lord Jesus Christ, but their own belly; and by good words and fair speeches deceive the hearts of the simple. For your obedience is come abroad unto all men. I am glad therefore on your behalf; but yet I would have you wise unto that which is good, and simple concerning evil. And the God of peace shall bruise Satan under your feet shortly. The grace of our Lord Jesus Christ be with you. AMEN."

1. The **PROBLEM** – *"them which cause divisions and offenses contrary to the doctrine which ye have learned"*

   "divisions" – Greek: *dichostasias*
   - The opposite of unity - Ephesians 4:1-3

478

"offenses" – Greek: *skandala* – the word refers to a scandal, trap, or snare, causing a fall.

(1)   As to their <u>MESSAGE</u>

"contrary to the doctrine which ye have learned" – the word *"doctrine"* is singular, but the words *"divisions"* and *"offenses"* are plural!

(2)   As   to   their   wicked <u>MOTIVATIONS</u>

"they that are such serve not our Lord Jesus Christ, but their own belly."

Similar words are found in Philippians 3:17-19: *"Brethren, be followers together of me, and mark them which walk so as ye have us for an example. For many walk, of whom I have told you often, and now tell you even weeping, that they are the enemies of the cross of Christ: whose end is destruction, whose God is their belly, and whose glory is in their shame, who mind earthly things."*

(3)   As to their <u>METHODS</u>

"and by good words and fair speeches deceive the hearts of the simple."

II Corinthians 11:3 states: *"But I fear, lest by any means, as the serpent beguiled Eve through his subtilty, so your minds should be corrupted from the simplicity that is in Christ."*

Colossians 2:4-8 adds: *"And this I say, lest any man should beguile you with enticing words. For though I be absent in the flesh, yet am I with you in the spirit, joying and beholding your order, and the stedfastness of your faith in Christ. As ye have therefore received Christ Jesus the Lord, so walk ye in Him: Rooted and built up in Him, and stablished in the faith, as ye have been taught, abounding therein with thanksgiving. Beware lest any man spoil you through philosophy and vain deceit, after the tradition of men, after the rudiments of the world, and not after Christ."*

2. The **PRINCIPLE** – *"mark them"* – it means "to look out for" or "to keep your eyes open (scope)."

"avoid them" – Greek: *ekklinete* – *"*keep on turning away*"*

II Thessalonians 3:14-15 – *"And if any man obey not our word by this epistle, note that man, and have no company with him, that he may be ashamed. Yet count him not as an enemy, but admonish him as a brother."*

Titus 3:9-11 – *"But avoid foolish questions, and genealogies, and contentions, and strivings about the law; for they are unprofitable and vain. A man that is an heretic after the first and second admonition reject; Knowing that he that is such is subverted, and sinneth, being condemned of himself."*

3. The <u>PURPOSE</u> – *"I would have you wise unto that which is good and simple concerning evil."*

The word *"simple"* refers to that which is "unmixed" or "harmless." It is similar to what our Lord Yeshua taught us in Matthew 10:16 – *"Be ye therefore wise as serpents, and harmless as doves."*

481

4. The __PROMISE__ – *"and the God of peace shall bruise Satan under your feet shortly"*

Romans 15:33 said: *"Now the God of peace be with you all."*

II Corinthians 13:11 says: *"Finally, brethren, farewell. Be perfect, be of good comfort, be of one mind, live in peace; and the God of love and peace shall be with you."*

Philippians 4:9 – *"Those things, which ye have both learned, and received, and heard, and seen in me, do: and the God of peace shall be with you."*

I Thessalonians 5:23 – *"And the very God of peace sanctify you wholly; and I pray your whole spirit and soul and body be preserved blameless unto the coming of our Lord Jesus Christ."*

The words *"bruise Satan"* **remind us of the words of Genesis 3:15** – *"And I will put enmity between thee and the woman, and between thy seed and her seed; it shall __bruise__ thy head, and thou shalt __bruise__ his heel."*

In Luke 10:17-20 our Lord spoke these words to the seventy who returned and said *"Lord, even the devils are subject unto us through Thy Name"* – He said to them: *"I beheld Satan as lightning fall from heaven. Behold, I give unto you power to tread on serpents and scorpions, and over all the power of the enemy: and nothing shall by any means hurt you. Notwithstanding in this rejoice not, that the spirits are subject unto you; but rather rejoice because your names are written in heaven."*

We need to <u>ACKNOWLEDGE</u> the blessing which others bring to our lives! Romans 16:21-24

"Timotheus my workfellows, Lucius, and Jason, and Sosipater, my kinsmen, salute you. I Tertius, who wrote this epistle, salute you in the Lord. Gaius mine host, and of the whole church, saluteth you. Erastus the chamberlain of the city saluteth you, and Quartus a brother. The grace of our Lord Jesus Christ be with you all. AMEN!"

　　1.　In terms of <u>HELP</u> – vv. 21-22

Timothy is separated from Lucius, Jason, and Sosipater, the ones Paul calls *"my kinsmen."* This might indicate that they had Jewish fathers. Acts 16:1 says: *"The came he to Derbe and Lystra; and behold, a certain disciple was there, named Timotheus, the son of a certain woman, which was a Jewess, and believed: but his father was a Greek."*

Perhaps Paul's physical condition (eyes – perhaps infected) made it difficult for him to do the actual writing of the epistle to the Romans. This would explain verse 22 and the remark about Tertius *"who wrote this epistle."*

2. In terms of <u>HOSPITALITY</u> – v. 23a *"Gaius, mine host, and of the whole church"*

I Corinthians 1:14 mentions a man named *"Gaius"* – baptized by Paul. Also, Acts 19:29 refers to a man named *"Gaius"* who was Paul's companion in his travels from Macedonia. Acts 20:4 mentions another *"Gaius"* from Derbe who was among the traveling companions of Paul. Another *"Gaius"* is mentioned in III John 1 whom John calls *"the well-beloved Gaius, whom I love in the truth"*

In III John, verses 4-8 speak of the relationship John had with a man named *"Gaius"*:

"I have no greater joy than to hear that my children walk in truth. Beloved, thou doest faithfully whatsoever thou doest to the brethren and to strangers; Which have borne witness of thy charity before the church: whom if thou bring forward on their journey after a godly sort, thou shalt do well: Because that for his name's sake they went forth, taking nothing of the Gentiles. We therefore ought to receive such, that we might be fellow-helpers to the truth."

3. In terms of <u>HEARING</u> of their salvation – v. 23b – *"Erastus the chamberlain of the city saluteth you, and Quartus the brother."*

Acts 19:22 mentions *"Erastus"* who joined *"Timotheus"* in going to Macedonia ahead of Paul. *"Erastus"* is also mentioned in Paul's last letter in II Timothy 4:20 when he wrote *"Erastus abode at Corinth."*

Many years ago it was my privilege to visit the ruins of the ancient city of Corinth. I had heard that there was some evidence of the name *"Erastus"* in the archaeological findings of that ancient city. I searched – unto I found an official-looking stone slab with the name *"Erastus"* on it – I was so excited!

I could not hardly believe that it was so, but here I was standing beside the evidence of a man named *"Erastus"* who was indeed a major official of that ancient city – Praise the Lord!

We need to __APPLY__ what we have learned and thus give glory to God!
Romans 16:25-27

"Now to Him that is of power to establish you according to my gospel, and the preaching of Jesus Christ, according to the revelation of the mystery, which was kept secret since the world began, but now is made manifest, and by the scriptures of the prophets, according to the commandment of the everlasting God, made known to all nations for the

obedience of faith: To God only wise, be glory through Jesus Christ forever – AMEN!"

1. By <u>RELYING UPON</u> God's power to establish you – v. 25a

2. By <u>RECOGNIZING</u> the means by which God accomplishes this in our lives – vv. 25b-26a

3. By <u>REMEMBERING</u> the purpose of it – v. 26b

4. By <u>RETURNING</u> all the glory to God – v. 27

There is no doubt about it – the Book of Romans is fundamental to our Christian faith and growth. Again, the central theme of the Book is:

RIGHTEOUSNESS BY FAITH

We have looked at the three major division of the Book of Romans:

THE PRINCIPLES OF THE RIGHTEOUSNESS OF GOD Romans 1-8

We learned that there are four major principles of our salvation:

CONDEMNATION
JUSTIFICATION
SANCTIFICATION
SECURITY

**THE PROBLEMS OF THE RIGHTEOUSNESS OF GOD
Romans 9-11**

**THE PRACTICES OF THE RIGHTEOUSNESS OF GOD
Romans 12-16**

May you be enriched in your knowledge of the true gospel of Jesus Christ our Lord, and may you be strong in the Lord and ready to defend what you believe — or better yet — WHO YOU BELIEVE!

SOLO DEO GLORIA!